FROM

UNKNOWN

TO

UNFORGETTABLE

'This book is a masterclass in start-up branding. Whether you are a seasoned founder, an aspiring entrepreneur, a start-up team member, or simply curious about how businesses work—this book is an accessible, essential read. Harsh has sought insights from some of the brightest minds in the space and put them together in a book that is not didactic. What's refreshing is how he brings in examples from different Indian companies, comparing and contrasting start-ups against long-established companies and showing us real world applications which I found valuable'—**Deep Kalra, founder and chairman, MakeMyTrip**

'Harsh has done a great job of bringing together insights from some of the brightest minds and remarkable new-age brands. This book offers many valuable lessons for those aiming to create a standout brand in an era when the market is more crowded than ever'—**Anand Deshpande, founder, chairman and managing director, Persistent Systems**

'By explaining crucial core concepts through relatable stories and examples, Harsh has crafted a wonderful book to inspire many new, budding, and young entrepreneurs into building great new start-ups and admirable brands over time'—**Supam Maheshwari, co-founder and CEO, FirstCry, and co-founder, XpressBees and GlobalBees**

'Harsh's book explores brand building in start-ups. He has garnered insights by direct interviews with investors and start-up CEOs. As India becomes one of the centres for start-ups across the world, the book is well-timed and should be read'—**Janmejaya Sinha, chairman, Boston Consulting Group (BCG) India**

'Every start-up aspires to build a powerful brand for itself. In this lucidly written book, Harsh Pamnani puts forward many of the key principles that lie at the foundation of creating standout brands. Drawing on the wisdom of many experts and his own rich experience, Harsh provides an invaluable guide to this essential subject. A must-read for entrepreneurs and marketers who wish to build great brands for their enterprises'—**Harish Bhat, former brand custodian, Tata Sons, avid marketer and bestselling author**

FROM
UNKNOWN
TO
UNFORGETTABLE

Stories *and* Strategies *to* Transform Your
Start-Up *into a* Trustworthy Brand

HARSH PAMNANI

PENGUIN
BUSINESS

An imprint of Penguin Random House

PENGUIN BUSINESS

Penguin Business is an imprint of the Penguin Random House group of companies
whose addresses can be found at global.penguinrandomhouse.com

Published by Penguin Random House India Pvt. Ltd
4th Floor, Capital Tower 1, MG Road,
Gurugram 122 002, Haryana, India

First published in Penguin Business by Penguin Random House India 2024

The views and opinions expressed in this book are the author's own and the facts
are as reported by him which have been verified to the extent possible, and the
publishers are not in any way liable for the same.

The contents of this book are based on interviews with various individuals as
well as information available in the public domain, with some creative liberties
taken while narrating incidents, actions, moments and dialogues. The contents
of the book are for informational purposes only and reflects the author's own
understanding and conception of the topics covered. Neither the publisher nor
the author makes any warranties regarding its comprehensiveness and disclaims
any responsibility or liability for the same. The objective of this book is not to
defame, malign or hurt the sentiments of any particular individual, organization,
community, region, linguistic group, caste, gender or religion.

Please note that no part of this book may be used or reproduced in any manner
for the purpose of training artificial intelligence technologies or systems.

ISBN 9780143463962

Typeset in Adobe Caslon Pro by Manipal Technologies Limited, Manipal
Printed at Replika Press Pvt. Ltd, India

www.penguin.co.in

Contents

To every entrepreneur who has touched my life, my mentors who have guided me through the ups and downs, my family members who have always stood by me and my five-year-old daughter Yashvi, who reminds me to be productive whenever she catches me spending time on social media

Preface

Dear reader,

Welcome to *From Unknown to Unforgettable: Stories and Strategies to Transform Your Start-Up into a Trustworthy Brand*! Your commitment to learning and growing your knowledge as a business enthusiast has brought you here, and I hope this book serves as a valuable resource in your quest to build a successful and enduring brand.

Why did I write this book?

Over the years, I've had the privilege of collaborating with numerous entrepreneurs and start-ups. I've witnessed the challenges they face in establishing and distinguishing their brands within competitive markets first-hand. Additionally, I've had the opportunity to teach the subject of start-up branding at several prestigious business schools in India.

The inspiration for writing this book arose from the repetitive questions I used to receive from my students and friends at start-ups. Sometimes, I knew the answers to their thoughtful questions, but many times, I felt the need to learn more in order to provide comprehensive responses. Then, destiny connected me to Manish Khurana, senior commissioning editor at Penguin Random House India. He encouraged me to deepen my learning on branding from start-ups' perspective and document my research in the form of a book that could benefit many start-up enthusiasts.

Writing a book is not an easy journey. I had to contact numerous founders, brand experts and investors for my research. I felt that getting their valuable time would not be easy and, as a result, I was hesitant to move ahead. However, when I discussed the idea of this book with numerous business school professors, entrepreneurs, MBA students and investors, I discovered that they all echoed the same sentiment: 'We have read a lot about American brands. We want to read about new-age Indian brands, deep research is missing on them. Go ahead and write it!' Then, the universe conspired to help me. Just as it takes nine months for a baby to develop in the womb of a mother, this book, largely based on primary research, took exactly nine months to complete.

In this book, I aim to demystify the process of turning a start-up into a renowned brand. I provide practical insights, strategies and tools to empower founders and marketers on their branding journey. Whether you're launching a new venture, scaling your start-up or rebranding an existing business, this book will be your trusted companion.

How to read this book?

This book is divided into four parts, each focusing on a different aspect of start-up branding. Here's a brief overview of the structure and contents of each part:

Part I: Investors' Perspective

In this section, we delve into the perspectives of two of India's leading start-up investors, exploring their insights and strategies for building strong brands that attract investment.

In the subsequent sections, various branding concepts are explained. Each chapter begins with perspectives from a renowned leader who has either created an admirable brand or assisted start-ups in brand creation. Then, each concept is explored contextually through case studies of admirable start-ups from diverse sectors.

Part II: Foundational Pillars

This part lays the groundwork for start-up branding, covering topics such as building a start-up's belief system and culture, which form the foundation of a strong brand identity.

Part III: Market Research and Opportunity Analysis

In this section, we dive into the critical aspects of market research and opportunity analysis, including leveraging insights, category creation, segmentation and achieving product–market fit.

Part IV: Brand Development

The final part focuses on the practical aspects of brand development, including brand positioning, design, consistency, communication, sales, distribution, brand portfolio management and the dynamics of environmental, social and governance (ESG) and corporate social responsibility (CSR).

As you read this book, I encourage you to engage actively with the material. Take notes and reflect on how you can apply the concepts and strategies to your own start-up journey. Each chapter is designed to build upon the previous ones, providing you with a comprehensive road map for building a successful and enduring brand.

Building a brand is not a one-time endeavour but an ongoing process of discovery and refinement. Moreover, what works for others may not work for you, so approach the material with an open mind and a willingness to embrace experimentation and iteration.

Embrace the journey and its challenges, and most importantly, embrace the opportunity to create something extraordinary.

Wishing you all the best on your start-up branding adventure!

Warm regards,
Harsh Pamnani
www.harshpamnani.com
harshpamnani@hotmail.com
https://www.linkedin.com/in/harshpamnani/

Introduction

India, with over 100 unicorns and thousands of innovative start-ups emerging from both big cities and small towns, has become one of the largest start-up ecosystems in the world. Many Indian start-ups are expanding globally, with some going public and generating wealth for their investors, founders and employees. Moreover, the rising popularity of shows like Shark Tank, along with numerous start-up awards and business podcasts, has inspired many young Indians to pursue entrepreneurship. The government is also implementing many initiatives like Make in India, Start-up India and Atal Innovation Mission (AIM) to foster entrepreneurship. Therefore, the Indian start-up landscape seems highly promising and is attracting many new entrepreneurs.

However, because of this promising new landscape, the market will inevitably see a crowding of start-ups. When a market gets crowded, customers (demand) have numerous choices, while start-ups (supply) face immense competition. However, a plethora of choices also leads to customer confusion.

To avoid this confusion and get the desired value, customers use brands as 'quality-guarantee' shortcuts to make choices. In fact, they may pay a higher price for a trustworthy brand even if an unknown alternative is available at a lower price. However, many entrepreneurs are clueless about how to turn their start-up into a renowned brand and, as a result, many promising start-ups fail due to the inability to build a recognized brand.

You might wonder why start-ups find it challenging to build a brand, despite the abundance of branding literature. Unfortunately, much of it focuses on examples of American brands. America and India are distinct markets, and strategies effective in the former might not be applicable here. Even if there is extensive literature on established Indian brands like TATA and HUL, it's crucial to recognize that these brands evolved over decades. The current era is different, and past strategies may not be relevant today. Moreover, what works for large organizations currently may not be feasible for start-ups due to resource disparities.

Nevertheless, many excellent blogs, media articles and podcasts extensively cover start-ups. However, their focus often centres more on 'what' was done rather than delving into 'why' and 'how', particularly about branding. Without understanding the proper context, replicating the same success factors or avoiding the pitfalls encountered by others may pose a challenge.

Regarding seeking advice from consultants and agencies, many founders either don't see the need for advice or fail to seek guidance from relevant experts. Possibly, they also get confused due to numerous branding terms, marketing channels and non-contextual advice coming from every direction.

This book aims to demystify the branding principles that help turn a start-up into an admirable brand. It not only offers advice, strategies and insights from industry experts such as investors, brand consultants and start-up founders well-versed in the Indian market but also features detailed case studies of many new-age, admirable brands. This comprehensive knowledge could prove invaluable for entrepreneurs and marketers attempting to build a standout brand in a competitive landscape.

The world of business and branding is vast and perpetually evolving. This is why, even as you turn the final page of this book, remember that learning is an ongoing process. Remain curious and continue to immerse yourself in more literature that can assist you in building a memorable brand.

PART I

Investors' Perspective

1

Investor Outlook on Start-Up Branding

Venture capitalists (VCs) invest in ideas that appear promising yet uncertain. By closely observing the journeys of numerous start-ups, VCs gain a deep understanding of why some become iconic brands while many others fail. It's essential to note that each VC may have a unique perspective, which is why I've gathered insights from two of India's leading VCs, who invested in different sets of successful start-ups.

Kanwaljit Singh (Kanwal), founder and managing partner, Fireside Ventures and early investor in boAt, Mamaearth, Paper Boat, Epigamia, Licious, iD Foods and YogaBar

I was curious to understand how Kanwal identified several iconic brands when they were in their nascent stage. He explained that his approach to selecting start-ups was, and is, rooted in one fundamental principle—putting the jockey before the horse. 'It's always the jockeys who change the game,' he said.

'I look for hunger, passion and vision in founders. In most of our successful investments, I've been confident that the founders would find a way to make things happen, even if they had to iterate.'

For instance, Kanwal backed Neeraj Kakkar when he was trying to build an energy drink brand called Tzinga, which didn't achieve the desired growth. However, Neeraj's unwavering commitment eventually led to the creation of Paper Boat. Similarly, when Kanwal decided to support Rohan Mirchandani, he was focused on crafting an ice cream brand called Hokey Pokey, which also encountered growth challenges. Nevertheless, Rohan's resilience ultimately gave rise to Epigamia.

Here are some of the lessons I learned from Kanwal:

Brand building starts from day one

Many entrepreneurs mistakenly confuse advertising with brand building, leading them to delay their focus on the latter. However, advertising represents only a fraction of the whole picture. Another common mistake is entrepreneurs assume that having a great product will automatically result in sales. In reality, as competition intensifies and more similar products flood the market, this essential question arises: How can you establish a genuine connection with consumers and make your product stand out? This is where the brand plays a pivotal role.

While each brand's growth strategy may display unique characteristics, the fundamental framework of brand building remains consistent. It all begins with a concentrated effort to identify the target consumer and acquire a unique insight into their needs and desires. This insight becomes the cornerstone of the product's distinctive value proposition. Once a start-up has confirmed a product–market fit with its consumers, it can explore the most effective approaches, which includes the selection of distribution channels, marketing strategies and engagement tactics, to reach its target audience.

Kanwal emphasized, 'Identifying the right purpose for your brand is crucial, and it can be beneficial from the very beginning, not just when your brand reaches a certain size and maturity.'

For instance, Slurrp Farm, a children's food brand, was founded by two mothers who noticed the widespread issue of unhealthy diets for kids around the world. They developed nutrient-rich snacks for children, and this commitment to their purpose has remained central to the brand's identity.

Kanwal also mentioned that insights are not always gathered through conventional market research. For instance, he enlightened me that many of his portfolio companies focus a lot on insight mining, wherein they go to large e-commerce sites and study their product reviews, after which they try to identify the gaps in the market and come out with products accordingly.

For example, the founders of boAt uncovered a valuable insight by analysing Amazon reviews, which revealed a common issue with Apple's cables—frequent breakage near the connectors. In response, they introduced a highly durable charging cable, competitively priced compared to other offerings. boAt's inaugural Facebook ad featured a damaged iPhone cable with the tagline: 'Tired of constantly replacing charging cables? Switch to boAt's indestructible charging cable.' To boost its appeal, boAt got its cable certified by Apple and offered a two-year warranty. This value proposition strongly resonated with buyers, resulting in an overwhelming success for the product.

Building consumer brands is becoming cost-effective and efficient

In the past, establishing a consumer goods brand in India was a laborious and capital-intensive endeavour. Traditional brands were designed to cater to a mass audience, requiring substantial investments in both production and marketing. These challenges were further compounded by the expensive distribution through numerous mom-and-pop stores. These small-sized stores with congested displays offered limited opportunities for consumers to discover new brands.

However, a significant transformation occurred with the introduction of modern retail that allowed consumers to explore various brands. The digital era brought even more profound changes. E-commerce made brand discovery more accessible, simultaneously revolutionizing distribution. Brands could now reach many PIN codes across the country from a single warehouse location. Capitalizing on the e-commerce infrastructure, numerous D2C (direct-to-consumer) brands have emerged, selling directly to their end customers instead of going through online or offline retailers.

E-commerce and D2C channels also allow testing the market. Companies often produce a limited quantity, list it online, assess the response and scale up if their product garners positive feedback or quickly withdraw if it doesn't. Additionally, advances in digital marketing and the rise of social media influencers provide brands with more efficient and cost-effective means to connect with customers, creating exciting opportunities for niche brands.

A crucial catalyst in this transformation has been the emergence of millennial and Gen Z consumers. They have exposure to global trends, disposable income, a willingness to experiment and an inclination to invest in innovative, high-quality and aspirational products. Kanwal said, 'In an online world, your products are constantly subjected to reviews. The quality is extremely critical in this case. Millennials and Gen Z consumers are ready to give you a try, but they are also the first ones to write you off if you can't deliver.'

Kanwal shared that when boAt launched earphones, the market was already saturated with low-cost brands as well as industry giants like Sony. However, what set boAt apart was a profound consumer insight; Indians have a deep affinity for bass, a preference deeply ingrained in our culture through instruments like the *tabla* and *dhol*. boAt fine-tuned its products to cater to this preference. Their superior-quality products with captivating audio and compelling designs were priced between affordable local brands and high-priced options. At the time, most companies primarily relied on offline distribution, with a dependency on distributors and retailers to communicate with their consumers. Conversely, boAt adopted a D2C model, facilitating direct contact with consumers. Moreover, instead of relying on performance marketing, boAt made significant investments in influencer marketing and cultivating a dedicated community of boAt enthusiasts. This approach successfully connected with millions of individuals who developed a strong affinity for the brand.

Consumer love is reflected in repeat purchases

Kanwal said, 'You can always entice someone with discounts or freebies for their first purchase, but if customers don't develop a connection with the brand, they won't return. If customers continue to buy from you regularly, it signifies their trust and affinity for your brand.'

An entrepreneur's continuous focus should be on understanding the value proposition they need to offer to keep customers returning. We are living in 'The Age of Responsibility', where modern customers prefer brands that not only offer quality products at competitive prices but also align with broader societal and environmental goals. Kanwal adds, 'With a sustainable offering, brands can attract two kinds of customers. Some are willing to pay a premium for a sustainable product, while others will choose it over another product—all other things being equal.'

I learned that brands should mirror the values that are most significant for their target audience. This alignment should not only be evident in their products, but also in how they are presented to the customer. This includes aspects like packaging, design, messaging and policies. However, ensuring authenticity is paramount in this endeavour.

For instance, Mamaearth was launched with MadeSafe certified, toxin-free products for kids. Moreover, its packaging is eco-friendly and recyclable. Additionally, they have planted over 5,00,000 trees and run a programme to recycle and reuse their bottles.

I also learned that lovable brands build bonds with their consumers through stories. Mamaearth's website highlights the founders' story—a husband-and-wife team inspired to start the company because they struggled to find suitable products when they had their first child. This story establishes an emotional connection with consumers, as the founders themselves experienced the issue and are addressing it as if it were for their children.

Brand building can help to align growth with profitability

When a business is in its early stages and aiming for growth, achieving profitability can be a challenge. However, it's imperative to recognize that if a loss-making business fails to transition into a profitable one in the long run, its survival may be questionable. To effectively align growth with profitability, start-ups should place a strong emphasis on unit economics from the outset, which primarily centres on the gross margin of individual products.

It's crucial to grasp that a product's pricing strategy significantly affects its unit economics. A product sold at a discounted price would yield less favourable unit economics than one sold at a premium rate. As Kanwal aptly states, 'It is unwise to assume that if your unit economics are weak at a small scale, they will miraculously improve as your business grows.'

When a company offers a product that genuinely resonates with consumers, buyers develop a deep connection with the brand and are often willing to pay an appropriate price. This connection can significantly enhance the overall economic health of the company. After start-ups have established a solid foundation with robust unit economics, they should shift their focus to performance metrics. These include customer acquisition and retention costs, as well as marketing and advertising expenses.

As customers wholeheartedly embrace the core product and brand story, their referrals and repeat purchases can significantly reduce customer acquisition and retention costs. Strong brand recognition can lower performance marketing expenses, which leads to accelerated growth and increased profitability.

Building the right team is crucial for upholding a superior brand experience

Scaling a business is a multi-faceted journey characterized by distinct phases, each with unique priorities and challenges. A common challenge that entrepreneurs face is not assembling the right team at the appropriate stage.

As Kanwal aptly pointed out, 'Some founders mistakenly believe they can manage all aspects of their business single-handedly for an extended period. However, this approach is flawed. As the business grows, complexities increase and any inefficiency within a business function can adversely impact the overall brand experience for consumers. Therefore, specialized talent is required to handle the increasing complexities.'

To attract the right team members who would help them successfully navigate each growth phase, founders should craft a compelling employee value proposition. However, attracting talent is only the beginning. It is essential to assess whether these team members can thrive in the start-up.

Sometimes, leaders transitioning from larger enterprises may not have the flexibility to adapt to the start-up setting. Kanwal rightly notes, 'Just as investors assess founders, they must similarly evaluate talent.' However, securing exceptional talent is just the beginning; founders must foster a workplace culture that enables this talent to thrive.

Anand Lunia, founding partner, India Quotient and early investor in Rebel Foods, SUGAR Cosmetics, ShareChat, Kuku FM, WebEngage and Lendingkart

I was keen to understand how Anand identified several iconic brands in their early stages. He explained, 'We focus on identifying market insights and finding the right founder-market fit. While selecting founders, we strive to ascertain their motivation for entrepreneurship. Are they merely following a trend because others are doing so, or do they possess a profound mission to address a problem that would keep them awake if left unresolved? We prefer to invest in entrepreneurs who are driven by a mission.'

Here are some of the lessons I learned from Anand:

Brand building is a necessity for start-ups, not a choice

Commonly, start-ups find themselves competing with established players who have already earned credibility in the market. This raises a pivotal question: Why would customers shift from a well-established player to an unknown start-up? Anand expressed, 'In a market filled with incumbents, start-ups cannot thrive solely by offering enhanced features and conveniences; brand building becomes an absolute necessity.'

Let us consider the early days of Myntra, when it had to compete with established retailers like Shoppers Stop, where shopping was associated with a certain status and top-notch experience. To attract customers, Myntra introduced incentives such as greater variety, a hassle-free return policy and better discounts. However, these benefits did not immediately replace the trust and social validation built up by Shoppers Stop.

Anand further underlined this point, saying, 'Start-ups don't have the luxury of time that legacy competitors have, so they must expedite the brand-building process. That's why many start-ups hire brand endorsers to leverage their credibility and build trust quickly.' Myntra, for instance, has collaborated with film stars, cricketers and influencers for several years.

Emphasizing the importance of brand trust, Anand explained, 'It is not just customers; suppliers too, need to trust the brand.' He cited the example of Holachef, once a portfolio company of India Quotient, that had to shut down due to operational challenges. Holachef was known for serving home-cooked food. In its early days, when the founder approached well-known chefs on collaborations, they were sceptical and questioned joining a new platform. Fortunately, Holachef received a small investment from Ratan Tata, significantly boosting its brand reputation. Once news of the investment spread, many chefs who had initially rejected the partnership changed their minds and chose to collaborate.

New trends create opportunities for new brands

Identifying and capitalizing on emerging trends to cultivate new opportunities can be a daunting task. However, doing so allows start-ups to avoid direct competition with established players and achieve significant benefits. Anand expanded on this and said, 'Not all of our investments in unexplored markets yield success; many bets fail. But some become admirable brands.'

Let's look at some of India Quotient's successful bets on start-ups focused on emerging trends.

In 2014, the rise of the selfie culture in India—driven by platforms like Instagram—created a potential demand for a wide variety of lipstick shades for spontaneous photoshoots. This provided the ideal setting for SUGAR to introduce a unique category of colour cosmetics in India.

Similarly, between 2015 and 2019, the price of gold almost doubled. Meanwhile, white-collar salaries stagnated, and tech salaries experienced limited growth. The affordability of gold suddenly became misaligned with people's incomes, prompting a growing number of individuals to turn to silver as a viable alternative. Seizing this exceptional opportunity, GIVA was launched and swiftly evolved into the fastest-growing silver jewellery D2C brand in the country.

In India, events such as the implementation of GST, demonetization and the Covid-19 pandemic have expedited the adoption of business software. However, a majority of the world's software originates in the USA, often carrying a steep price tag. This makes it less accessible to small businesses in regions like India, Vietnam, Bangladesh and Africa. Nonetheless, India, with its abundant talent pool and growing domestic market, was well-positioned to address this demand by nurturing budget-friendly B2B SaaS brands.

Anand explained, 'With this premise in mind, we invested in companies such as PagarBook and Vyapar, which are dedicated to digitizing India's MSMEs and supporting their growth. We see global opportunities for these brands.'

Nearly 90 per cent of India's population does not speak English but is rapidly coming online due to the availability of affordable internet and smartphones.[1] India Quotient is a pioneer in supporting social media and content firms that cater to this demographic. For instance, it was the first investor in ShareChat, India's largest social media platform for vernacular users. Additionally, it has backed Kuku FM, a leading vernacular audio content platform; FRND, an innovative audio-dating platform in multiple Indian languages; and Lokal, a news and classifieds platform in regional languages.

Strike a balance between storytelling, personal branding and business building

In the start-up world there is the widely held belief that founders must possess effective storytelling skills and a strong personal brand. These attributes are essential to attract talent, raise funds and engage buyers. However, some founders mistakenly give greater importance to these elements than the actual process of building a company.

Anand emphasized, 'Mere words and narratives, no matter how compelling, are insufficient. The crux of the matter lies in authenticity, which emanates from actions. Sometimes, actions themselves convey the story.'

Before founding India Quotient, Anand served as a partner at Seed Fund, an early-stage fund that invested in redBus. Anand recalled, 'Despite securing substantial funding, redBus founder Phanindra Sama chose to visit our Mumbai office taking a local train instead of a taxi. When I inquired why he had done so, Phanindra explained that his company made only Rs 50 per ticket, hence travelling by cab was a luxury they could not afford. It was Phanindra's action that conveyed the story of how the company managed its finances, as well as its culture of frugality.'

Anand also cautioned that founders can become obsessed with cultivating a positive image in the market by promoting favourable narratives, while neglecting stakeholder satisfaction. In cases where suppliers, employees and customers are left dissatisfied, negative narratives can emerge in the media, casting doubt on the authenticity of the founder's stories.

These days, founders are often focused on building their personal brands. Anand said, 'Some people think content creation and social media presence can help build their personal brand. This can be good for getting likes and views. But from an investor's perspective, a personal brand is created by delivering results and giving returns.'

Additionally, entrepreneurs often confuse personal branding with thought leadership, yet these are two distinct concepts. Personal branding revolves around what an individual is known for, their public image and their interactions with others. Conversely, thought leadership relates to the profound knowledge and insights a person contributes to their industry or field. Anand remarked, 'When someone shares their journey on a podcast, it can be perceived as a form of personal branding. However, Zerodha's founder, Nithin Kamath, sharing his insights on trading and nurturing fintech start-ups, exemplifies the essence of thought leadership.'

The relevance of personal branding and thought leadership varies depending on the industry. For instance, in fashion and cosmetics, the founder's personal brand holds importance, while in consulting, thought leadership is more critical. However, outstanding businesses can be constructed without the founder placing excessive emphasis on personal branding. Swiggy and CaratLane, for instance, stand as prime examples where the founders have built robust businesses and corporate brands without high media presence.

It is also important to recognize that over-reliance on the founder's personal brand can have drawbacks. Founders, like anyone else, experience both highs and lows in life. This is why a business should strive to establish a unique identity, separate from the personal brand of its founder. A notable example of this is CRED. Initially, Kunal Shah's personal brand played a significant role in building CRED's reputation. However, as time passed, CRED managed to develop a strong identity that was distinct from the founder's personal brand.

A start-up brand should not try to please everybody

Observing the growth of other companies and having access to significant funding creates the temptation to rapidly scale up. However, before venturing into new markets, start-ups should prioritize achieving product–market fit and reducing customer acquisition cost within their initial segment. As Anand suggested, 'To achieve this, you should be in love with your segment and be ready to dedicate yourself to solving its needs. Once you start seeing significant pull within your initial segment, you can then consider expanding to additional markets.'

For example, in India, major financial institutions prefer to cater to large corporations, while regional lenders mainly focus on the bottom of the pyramid. Lendingkart targeted graduates aged twenty-three to forty-five, who operate small businesses such as coaching centres, computer shops and academic bookstores. These entrepreneurs typically seek smaller loans of shorter duration, primarily to meet their working capital requirements. Anand notes that Lendingkart has diligently maintained its exclusive focus on serving MSMEs for nearly a decade. It deliberately passed up various diversification opportunities. Anand affirmed, 'Lendingkart's unwavering dedication to a specific segment and product specialization significantly strengthened its brand. It has become synonymous with MSME lending.'

Craft your brand associations strategically

Associations play a pivotal role in crafting a brand's identity. By carefully cultivating the right associations, businesses can distinguish themselves in a competitive market and effectively communicate their unique value proposition.

For instance, by 2014, Flipkart had established itself as India's leading e-commerce brand. In the same year, Lendingkart emerged to offer financial support to MSMEs, specifically targeting e-commerce sellers. Following a pattern akin to Flipkart, Lendingkart included 'kart' in its name, establishing an immediate connection with the e-commerce industry. In another example, SUGAR Cosmetics chose to manufacture its products in Germany, capitalizing on the country's renowned reputation for quality and precision. The incorporation of the 'Made in Germany' label significantly enhanced the brand's appeal.

Speaking of his own entrepreneurial journey, Anand reflected, 'When we started, the market had renowned international funds like Sequoia and Accel. To set ourselves apart, we focused on highlighting our deep understanding of India. The name 'India Quotient' highlights our commitment to India and our desire to back founders building India-centric businesses. We aim to ensure that every founder meeting us recognizes our expertise in India-centric trends and insights.'

PART II

Foundational Pillars

2

Building a Start-Up's Belief System

If you sell what you do, you're a vendor. If you sell why you do it, you're a brand.

—Simon Sinek, author and speaker

A company's belief system is built on key elements such as *purpose, vision, mission and values.* Purpose is the fundamental reason for a company's existence, extending beyond making profits. Vision represents an aspirational future that people can see, while mission outlines the actionable steps employees can take to contribute to that vision. Values are the foundation for the company's culture, guiding its actions and decisions.

I had the privilege of discussing this topic with one of India's most respected brand gurus—**Kiran Khalap, co-founder & MD of chlorophyll, India's first end-to-end brand consultancy firm.** He has played a pivotal role in crafting growth strategies for over 400 brands. Notably, he served as the chairman of the committee that shaped the Aadhaar brand for the Government of India.

Here are some lessons I learned from Kiran:

Start-ups should validate their belief system with their target audience

Some years ago, Kiran conducted a workshop for 150 CEOs and CFOs at IMA India. During the session, he presented a task where attendees were asked to match ten famous Indian brands with their respective vision statements. None of the leaders could correctly match them, as the statements appeared rather similar and difficult to relate to.

Kiran pointed out that many organizations develop belief systems internally, lacking external feedback. This often leads to vague, disconnected statements that hold little meaning for both internal teams and external audiences. He also noted that vision and mission statements are losing their relevance due to their lack of relatability with the audience. He advises that start-ups should not define their belief system in isolation. Instead, its relevance should be tested with their target audience. It's also important to ensure that the belief system is clearly documented. Regular communication, especially during the induction process, is crucial for new employees to grasp the essence of these beliefs. Implementing strategies that reward adherence to the belief system while discouraging contrary actions is equally important.

Brand purpose should be beyond category

Kiran cautioned, 'A well-defined brand purpose should not be confined to a specific category. It should enable a brand to enter diverse categories while staying relevant and meaningful to its audience.'

For instance, let's consider a start-up focused on producing sustainable clothing. If the start-up's purpose is confined to 'creating environmentally friendly clothing', it could find itself restricted to the clothing category. However, if its purpose was to 'advocate sustainable living', the start-up could expand beyond clothing to venture in sustainable accessories, eco-friendly home products, or community initiatives centered around sustainable practices.

Brand purpose should be backed by a story

In one of the most popular TED talks of all time, *'How Great Leaders Inspire Action'*, Simon Sinek said, 'People don't buy what you do. They buy why you do it.' The 'why' is the purpose! Kiran expanded on this point saying, 'To make a lasting impact on your audience, conveying your brand's purpose is crucial. And to make it relatable, backing it with a compelling story is equally important.'

For example, Ritesh Agarwal, CEO and founder of OYO, often shares a personal story that was the catalyst to his entrepreneurial journey. During his travels across India, he witnessed a significant gap in the availability of affordable and reliable budget accommodations. This first-hand experience ignited his strong motivation to provide standardized and affordable accommodations for budget-conscious travellers. The story does not have to be personal; even a philosophical or mythological tale can vividly bring your purpose to life.

Brand purpose is the foundation for crucial brand assets

Kiran mentioned, 'Once you have defined the purpose, everything, including brand communication and brand behaviour, should reflect it.' The purpose informs the development of visual elements like the logo, which represents the brand visually and acts as a symbol of its identity. Similarly, it influences the creation of a tagline, as well as new product development, service standards and metrics of success.

chlorophyll has collaborated with two prominent mutual fund companies in India. When Sandeep Tandon and his team approached chlorophyll, expressing their aspiration to create a unique finance company, Kiran inquired curiously, 'What makes it unique?' Sandeep responded that their distinctiveness lay in providing measurable advice and avoidance of the term 'market sentiment'. If market sentiment was crucial, they intended to incorporate it as a variable in their equations. Subsequently, chlorophyll devised the brand name 'Quant', symbolizing measurability, and crafted a logo that integrated geometric symbols into each alphabet.

On another occasion, when the late and legendary Parag Parikh, and his team, approached chlorophyll, they spoke of their dedication to Warren Buffett's investment philosophy—focus on diligent research and investment in enduring companies rather than responding to market fluctuations. In response, chlorophyll crafted the PPFAS logo—a tortoise, paired with the tagline 'There's only right way'. Kiran elucidated this saying, 'The tortoise embodies "slow and steady wins the race", symbolizing the brand's commitment against seeking quick gains.' The visual thus encapsulated the core of the brand.

Customize values and make them relevant across employee levels

Values are fundamental to a business' operations. Kiran outlined the four kinds of values that exist within companies:

- Core values established by the founder are essential for a company's existence. They are non-negotiable and must be upheld at all times.
- Aspirational values come into play when a company recognizes the need to adopt specific behaviours to remain relevant. For instance, in the age of social media, agility can be a crucial value to incorporate.
- Permission-to-play values are necessary for a company to be considered a player in a particular industry or category.
- Accidental values inadvertently become part of the company culture due to the actions or preferences of individuals in leadership positions. For example, everyone starts wearing black ties because the CEO does.

The significance of values varies across different employee levels within a company. Back in 2004, while working on an employer branding project for Infosys, chlorophyll engaged in discussions with the company's leadership regarding the practical implementation of their values. Kiran found that value of fairness held more weight for department heads who primarily focused on employee welfare, compared to junior employees primarily involved in coding tasks. The company also values excellence. However, Kiran noted that the meaning of excellence differed among employees across lower, middle and upper management. chlorophyll suggested Infosys to assign varying weights to their values, aligned with their importance across different organizational levels.

Kiran also highlighted the irony of companies claiming specific values when their behaviour contradicted them. For instance, a company proclaiming trust in its employees while chaining the drinking cup to the water cooler, or advocating equality while maintaining separate washroom for different tiers of employees. 'These inconsistencies are great signals to understand a disconnect between companies' verbal commitments and observable behaviours,' Kiran said.

Protect the core while adapting to market changes

There are remarkable similarities between human beings and brands. Both encompass unchanging as well as evolving aspects. Consider Mahatma Gandhi's clothing evolution. During his tenure as a lawyer in South Africa, he donned a three-piece suit, while in India he embraced a simple dhoti as a freedom fighter. However, his unwavering belief in the equality of all humans and his non-violent struggle against inequality remained constant across both periods.

Similarly, one of chlorophyll's clients exemplifies this concept of continuity amid change. With a history spanning about 1400 years, Eternal Mewar is the oldest brand in the world. It epitomizes the unwavering commitment of the Maharana of Mewar's family to custodianship. It signifies maintaining and passing down Mewar's heritage, traditions and legacy to future generations. While Mewar's adversaries changed from the Mughals to the English, the governance structure changed from kingdoms to the Indian Republic, and sources of revenue changed to hospitality, their core purpose was upheld by seventy-six generations, even amidst significant changes. The brand remains relevant to people who value the importance of cultural preservation.

Kiran stressed the underlying message saying, 'Every brand has both the changing (communication, segments, products) and the unchanging (name, purpose, values) aspects. They must guard the unchanging aspects and manage the changing ones.' When a brand's guiding philosophy remains steadfast over time, it helps establish consumer trust and loyalty.

Case Studies

Note: These case studies focus on *purpose, vision* and *mission.*
Values are covered in the case studies on culture.

How STAGE OTT Is Preserving the Linguistic and Cultural Diversity of India

India is a diverse country with twenty-two official languages,
including Hindi, Bengali, Gujarati, Malayalam, Marathi,
Punjabi, Tamil and Telugu. However, India's linguistic
diversity extends beyond these official languages to encompass
thousands of dialects. For instance, in Haryana, people
predominantly speak Haryanvi. Similarly, Uttar Pradesh is
home to various dialects such as Bhojpuri, Bundeli, Awadhi
and Braj. In Bihar, one finds Maithili, Magadhi, Angika and
Bhajika spoken widely.

The diverse populations speaking these dialects have
unique aspirations, local issues and specific content preferences.
However, there has been a lack of an entertainment industry
that specifically caters to these diverse audiences. STAGE
OTT was established in 2019 to bridge this gap. Its mission is
to develop premium, relatable content for Bharat, consisting of
India's dialect-speaking populations residing in villages, small
towns and migrant neighbourhoods in large cities.

Envisioning the creation of India's largest dialect-based
OTT platform, STAGE founders Vinay Singhal, Shashank
Vaishnav and Parveen Singhal, identified fifty of India's
main dialects. They studied the demographics, income levels,
audience sizes and the people associated with each dialect.
Emphasizing the importance of thorough research, Vinay said,

'To effectively cater to the local context, it is crucial to engage with the community and foster a genuine understanding of their needs and preferences.'

During their research, the trio recognized the significant role of Jio in bringing internet access to rural India. They also noted that content creators often prioritized the creation of high-quality content for urban audiences, resulting in rural viewers being offered substandard content featuring mindless and sleazy themes, or low-quality dubbed versions of popular shows. Vinay believes informative and inspiring content can improve people's thoughts and lives. Hence, he emphasizes the importance of giving equal respect and attention to rural audiences when it comes to content creation.

Additionally, the STAGE team discovered that local dialects were not widely accepted in the large cities and were often associated with a lack of education or progress. This led to many people living in rural India feeling inferior while speaking in their local dialects with people from cities. Shashank stated, 'Suppression of dialects becomes suppression of the people who speak them.'

Vinay observed that while film heroes are often regarded as role models, the lack of a dialect-based film industry meant that actors who spoke in local dialects were rarely seen on screen. STAGE aims to change this by creating on-screen actors who express themselves in their native dialects. The trio believe that such performers can inspire other individuals to showcase their identities confidently. 'We create and publish content, but our actual product is not content—it is the dignity of the user,' said Shashank. Parveen added, 'We are driven by the core purpose of giving back their pride and dignity to the dialect-speaking population of India.'

How Icertis Is Helping Companies Maximize the Value of Their Contract Data

A contract is a legally binding agreement between two or more parties. A Fortune 1000 company could typically manage anywhere between 20,000–40,000 contracts. As companies grow, these contracts become interlinked and evolve in complexity, making it increasingly challenging to monitor their clauses and implications. Moreover, any oversight on crucial contract data can result in missed revenue opportunities, non-compliance and unforeseen risk.

To navigate this complexity, Contract Lifecycle Management (CLM) solutions are essential, and Icertis is the undisputed leader in the $30 billion CLM category.[1] Presently, Icertis stands as one of the world's fastest-growing companies, trusted by over thirty of the Fortune 100 companies and numerous other renowned brands.

Icertis was founded in 2009 by Samir Bodas and Monish Darda. Although the company aimed to leverage the emerging cloud computing wave, its founders were initially unsure about the specific problem to address. They embarked on an exploratory journey, experimenting with various ideas to find the right product–market fit. Looking back on those formative years, Monish acknowledges the role of serendipity in shaping their path forward.

Microsoft, a strong advocate for cloud computing, recognized Icertis' commitment to this technology. In 2012, Microsoft faced the challenge of managing an extensive volume of contracts involving over 1,15,000 employees, 6,50,000 partners and numerous customers across 100 countries. The absence of a centralized repository for contracts, combined with a complex and time-consuming process, presented significant obstacles. One of Microsoft's executives suggested Icertis explore the development of a cloud-based contract management solution for them. Reflecting on the outcome, Monish said, 'Our solution led to 83 per cent faster contract turnaround time and one million legacy contracts digitized. Considering the success achieved in contract management through our cloud platform, we decided to expand our platform's vision in this area.'

Monish also highlighted the significance of contracts in business operations. He said, 'Every dollar in and out of a company has a contract behind it. A company hires employees and has to pay them salaries, resulting in an employment contract. It engages in buying things, leading to procurement contracts. Sales involve sales contracts, and leasing requires leasing contracts. Even renting a car involves a rental contract. Essentially, any financial transaction in a company is backed by a contract.' Monish added, 'We realized that by enhancing companies' contracting processes, we could streamline their financial flows, providing them a significant advantage.' This insight led the founders to establish Icertis' overarching vision—'Transform the foundation of commerce'.

Discussing Icertis's mission, Monish explained, 'We realized that to transform the foundation of commerce for all kinds of companies everywhere, we would need to become the contract management platform of the world.' Consequently, Icertis adopted the mission statement—'Be the contract management platform of the world'.

Icertis' purpose statement is: 'Build trust, strengthen bonds, and create a better world'. Monish explained its meaning saying, 'Our purpose statement logically extends the value proposition of the Icertis Contract Intelligence (ICI) platform. ICI uniquely structures and connects contract data, ensuring the intent of every contract is correctly recorded and fully accomplished. This helps companies keep their promises to their customers, partners, employees and each other.'

He expanded on this to say, 'When companies keep their promises, it **builds trust** between organizations and people and **strengthens the bonds** that form the foundation of commerce and society, ultimately helping to **create** a more ethical, equitable and sustainable **(better) world**.'

Monish believes that offering a best-in-class product that brings value to the customer is essential. However, it is not the only thing one must consider when starting a company. If one intends to build a company to go far, understanding its purpose, vision and mission, while focusing on establishment of a values-driven culture, is essential.

How Sirona Is Bridging the Gaps in the Women's Hygiene Market

In 2013, Deep Bajaj embarked on a weekend road trip from Delhi to Jaipur with his wife, Rashi. During this multi-hour journey, Rashi refrained from drinking water to avoid the discomfort of using public restrooms. Despite stopping at multiple petrol pumps and restaurants along the way, the absence of clean and satisfactory restroom facilities made her increasingly uncomfortable and dissatisfied. Deep noticed a striking variance in the restroom experience for men and women during this trip. Men could relieve themselves without direct surface contact by standing, while women had to clean seats or find ways to sit comfortably.

The situation escalated when Rashi became pregnant, making it even more challenging for her to use public restrooms. Deep also noticed that his mother, who had arthritis, faced similar difficulties. This led him to wonder why there couldn't be some way for women to relieve themselves while standing, just as men do. He was surprised to discover that while there were numerous feminine products in the beauty and cosmetics category, there seemed to be a dearth of innovative products in the feminine hygiene category. The market primarily consisted of sanitary pads, with minimal offerings to address other period-related issues such as pain, rashes and disposal. This realization prompted Deep to launch Sirona with a purpose to make feminine hygiene more convenient and dignified.

In 2014, through research and extensive experimentation, Deep developed the company's first product—PeeBuddy, India's first portable, disposable and funnel-shaped female urination device. In 2015, he obtained a patent for the design. In the first year after its launch, Deep reached out to friends and family for feedback. Deep said, 'Once the reviews started coming in, we knew we were on the right track.'

Although the product gained acceptance, finding a distribution channel to reach the masses was difficult, even in Delhi NCR. Medical stores, typically run by men, hesitated to stock the product due to the taboo associated with female urination devices. Distributors also turned it down as they could not understand the product. They did not consider it a serious product, especially since it had 'pee' in the name.

To overcome this ingrained mindset challenge, Deep and his team sought the support of doctors, who began recommending the product to their patients. The team also began listing PeeBuddy on e-commerce websites and promoting it through social media. Deep emphasized, 'Being a digital-first brand offers the advantage of gaining immediate consumer insights and rapid data acquisition from online platforms.' Customers could openly express their opinions online when they encountered issues or were dissatisfied with a product. Conversely, they enthusiastically shared their delight in discovering a problem-solving product that had transformed their lives. E-commerce platforms also provided valuable data on sales, geography, demographics and more, offering deep insights into customer profiles and purchasing preferences.

Building on the success of PeeBuddy, Sirona shifted its focus to menstrual hygiene. On average, menstruating women are estimated to use between 8000 to 17,000 sanitary pads during their lifetime.[2] The collective impact on landfill waste becomes significant when we consider the global population and the widespread reliance on disposable menstrual products.

To address this issue, Sirona introduced the menstrual cup, a compact, bell-shaped device designed for insertion into a person's vagina to collect menstrual blood. These cups are typically made of medical-grade silicone, ensuring safety and ease of use during menstruation. Notably, these cups can hold twice as much liquid as sanitary napkins and tampons. Their remarkable durability, lasting up to ten years, makes them both environmentally friendly and cost-effective. Moreover, menstrual cups offer unparalleled freedom of movement, eliminating concerns about leakage or discomfort during activities like swimming, trekking, exercise and sports.

As Sirona's dedication to the addressal of feminine hygiene concerns became apparent, female customers began sharing with the company additional challenges they faced. Most women used hot water bags or painkillers during menstruation to alleviate pain and discomfort, particularly at night. However, this was not always effective. In response, Sirona introduced India's first herbal pain relief patch, providing relief from pain for up to twelve hours. More importantly, this innovation allowed women to sleep more comfortably and perform better during their periods.

Deep said, 'Our mission is to positively impact women's lives by offering products that solve unaddressed feminine hygiene issues and share unbiased information that empowers them to make the right decisions. Before introducing any product to the market, we conduct thorough research and testing to ensure that the product is well-received and accepted by consumers.'

During one of the focus group discussions, young mothers shared their experiences with home pregnancy testing, describing it as cumbersome and annoying. The existing process required a woman to urinate into a bottle or container and then transfer a few drops of urine onto a plastic testing cassette using a dropper. This method resulted in excessive plastic usage as each pregnancy test involved multiple plastic components. Additionally, the use of numerous elements made home pregnancy testing expensive, while sometimes affecting the accuracy of the results.

'We decided to delve deeper into the process and realized that we could significantly streamline it by integrating HCG* test strips with PeeBuddy, simplifying the entire process in terms of usage, while reducing wastage. With PeeBuddy PregRx, women can now conveniently conduct pregnancy tests anywhere without needing additional accessories,' Deep explained.

The company has expanded its product range to include wet wipes, underarm sweat pads, oxo-biodegradable† disposal

---

* HCG is a hormone. Its presence in a woman's urine can be an indicator of pregnancy.

† Oxo-biodegradable refers to a type of plastic that is designed to undergo a process of degradation when exposed to oxygen, ultraviolet (UV) light and heat.

bags for sanitary waste and a complete range of hair removal products, including creams, face razors and body razors.

Sirona has rapidly risen as a prominent brand dedicated to addressing women's hygiene needs, spanning puberty to menopause. The brand has not only shattered taboos but also revolutionized the feminine hygiene landscape. Deep affirmed, 'Our vision is to eliminate the stigma surrounding menstrual hygiene and redefine femininity for the modern era.' In the past, women's health and hygiene were rarely talked about openly, related to whispers and myths. Sirona has changed that, openly encouraging women to prioritize their well-being.

3

Building a Start-Up's Culture

Culture eats strategy for breakfast.

—Peter Drucker, business thinker and author

The culture of any organization is built on its values, which act as a moral compass, guiding employee interaction within the organization, with customers and with stakeholders, as well as their approach to work. In start-ups, where the influence of a brand name is less, culture becomes crucial in defining the company's identity and attracting employees to the work.

I had the privilege of discussing this topic with **T.N. Hari, former head of HR at BigBasket, and co-founder of Artha School of Entrepreneurship**. He has helped shape five successful exits in different industries, including an IPO on NASDAQ. He is also a strategic advisor to Fundamentum, a growth stage venture capital fund, and one of India's leading business authors.

Here are some lessons I learned from Hari:

The culture of a start-up is synonymous with its founders

In early-stage start-ups, the culture often mirrors the personalities of the founders. Their preferences and expectations shape hiring decisions and significantly impact how employees are treated. A founder's actions—encouraging critical thinking, dismissing employee opinions, promoting teamwork, or exhibiting favouritism—are visible to all and profoundly influence the company's culture. Hari said, 'By modelling desired behaviours and encouraging others to do the same, founders can foster a strong and positive company culture.'

This point can be illustrated with an example from the movie, *Chak De! India*. In the film, the issue between the two key players, Preeti Sabharwal (Sagarika Ghatge) and Komal Chautala (Chitrashi Rawat), arose due to their competitive nature and desire to be the team's top striker. Both players were highly skilled and had strong personalities, which led to friction on the field. Other players frequently discussed their rivalry, which affected team cohesion. Kabir Khan (Shah Rukh Khan), the coach of the Indian women's hockey team, resolved this issue by emphasizing the importance of teamwork over individual glory. Ultimately, the players realized that cooperation is essential for the team's success, and they focused on working together rather than outperforming each other, strengthening the team's overall performance and setting an example for everyone. This example illustrates that culture is not about what is said or displayed on walls, but rather about the consistent behaviours demonstrated by key leaders in the company.

Reflecting further on the role of founders, Hari added, 'Founders should have the humility to understand that nobody, including themselves, is perfect. As start-ups grow, founders too need to improve and evolve as leaders and individuals. They have to be open-minded to learning from their mistakes and from feedback given by more experienced individuals such as investors, advisors, veteran entrepreneurs and experienced employees.'

Every company's culture is unique and should be handled carefully

The culture within a start-up is greatly affected by the nature of the industry it operates within. For instance, the culture of a manufacturing company is different from that of a technology company. Attempting to replicate one company's culture in another often leads to inefficiencies and/or failures. Hari clarified this point by citing examples from BigBasket and Daksh where, as the HR head, he was responsible for shaping the culture.

BigBasket is a low-margin grocery delivery business, where 75 per cent of the workforce is blue-collar. The company focuses on recruiting people who may not have specialized skills, advanced education or extensive experience but possess the general skills and abilities necessary to perform the tasks required for the job. It implements strong processes and nurtures its employees to become outstanding performers. Here, people are not fired solely based on performance; even if an employee fails, they are given the opportunity of moving to a different role. Moreover, language proficiency, particularly in English, is not a prerequisite as long as the individuals can execute their tasks effectively.

Unlike many companies with an experimental and quick-fail approach, BigBasket takes a more calculated path, expanding into new ventures only when there is a compelling necessity. 'When everyone was talking about ten-minute delivery, BigBasket didn't opt for that because we couldn't see a compelling need,' Hari explained.

In contrast, Daksh (a renowned BPO acquired by IBM in 2004) had a markedly different culture. It prioritized hiring from prestigious educational institutions and top companies, offering high salaries to attract top-tier talent. Here, achieving performance benchmarks in a specified timeframe was essential. This culture resonated with their high-margin business model, emphasizing communication skills and pedigree.

Hari emphasized on this point and said, 'Everybody is different. Each of us is unique. You cannot be who I am, and I can't be who you are. The same applies to companies. Company cultures vary significantly; each is unique. There's no absolute good or bad. Both organizations—BigBasket and Daksh—designed their cultures according to their sector needs and achieved the desired growth.'

It is important to note that companies in the same industry can also have different cultures based on their specific objectives, leadership styles and employee demographics. Hari cautioned that start-ups sometimes recruit accomplished leaders from different companies or industries who seek to promptly overhaul the start-up culture using their own ideologies and prior experiences. These endeavours frequently backfire, causing discomfort among employees who struggle to adapt to the sudden cultural shift.

As start-ups expand, their culture must evolve in tandem

It's crucial for companies to regularly assess and nurture their culture to ensure it remains aligned with their evolving vision, while supporting the well-being and productivity of their employees.

We can better understand this point using the example of MakeMyTrip (MMT). During its early stages, MMT focused on selling air tickets in a market where airline suppliers were limited and competition was fierce. However, the uniformity of air tickets across all sales channels created a commodity-like business landscape, leading to low negotiating power for MMT. Despite amassing a large subscriber base, profitability remained a challenge.

But this significant subscriber base became invaluable when MMT expanded into the hotel industry. Unlike the few suppliers in air ticketing, the hotel sector had many providers, requiring robust negotiation and onboarding processes. Additionally, scaling up technology integration with thousands of hotels posed significant technological and operational hurdles. This shift demanded new processes and people with different capabilities.

Hari emphasized, 'During such scenarios, a founder's role in overseeing the integration of external talent from diverse cultures with internal talent and processes is crucial. Simultaneously, it's essential to instil new processes and ideas that align with the requirements of the new business.'

Further expansion occurred when MMT acquired brands like Goibibo and redBus. These additions introduced teams from different cultures, suppliers with other processes and customers with varying expectations. Hari said, 'For successful mergers and acquisitions, mutual respect is critical for both companies, especially between the senior management teams.' He believes that any sudden change in reporting relationship from one organization to another can lead to chaos. Hence, it is essential to maintain the existing reporting structures, except for the top management, for at least twelve months.

Balance haste with thoughtfulness when hiring or firing talent

Hiring external talent often becomes necessary for any rapidly growing start-up. During the recruitment process, founders tend to seek leaders with experience in managing large-scale operations, assuming that managing scale equates to an ability to build for scale. However, these are distinct skills.

In a scaled environment, leaders often oversee a sizable team that resolves issues before they reach the top management. Consequently, they might lose their hands-on problem-solving abilities within their specific functions. However, in a start-up, leaders must be prepared to engage from the ground up and take responsibility for building for scale. Hari told me, 'This requires skills that many haven't acquired, as their experience primarily lies in managing scale, not building it.' He emphasized that when assessing a leader's ability to build for scale, founders must seek traits such as first-principles thinking, problem-solving skills, a keen interest in fundamental concepts and a childlike curiosity to understand the business.

Moreover, integrating external senior hires with internally nurtured teams can be a challenge. The clash between these groups can lead to the downfall of a promising start-up. That's why, when interviewing for senior roles, it is crucial to assess whether the candidates can appreciate the work done within the company and integrate well with the existing employees and earn their respect.

'I've seen so many lateral hires from large companies fail because they have lost their ability to be hands-on. As a result, their teams in start-ups, who were hands-on, lost respect for them. I think leaders joining start-ups should be hands-on and bring certain additional perspectives that the existing employees don't have,' Hari said.

The way a company handles employee terminations speaks volumes for its culture. Hari emphasized that unjustified firings can severely damage the reputation of a start-up and its ability to attract future talent. The process should stay transparent and non-toxic, even during layoffs tied to performance, integrity issues or a downturn. Hari underlined this point saying, 'Founders must communicate the genuine reasons behind layoffs. If financial constraints are the cause, attributing the layoffs to individual performance is dishonest and can damage the company's brand image.'

Hari also stressed the need to treat departing employees respectfully, saying, 'Existing employees and the market observe the departure process. Securing the loyalty of the remaining employees post-layoffs and alleviating their concerns is vital. To achieve this, founders should organize a town hall to directly address the remaining team members, reassuring them that the layoffs have concluded, while reaffirming their commitment to hard work and cost management, thus reinforcing the message that the business will continue to grow.'

Comprehend culture but avoid excessive promotion, and ensure it is documented

Based on their approach to culture, start-ups can be classified into three types:

1. **Clueless about culture:** These start-ups have no clear understanding of their culture. They may not prioritize or even acknowledge the importance of having a culture.
2. **Appreciate the importance of culture:** They deeply understand their culture but talk about it in a subtle way to get the message across without making anyone feel excluded. They accommodate diverse candidates and remain open to learning new things to improve their culture.
3. **Showcase cult-like culture:** They consider their culture the greatest and over-popularize it, creating a sense of exclusion by essentially saying, 'If you don't fit into our culture, you don't belong here'. But this approach has its pitfalls. For example, if a start-up over-emphasizes that it rewards everyone equally, top performers may feel disinclined to being part of such a flat culture. Also, such start-ups may not be able to attract diverse candidates and may face difficulty in adapting to changing circumstances.

For start-ups, Hari advocated for the second type. As business grows, founders may not always be available to demonstrate culture through their behaviour. Therefore, having a written record of core values becomes beneficial for maintaining consistency in culture as the company scales. To make organizational values relatable to employees, they must be explained through examples. For instance, if integrity is a core value of a company and it is not explained correctly, employees could think that if they are not stealing money, they are demonstrating integrity. However, integrity may also mean giving credit to peers for their work, even when they are not present.

Hari added, 'To drive culture effectively, it has to be integrated into company policies over time. For instance, if fostering an employee-friendly environment is a cultural goal, the company's policies must align with that objective. This ensures that the desired culture is embedded in the daily operations and practices of the organization.

Case Studies
How Fractal Built Its Culture

Fractal, an Indian unicorn renowned for its analytics and AI expertise, shines as a 'Made in India' brand, serving many prestigious global brands. Srikanth Velamakanni, co-founder at Fractal, believes that one of the key factors that sets Fractal apart from its competitors is its distinctive culture. He emphasizes that in the realm of B2B, the individuals who comprise a company play a pivotal role in shaping its reputation. They act as ambassadors, representing the brand during client interactions. He said, 'How employees conduct themselves reflects the values and culture that the company upholds. Clients consider a company's culture when it comes to forging long-lasting partnerships.'

But it's important to note that Fractal wasn't always as focused on its culture as it is now. From its inception in 2000 until 2007, the leadership did not prioritize building a strong organizational culture. Srikanth said, 'Back then, when the company was small, and everyone worked from a single office, we believed that if everyone worked well together, the culture would take care of itself. So, we remained focused on growing the business.'

By the end of 2007, Fractal had grown to a team of 100 people. However, this growth came with its own set of problems. While the company was expanding to different countries and hiring new people, a few of the co-founders left. These exits led to misunderstandings that threatened to disrupt the company's progress. Furthermore, because Fractal was renowned for its expertise in analytics, other companies aggressively attempted to recruit their employees. This brought its own considerable pressure to the leadership. Srikanth remembered this phase: 'We lost 25 per cent of our team. It was like starting almost from scratch.'

The growing issues made both Srikanth and Pranay Agrawal—co-founder at Fractal—realize that they needed to fix the company culture. Srikanth explained, 'A company's culture is deeply connected to its core values. So, the leadership team spent five days figuring out what the company's core values should be.'

Srikanth recognized that merely displaying company values on the wall was not sufficient. He believed that it was crucial for everyone in the company to not only comprehend these values but also apply them in their daily work. To achieve this, discussions about the values took place during significant gatherings like town halls and team meetings.

To gauge how well employees understood these values, Fractal introduced a 'values audit'. Every quarter, all employees were asked to share their opinions to determine if the company was genuinely embracing these values. They used a rating system from one to ten for each value. The results consistently showed ratings of around 6 to 7. It was soon found that employees found it somewhat challenging to recall or explain these values. This indicated that substantial work was still required to deeply integrate the values into the company's everyday operations.

A few years later, Srikanth came across *The Advantage* by Patrick Lencioni—a book that transformed his perspective. He realized that using action-oriented language rather than abstract nouns made values much easier to grasp. For instance, 'integrity' is an abstract concept, but 'act with integrity' shows precisely what it means in action. Srikanth promptly gathered Fractal's executive team for a workshop to rephrase and clarify their values so that more people could understand them. Srikanth explained, 'It took an entire year to implement, explain and test our new values because values hold immense importance. We couldn't simply replace them overnight.'

However, this was just the beginning of their transformation journey. Srikanth and Pranay recognized the necessity of establishing a comprehensive framework to ensure the well-being of their employees. This realization led to the creation of the 'People Principles'. These consisted of seven guiding principles that revolved around trust, transparency and freedom. Srikanth explained, 'The primary objective of these principles is to minimize professional stress for our employees as much as possible.'

Under the 'People Principles', employees have the autonomy to modify company policies, select their preferred roles, projects, managers and mentors, and even change career tracks. They are empowered to set their own targets and determine their goal achievement percentages, which serves as the basis for salary increments and variable pay. Additionally, Fractal does not question employees' reimbursement bills. The key is trust. The company offers flexible work arrangements, with no fixed 'in' or 'out' times, and allows employees to work from home.

To keep employees well-informed about company affairs, weekly seventy-five-minute town hall meetings are conducted. Here, the CPO and CEO address employee questions and provide updates on the latest developments. Srikanth emphasized, 'What we share with our Board, we also share with our people.'

Srikanth wants Fractal to be the BMW of analytics. He said to me, 'If we take great care of our people, they will take care of our clients.' To maintain a client-centric approach, all meetings at Fractal, whether they are board meetings, town halls or team meetings, commence with the presentation of the Net Promoter Score (NPS). This score provides valuable insight into clients' genuine perceptions of Fractal's services, highlighting the company's commitment to evaluating its success through the eyes of its clients. Additionally, Fractal conducts weekly sessions to discuss the latest industry trends and strategies to address client issues.

Fractal has established specific practices for onboarding new employees and managing departures. One notable practice is the 'exit town hall'. When a number of employees are leaving Fractal in a given month, the leadership assembles them for an open conversation. During this session, departing employees are encouraged to freely express their reasons for leaving, and provide feedback on what did not work for them at Fractal, along with suggestions for improvement. Fractal values this feedback and uses it to enhance its practices.

Srikanth emphasized the importance of treating departing employees with care, stating, 'How we treat people on their way out is crucial because they remain influential as brand ambassadors. They should feel positive about their time at Fractal from the moment they join, throughout their tenure, and even after they leave.'

Furthermore, Fractal introduced a range of employee benefits, including free meals and employee stock options. The combined impact of these initiatives led to a significant decrease in attrition rates and substantial revenue growth for the company.

As of August 2023, Fractal has been on the Great Places to Work list for the last six years.[1] Srikanth affirms, 'Culture is the sole differentiator in the long term, and it should not be underestimated. Competitors can replicate someone's strategy, tactics, products, or intellectual property. However, replicating someone else's culture is exceptionally difficult.'

How Licious Created a Rewarding Workplace for Its Employees

Licious is a versatile organization that operates in multiple sectors, including agri-business (meat production), FMCG (meat processing and packaging), brand development (striving to become India's favourite food brand), R&D (continuous product innovation), a tech platform (D2C business), a complex supply chain (sourcing meat from various suppliers), logistics (ensuring last-mile delivery to customers) and retail (experience centres). Managing such a diverse organization with innovative practices requires top-level talent from different fields.

Recognising early on that the sector would require Licious to be a talent factory rather than simply sourcing from an existing talent pool was crucial. Licious' co-founders Abhay Hanjura and Vivek Gupta set aside 20 per cent of the company on Day 1 as an ESOP pool. Abhay explained this saying, 'We realised that without fancy titles and large pay checks, we had a unique dream. To get people to participate in it, we needed to make a serious commitment to long-term value creation.'

Vivek added, 'To build a transformational, category-leading food brand in one of the most complex and underserved sectors, required high calibre talent with a lot of conviction.' In its early days, Licious faced challenges in attracting the desired talent due to the stigma associated with the meat industry. Nevertheless, the founders undertook significant efforts to clarify why and how Licious aimed to revolutionize one of the oldest and largest food categories for the better. This narrative of purpose proved instrumental in helping potential employees see that joining Licious meant becoming a part of a significant industry transformation.

Licious has been very careful in selecting talented individuals at all levels. Abhay mentioned, 'Our journey is far from ordinary; it's a long path filled with challenges. We're not here to do what's already been done; we're here to build for the future. So, we look for individuals who thrive in uncharted territory, who discover their true potential even in moments of failure, and who emerge with remarkable stories of hard-fought victories. We prefer people who think of themselves as the authors of their destiny, not victims of circumstances.'

One of the qualities Licious seeks in individuals is an obsession for quality. They should also have a real interest in understanding meat and its various products. Regardless of their job title and role, every selected candidate is provided with the opportunity to visit the Licious factory before joining. This helps them learn about the unique nature of Licious meat and how it is processed.

Once these talented individuals join the company, Licious focuses on providing them with the right environment to thrive in their roles. Vivek emphasized this point saying, 'Licious isn't striving to be just another big corporation; instead, it's committed to creating a genuine space where individuals can be themselves, work together, and find creative solutions that leave a lasting impact.' Abhay added, 'Licious fosters an enjoyable work environment, where problem-solving is a source of joy rather than feeling like a burden.'

Since Licious is pioneering many aspects of the meat industry, not only in India but worldwide, failures are bound to happen. In accordance with the founders' philosophy, Licious has a unique approach to dealing with failures. Even significant failures are not met with punishment; instead, the entire organization supports the individual facing the setback, encouraging them to turn the experience into a stepping stone to success.

However, when it comes to the quality of thinking and action, Licious maintains unwavering and non-negotiable standards. Whether these pertain to products, services or technology, Licians (employees at Licious) leave no stone unturned to consistently deliver the highest quality. Abhay said, 'Quality is at the core of consumer trust. We hold ourselves to an exceptionally high standard to provide the superior quality consumers deserve.'

One of the core values at Licious is an unwavering commitment to treating everyone, regardless of their level or role, with utmost respect and dignity. In many societies, including India, 'butchers', despite their significant expertise in meat and understanding of customer preferences, often do not receive the recognition and respect they deserve. In a move to change this norm and showcase profound respect for the profession, Licious has rebranded the title of 'butcher' to 'Meat Technician'. With this new title, individuals can now speak about their roles with enhanced confidence, recognizing the importance of their work in delivering quality meat products to customers.

Moreover, Licious offers substantial career growth opportunities for its Meat Technicians, offering skill-based roles and a corresponding pay structure. These roles include Meat Handlers (individuals responsible for packing), Meat Processors (occupying a semi-skilled role responsible for processing) and Meat Artists (highly skilled individuals responsible for cutting meats to meet various regional requirements).

Furthermore, there are pathways for further advancement within the company, enabling individuals to progress into managerial and executive positions. Naveen Kumar, head of

Human Resources at Licious, emphasized this aspect, 'We don't define Licians' growth prospects by their existing roles, past experiences, or educational backgrounds. If there's potential and a determination to make a difference, we'll take chances. If a Lician can perform three roles effectively, we'll entrust them with a fourth.'

Licious strongly believes in the significance of food and health for everyone. It provides snacks and lunch for all its employees. Most of the company's meat technicians come from small towns and villages. Recognizing that they live away from their homes, the company goes the extra mile by providing dinner, ensuring their nutritional needs are met.

Furthermore, Licious extends its care through additional benefits such as insurance, medical coverage and learning opportunities, available to all its employees. Naveen elucidates the company philosophy, stating, 'We firmly believe that if we take care of our people, they will also reciprocate with their best efforts for the organization.'

Like the meat technicians, Licious also has another important blue-collar workforce—the delivery personnel. Each Licious delivery person approaches their role with the mindset that they are delivering something special to enhance an occasion in the customer's life. They undergo extensive training about Licious' products to ensure they can respond to any last-minute customer queries. Moreover, they receive training on how to interact respectfully and authentically with customers. In cases where Licious delivery personnel hail from a specific area, they are typically assigned orders in that vicinity. This strategic allocation helps them save time in locating the delivery destination. Furthermore, by consistently delivering orders in their own area, they have the opportunity to establish a rapport with repeat customers.

Abhay highlights Licious' performance evaluation approach, saying, 'In our assessment, we place equal value on two aspects: first, the achievement of goals, which is the "what" of delivery, and second, living our values at work, which represents the "how" of delivery. To ensure objectivity, we gather feedback from all relevant stakeholders who collaborate with our team members.' Naveen adds, 'Licians are recognized with value cards when they exhibit specific behaviours. We also gather feedback on our policies and collect their Net Promoter Score (NPS).'

Licious is apparently the first Indian start-up to offer Employee Stock Ownership Plans (ESOPs) to blue-collar employees, in addition to the corporate workforce. Vivek stated, 'This initiative fosters an ownership mindset in every Lician.' After the one-year period, Licians also have the option of anytime liquidation of ESOPs without any associated terms and conditions. The company sets aside a pool of secondary funds every year to enable anytime liquidation.

Vivek added, 'At Licious, we have been experiencing unprecedented growth in a highly unorganized market. Our employees' contribution to this growth trajectory has been significant, and incentivizing them well is among our priorities. We are committed to helping Licians meet their personal and financial goals through wealth creation as we organize the market. Making vesting and buying ESOPs anytime signifies our dedication to the same. It is the kind of wealth creation opportunity for employees that India has not seen before.'

It is inspiring to see that Licious has positively impacted the lives of numerous employees, including blue-collar workers by providing them with a great workplace and opportunities to build wealth. Vivek emphasizes, 'We are not perfect, but every day as we travel to the office, our goal is to move closer to perfection in everything we do—be it serving our customers, supporting our employees or contributing to the environment.'

How BigBasket Built a Customer-Centric and Employee-Friendly Culture

Hari Menon, co-founder and CEO of BigBasket, said, 'Grocery is a consumer business, and in the consumer business the single most important thing is the consumer experience. Therefore, from day one, their happiness has been our priority. In our culture, we prioritize integrating consumer sensitivity across our workforce.'

But before delving into the BigBasket culture, let us spend a moment on its core values, which help its teams deliver on the cultural aspect. Hari explained, 'We need to become stronger and bigger in a peaceful and harmonious manner. Therefore, following these values is extremely important for us.' The primary value treasured at BigBasket is respect for people. 'Respect for people is often discussed in organizations but poorly practised. In some environments, individuals experience or witness yelling, screaming and demeaning behaviour in front of peers. This is unacceptable to us. We do not tolerate anger, shouting or disrespect toward anyone, regardless of their level or capabilities. Fundamental respect is a necessity for every human being,' Hari stated emphatically.

The second core value significant to BigBasket is integrity. Hari said, 'Integrity goes beyond honesty regarding financial matters. For us, it's about truthfulness in every aspect. For instance, it's crucial for our people to have the courage to say "I don't know" when they genuinely don't have the answer. Equally important is acknowledging and crediting others for their contributions, even in their absence.'

The third value at BigBasket is transparency. Hari explained, 'We value complete openness and accessibility. Initially, our offices lacked cabins to foster approachability. While this setup was appreciated, we recognized the importance of personal space for thinking. Thus, we introduced cabins, not for constant occupancy, but to offer moments of solitude when needed. Despite having titles, we maintain a flat organizational structure.' Hari further explained, 'All key metrics, from operational performance to the NPS score, are openly displayed not only at our corporate offices, but also in our warehouses. This transparency ensures that our employees remain motivated and informed about the company's performance, particularly in terms of customer satisfaction.'

And finally, the fourth value inculcated in the company culture is humility. As Hari explained, 'For us, humility is all about being real and genuine, even when we speak to the media.' He added, 'No one tries to make themselves bigger than what they really are. We are not here to win accolades or take shortcuts; we are here to solve customers' problems and do something meaningful for them.'

Talking further about BigBasket culture, Hari noted the importance of bringing ownership to every role, even when individuals may not completely control certain aspects, 'The expectation to own something beyond one's control may be uncomfortable. However, to get something done for the customer, multiple teams and functions have to work together, and we need people to step up and try to make things happen, no matter what. This approach cultivates an accountability mindset, encouraging individuals to take ownership rather than adopting a "not my job" mentality.'

Hari shared that many projects at BigBasket have highly aggressive timelines, saying, 'In the face of tight deadlines, people commonly experience anxiety. Therefore, we highlight the fundamental purpose behind setting ambitious targets while affirming our confidence in their attainability. To ease concerns, we clarify that falling short of these goals won't incur negative consequences. However, it remains paramount to demonstrate effort and commitment in reaching them.'

BigBasket has over 35,000 employees, 75 per cent of whom are blue-collared, including packers, stackers, delivery boys, etc. They are expected to come to their respective offices at 6.30 a.m. and deliver orders by 7 a.m., with a smile. If on any given day, thirty people do not turn up, the company cannot make their deliveries efficiently. As Hari said, 'From our warehouse to our last-mile delivery, BigBasket is a very operationally intensive business, and we need to be sure that employees at all levels are motivated.'

In terms of rewards and recognition, BigBasket has implemented a robust system to acknowledge and appreciate its employees. Every month, the top 20 per cent of employees in each region are rewarded for their exceptional performance, while the bottom 20 per cent are provided with valuable training opportunities to improve their skills. Additionally, the company hosts quarterly BB Rockstar awards at the regional level, where the leadership team from the Head Office personally visits to present these accolades. Furthermore, BigBasket conducts an annual national BB Rockstar award ceremony, honouring the top thirty employees across the country. These deserving winners, accompanied by their families, are invited to the corporate office in Bengaluru, to attend the prestigious Annual Day event, where they receive well-deserved recognition on stage amid the thunderous applause of their peers.

BigBasket also runs a Trust for the blue-collar workforce. Employees who have spent over twelve months at the company are eligible for educational assistance (reimbursement of school and college fees, cost of textbooks, etc.) for themselves and their families. The company also helps its employees identify suitable vocational courses to enhance their employability, while also aiming to create jobs for the dependents of employees.

Given that many blue-collar workers in cities like Bengaluru and Delhi come from rural areas, access to clean drinking water, safety measures and hygiene is an important concern. In response, the company actively ensures these essential aspects for its employees.

The company has also started a programme called Neev, in which top-performing seniors (Team Leads), handhold new employees for sixty days to get them up to speed. To keep the motivation levels of Team Leads high, they are incentivized with several benefits. Apart from Neev, the company has several other employee training programmes.

One of the essential learnings I took away from my discussion with Hari was that building a culture is not a quick-fix job, but a daily responsibility for the leadership. When team members do not align with the culture the leadership strives for, it poses a challenge. Hari suggests there are two approaches to handling such a situation. First, investing time and effort to bridge the gap and finding common ground is crucial. This involves open and constructive conversations to understand each other's perspectives and beliefs. While it may require patience, achieving alignment is beneficial for everyone involved. Second, it is equally important to recognize when it is best to part ways. If someone consistently cannot align with the organization's core principles and values, it can create friction and hinder progress. Though such a decision is always difficult, it is sometimes better to part ways early than to compromise the overall culture and vision of the company.

PART III

Market Research and Opportunity Analysis

4

Leveraging Insights to Uncover Hidden Opportunities

Great insight comes from seeing something as odd and finding out why.

—Philip Kotler, author, consultant and professor,
Kellogg School of Management

Insight goes beyond surface-level observations, delving into the motivations, preferences and needs that drive consumer behaviour. Insights empower businesses to create valuable products that align with consumer desires and craft compelling marketing messages that deeply resonate with their audience.

I had the privilege of discussing this topic with one of India's most respected experts in consumer knowledge, **Dr Vispy Doctor, chairman of the Ormax Group of Companies**, which includes **Ormax Consultants, India's first qualitative research firm, and Ormax Media, one of the largest media**

research companies in India, among other firms. Ormax has been instrumental in creating numerous iconic brands, including Fogg, Moov, Krack, Thumbs Up, Urban Company, Cadbury's, Titan, Pidilite and many others.

Here are some lessons I learned from Vispy:

Understanding consumer needs is key for generating meaningful insights

Vispy said, 'The term "insight" is often used loosely. Frequently, what is referred to as insights are merely observations or thoughts. True insights need to be revelatory—they should uncover something that's previously unrecognized. They ought to create an "aha!" moment, offering perspectives people hadn't considered before.'

Insights often stem from unmet needs in consumers' lives. By gaining a profound understanding of these needs, the challenges that consumers encounter and the solutions they actively seek, businesses can cultivate valuable insights. Typically, there are four types of needs:

Satisfied needs: These needs are already satisfied, and as a result, they may not lead to insights, given that the consumers' requirements are already met. For instance, a smartphone equipped with an excellent camera, sufficient storage, long battery life and desired apps and features would typically meet the expectations of most individuals. Consequently, they might not express dissatisfaction or actively pursue innovative ideas for revolutionary changes.

Unsatisfied needs: These needs persist due to shortcomings in the available solution. For instance, Iodex provided pain relief, but consumers found its sticky texture and strong odour discomforting. This led to the emergence of Moov, offering a non-sticky, odourless alternative.

Realized needs: These needs are widely recognized and prompt proactive searches for solutions. Paras Pharma, for instance, developed Itch Guard to tackle the prevalent issue of itching caused by fungal infections. The product is tailored to provide discreet relief, considering the social stigma associated with scratching in public.

Unrealized needs: These needs aren't consciously recognized until a solution is presented. For example, until Apple unveiled the iPod, people hadn't realized their desire for a portable music player capable of storing thousands of songs.

Vispy added, 'The strength of a profound insight lies in sparking the consumer sentiment of "I want this".'

Insights are not static; they evolve over time

Consumers constantly evolve, and businesses must identify shifts in consumer mindset and adapt their products and communication strategies accordingly.

For example, Thums Up made its market debut in 1977 as a party drink, with communication focused on 'food, friends and Thums Up'. However, this generic positioning did not deliver the desired results. Recognizing the need for change, Thums Up shifted gears and associated itself with manliness and macho-ness.

During this period, India faced significant financial strain and job scarcity. Thums Up's advertisements depicted the dissatisfaction of the Indian populace through the portrayal of the 'angry young man', intertwining anger with the imagery of manliness and macho-ness. This strategic move propelled Thums Up to remarkable popularity and market share growth.

However, with the liberalization of India, these ads lost their appeal. The Thums Up team sought advice from Vispy. Ormax's research unveiled that the dismantling of the License Raj led to increased job opportunities, bringing about a shift in people's sentiments. Consequently, Indian consumers were no longer as discontented, making Thums Up's association with the angry young man outdated. Vispy commented, 'Consumers had evolved, but Thums Up's proposition had not.'

Based on Ormax's advice, Thums Up transitioned its communication from anger to bravery, representing an alternative facet of manliness and macho-ness. The Thums Up campaigns began portraying 'courage within a person', which deeply resonated with the audience and proved immensely successful. Vispy said, 'Bravery also lost its appeal after a few years. So, we repeated the exercise and redefined the proposition.'

Insight can create a new leader even in a crowded market

By thoroughly understanding consumer needs, preferences and pain points, businesses can discover unique opportunities, differentiate themselves from competitors, and become more relevant to consumers.

For example, in India, there was a lack of established perfume brands, and people primarily used deodorants as a substitute. Before 2011, HUL's Axe was the market leader in the crowded deodorant industry. Darshan Patel, the founder of Vini Cosmetics, assigned Vispy with the task of identifying an opportunity for another deodorant brand. Ormax's research revealed that while people were satisfied with the fragrance and pricing of their deodorants, a common complaint was that 'deodorants get over fast'.

Most deodorant brands in the market were using aerosol pumps, which relied on compressed gases to propel the liquid as a fine spray. In contrast, Vini Cosmetics decided to use non-aerosol pumps that didn't rely on compressed gases. Instead, they functioned through manual pumping to dispense the liquid. This innovation ensured that their deodorants lasted for forty days, double the duration of competitors that typically lasted for twenty days.

While everyone else was marketing their deodorants based on smell, Darshan Patel decided to focus on longevity. Fogg was launched at the end of 2011 with the tagline *'Bina gas wala spray'* (deodorant without gas). Thanks to its unique formulation and extended longevity, Fogg quickly became the largest-selling deodorant in India.

Insight-based communication can make a brand more memorable

Ideas rooted in insights can enhance communication, making it more compelling and relevant. One afternoon, Darshan Patel recognized that highlighting his deodorant's reduced gas content could boost sales. To showcase this, he sprayed deodorant from two cans—Fogg and another brand—into separate glasses. The Fogg glass visibly filled with each spray, while the other barely did, revealing the dissipated gas.

This simple yet impactful demonstration could have conveyed to the target audience that they were receiving greater value. Capitalizing on this experiment, Fogg's advertisements amplified the message, swiftly catapulting Fogg into overnight success and establishing it as India's largest-selling deodorant brand within just two years.

Keenly observing people in everyday life can spark new opportunities

In established categories, consumer viewpoints are often based on their experiences and preferences. However, people may struggle to articulate their thoughts clearly. Observing people's behaviour across various settings, such as shopping venues or home environments, can help overcome this challenge. After compiling observations, it is beneficial to ask qualitative questions to delve deeper into the consumer mindset.

For instance, Darshan Patel, while working with his family business Paras Pharmaceuticals, made a keen observation at Mumbai's Churchgate station. He noticed numerous women with cracked heels, which not only affected their appearance but also posed risks of pain, infection and discomfort while walking. This observation became the catalyst for the inception of Krack cream.

Notably, the initial act of noticing cracked heels is a common observation that many people could have made. However, the process of uncovering hidden pain points and realizing the absence of effective solutions were crucial steps that transformed a mere observation into a valuable insight.

Vispy said, 'Many start-ups begin with ideas, technology, funding, drive and passion but often lack a deep understanding of their consumers. However, successful start-ups begin their journey with an insight. It is this deeper understanding of consumer needs and the ability to identify untapped opportunities that sets successful businesses apart.'

Case Studies

How SUGAR Accelerated Its Growth Using Consumer and Category Insights

In 2012, the availability of beauty products in India was limited, with traditional players mainly targeting women over thirty. Additionally, platforms like Nykaa had not been launched yet. Motivated to fill this gap, married couple Vineeta Singh and Kaushik Mukherjee embarked on creating FAB BAG, a beauty discovery and subscription platform that offered carefully curated bags filled with top-rated products from international brands for women aged twenty-one to thirty, residing in metros and tier-1 cities.

By 2014, the company had achieved profitability, generating nearly $1 million in revenue with a subscriber base of 15,000 women. Despite this success, scaling the business presented a formidable challenge due to the high costs associated with acquiring new customers.

One day, while conducting an in-depth analysis of the FAB BAG subscriber data, Vineeta identified a prevalent customer request—for transfer-proof, long-lasting make-up that did not leave marks on cups or clothing and was ideal for extended wear throughout the day. Kaushik remarked, 'We recognized that while the formulations of many international brands were excellent, they were not specifically designed for the diverse skin tones of Indian women and the unique weather conditions and pollution levels in India.' This core realization ignited a spark in the duo to pivot from being a subscription partner of international brands to manufacturers of budget-friendly make-up products for a younger audience. They aimed to cater to local preferences with long-lasting, transfer-proof formulations. Thus, they launched SUGAR in 2015.

Make-up can be broadly categorized into four main areas: nails, eyes, face and lips. While there are popular products across all age groups, specific categories tend to be more favoured among particular age groups, influenced by factors such as ease of use, familiarity and the level of make-up expertise. Nail polish and eye make-up, like kajal, are commonly used by teenagers and young adults. On the other hand, lipstick is often a symbol of a more mature make-up user and is typically associated with preparing for special occasions. Face make-up, encompassing products such as primer, compact and foundation, demands more knowledge and involvement. It is more nuanced and is generally preferred by individuals aged thirty and above. By this age, users have typically acquired enough experience to apply and manage their make-up effectively.

Recognizing that a woman's make-up journey often starts with kajal, SUGAR initially prioritized it, specifically targeting women in the eighteen to twenty-five age group. The kajal and eyeliner categories are highly competitive. What set SUGAR apart was its decision to manufacture the product in Germany, but specifically formulated for Indian consumers. 'Back then, many customers bought their make-up abroad or asked family members travelling overseas to bring back products. Given this context, we decided that we would manufacture our products at the state-of-the-art facilities in countries like Germany and Italy,' Kaushik explained.

The 'Made in Germany' label lent the product the allure of quality and craftsmanship, creating a strong appeal among customers. SUGAR initially targeted FAB BAG's subscriber base to gauge their response, which was overwhelmingly positive.

In 2016, SUGAR launched a long-lasting liquid lipstick that could last for ten to twelve hours, reducing the need for frequent reapplications. This product became popular among younger users who have active lifestyles that require durable make-up. Encouraged by the positive response, SUGAR attempted to market this unique product to women over thirty. However, they soon discovered that the product's appeal was not universal across all age groups. Women over thirty, especially those over thirty-five, reported a slight drying sensation when the liquid lipstick set on their lips. Further research then revealed that as people age their skin tends to lose hydration, making it less supple. The SUGAR team also came to realize that as women age, their make-up preferences lean more toward comfort. Products that are easy to wear, feel weightless on the skin, and do not cause discomfort or dryness, are more appealing, even if they faded sooner. Kaushik said, 'This insight helped us realize that recognizing distinctions in the preferences of different target segments is a crucial aspect of product development in the beauty industry.'

SUGAR has positioned itself as an innovative brand in the beauty industry. To consistently introduce new products, the team actively engages with customers to understand their evolving needs while closely monitoring global trends, ranging from the latest New York fashion runway looks to viral TikTok trends. The insights gathered from this broad environment serve as the foundation for identifying potential product ideas.

A few years ago, the SUGAR team researched into where globally recognized make-up brands made most of their profits. Interestingly, a large portion came from sales of foundation as it forms the base of make-up. However, foundation did not sell as well in India, even from the larger legacy brands. This discrepancy intrigued the team, leading to further consumer insight studies.

They found that the main challenge consumers had with foundation was blending it properly to suit their skin tones, which typically requires a separate blending brush. But, in India, consumers were reluctant to purchase an additional product just for blending. Instead, they tried to blend the foundation using their fingers, which often did not give the desired result, causing consumers to believe the foundation was not suitable for them. SUGAR came up with the solution of a dual-ended functionality stick, with foundation on one side and a high-quality brush on the other. This design allowed users to apply and blend the foundation seamlessly with a single product. SUGAR launched the product in twenty-two shades, catering to a wide range of skin tones, from light to deep. They educated consumers about the product through various influencer and content marketing strategies.

SUGAR's products were widely available in high street stores, kiosks in shopping malls and shop-in-shop at large-format retailers such as Shoppers Stop and Lifestyle. 'We invest heavily in creating our own video content,' Kaushik said, 'which plays on a loop on screens in retail locations. When customers see these videos, they often become curious and want to try the product.' Despite being priced at a premium, the foundation-applicator stick became a bestseller.

Over the years, SUGAR has successfully developed and marketed over 500 products, manufactured in state-of-the-art facilities in Korea, Italy, India, the USA and Germany, catering to a wide array of beauty needs in the sixteen-to-forty-year age group. Kaushik said, 'Different countries are known for their expertise in different products. We partnered with some of the best manufacturers in their respective countries and even started production in India.'

He shed light on the rationale behind launching such a diverse range of products, explaining that perceptions of make-up have significantly evolved. Once viewed as an occasional adornment, make-up has become an indispensable part of many women's daily routines. This shift is mainly due to the significant rise in women joining the workforce over the past decade. It is common to see women wearing basic make-up—kajal, nail polish and perhaps a subtle nude lipstick—not because they are dressed for a party, but because it boosts their confidence and enhances their overall work presence.

Due to the influence of social media and selfie culture, the traditional age barrier for make-up use is also dissolving, with make-up use becoming more regular and less occasion-based. Recognizing this trend, SUGAR has crafted a range specifically for a younger demographic. This line offers alcohol-free, safe, vegan make-up, suitable for teenagers.

In addition to make-up, there has been a surge in the investment in skincare. Sunscreen, for instance, not only acts as a protective layer against harmful UV rays, but also doubles as a moisturizer, providing multiple benefits to the skin. Anti-ageing products are now seen not just as corrective but also preventive solutions. They are being recommended for incorporation into a woman's regular skincare routine from the mid-twenties, offering benefits before signs of ageing become apparent. Kaushik said, 'Brands like ours have greatly benefitted from these trends.'

SUGAR has adopted a meticulous and strategic method for launching new products. Unlike traditional brands that release products in general and modern trade stores, SUGAR initially launches only 5000 units of any new product on its D2C platform. Here, customers are provided with a brief yet detailed questionnaire, asking them to rate the product, similar to how they would rate an Uber ride. If the rating exceeds 4.5, the product is produced on a larger scale and distributed through offline sales channels.

Physical stores allow customers to test products before making a purchase, which can significantly enhance customer satisfaction and loyalty. SUGAR decided to experiment by opening its own store in 2019. 'The aim was not only to increase brand visibility but also to create a controlled environment for showcasing and selling our products,' Kaushik explained. The first store was opened in a 200 square feet area in a mall in Kolkata on a trial basis. To the team's surprise, the store achieved operational break-even within just four months and capital expenditure break-even at about eleven months. This success prompted them to delve deeper into what made this store work effectively. The outcome was an understanding of the concept of the price-to-volume ratio, which illustrates a product's potential income relative to the space it occupies. For example, a small, high-value item like a diamond often generates more revenue per unit of space than larger items such as furniture.

Kaushik elaborated, 'Like diamonds, SUGAR products are compact but carry significant value. This allows the brand to make efficient use of limited space.' Recognizing that they did not require large spaces, the SUGAR team targeted smaller stores that others had overlooked due to their size. SUGAR thus established its presence in these spaces and thereafter observed strong sales. Additionally, the pressure to reach break-even was also less due to carefully optimized rents. As of December 2023, SUGAR has opened over 200 stores. 'Tier-2 and 3 India is where most of our growth comes from,' said Kaushik. 'We are the first make-up brand to set up standalone stores in many of these places. We have women coming to learn how to use make-up. These are all aspirational consumers on the back of which the brand has grown over the years.'

SUGAR has a network of approximately 3000 beauty advisors representing the brand at its stores. The company has implemented a system whereby these beauty advisors receive regular updates via WhatsApp. The updates typically include short videos, ranging from thirty to sixty seconds, that outline a specific product's unique selling proposition (USP), and guidance on how to use the product. SUGAR also provides beauty advisors with an opening script that they can use to engage customers and pique their interest in the products. Kaushik added, 'While we also conduct training sessions via Zoom, we regularly share small content bytes, allowing our beauty advisors to consume information at their own pace.'

While SUGAR is a start-up with ambitious growth targets, the company does not believe in compromising its brand image by achieving growth through discount-based sales. 'Giving discounts can boost sales in the short term, but it tarnishes the brand image in the long term. We neither allow our retail partners to sell our products at heavy discounts nor do we permit our sales team to commit to any discounts beyond 10 per cent in the market to achieve their sales targets,' Kaushik asserted.

As a rapidly growing start-up, SUGAR receives numerous ideas from its team members. However, the company exercises caution before acting on these as every idea development requires resources. Kaushik elaborated, 'We encourage experiments, but before initiating one, there has to be a clear objective in mind. I often remind my team that the worst outcome isn't failure, but not being able to recognize whether you've failed.' He added, 'We urge our team to commit their goals in writing, not for leadership to review, but for their own reference. They are encouraged to justify their actions and decisions based on these self-set goals. This practice fosters ownership and introspection, both of which are crucial for growth and improvement.'

Based on such values, SUGAR has become the third-largest and the fastest growing cosmetic brand in India. As of December 2023, its products are widely available through its official website, app, popular e-commerce platforms and over 40,000 stores, including its own. The brand continues to remain steadfast to its commitment of providing world-class make-up products that celebrate individuality, inspire confidence and redefine beauty products for Indian women.

How CaratLane Understood the Market and Category Dynamics

In India, jewellery holds significant cultural and traditional importance. It symbolizes not just fashion, but also wealth, power and status. Indian women adorn themselves with an array of pieces, including maangtikas, nose rings, necklaces, earrings, mangalsutras and bangles. The country's jewellery market is diverse—from small-scale jewellers operating individual shops, larger brands running multiple outlets within a city to even a few national brands. The business model of traditional jewellers typically involves establishing extensive stores with vast inventories, leading to high capital expenditures. To maximize their profit margins, they predominantly focus on higher price points, particularly in the wedding jewellery segment. As a result, their business model can often become inefficient.

In the early 2000s, Mithun Sacheti, a member of the business family that operates the renowned jewellery brand Jaipur Gems in India, was in the USA. While studying gemology and working there, he observed the growth of online jewellery brands like Blue Nile, which were leveraging the power of the internet and technology to create more efficient business models, enabling them to scale up rapidly.

Through his experience in the USA, Mithun realized that it was easier to sell a solitaire (a type of diamond) online. Diamonds are graded using a standardized system called the Four Cs (Carat, Cut, Clarity and Colour), which allows buyers to assess their quality without physical inspection. Mithun even witnessed a customer purchasing a $30,000 solitaire online without seeing it. He believed he could replicate this online solitaire sales model in India without holding any inventory and by maintaining extensive supplier relationships.

Although Mithun was knowledgeable about jewellery, he wasn't very familiar with the technology. Therefore, he brought Srinivasa Gopalan on board as a co-founder. In 2007, they began working on their e-commerce platform, and by 2008, they had launched CaratLane. Shortly after, Avnish Anand, the current CEO, joined as the company's first employee. During a market survey, the team discovered that the demand for loose solitaires in India was not as significant as they initially thought. They realized that they needed to change their strategy and first build a jewellery business.

Meanwhile, the team discovered that many young women in India were not wearing jewellery but storing it in bank lockers. Avnish explained, 'Many women inherit or receive jewellery as a gift from their parents or elders. By and large, it does not align with contemporary fashion trends or suit occasions where women prefer to wear modern pieces, leading to jewellery ending up in lockers.'

The team also observed that due to increasing disposable incomes and evolving fashion trends, there was a growing demand for affordable jewellery for everyday use, such as in the workplace, at parties and outings. However, due to jewellers' focus on expensive pieces, there was a lack of beautiful jewellery at lower price points, below Rs 30,000. Avnish said, 'We saw an opportunity to create beautiful designs at lower prices.'

Moreover, the team decided to focus on diamonds rather than gold. Several factors contributed to this decision. First, at that time, very few jewellers in India were focusing on diamond jewellery, creating a whitespace. Second, competing in the plain gold jewellery market with traditional jewellers was challenging as the price of raw gold was well-known to customers and profits mainly came from making charges. Last, diamonds offered better profit margins compared to gold, which helped create a healthier business model.

Mithun's expertise in design and manufacturing helped CaratLane prepare designs at low price points. Notably, CaratLane holds the distinction of being the first company in India to introduce beautifully designed diamond jewellery priced under Rs 30,000.

One of the most significant challenges CaratLane encountered was building trust in a market predominantly dominated by established family jewellers. People often prefer buying from family jewellers they've trusted for generations, and they are wary of trying new brands. Tanishq managed to stand out in the market due to factors such as the backing of the TATA brand, along with the introduction of the karatmeter, a device designed to accurately measure the weight and purity of gold. In contrast, CaratLane didn't have resources or a business model similar to that of Tanishq's.

To overcome the trust issue, CaratLane's team meticulously focused on every minor detail that could help build trust. For instance, they introduced convenient options such as cash on delivery (CoD) and a try-at-home service. This allowed customers to choose pieces online and inspect them at home before making a purchase. They also formulated comprehensive policies, particularly for exchanges or returns, to inspire customer confidence.

Recognizing that image quality shapes customer perception and helps build trust, CaratLane made considerable efforts to produce high-quality images of their jewellery. They established a fully operational call centre to address customer queries promptly and even invited customers to visit their office in Chennai, further enhancing customer confidence in the brand.

Regarding payment gateways, despite the presence of many new-age players like CC Avenue with faster setups, CaratLane pursued HDFC for two months due to the bank's trustworthy image. They even made a security deposit to secure HDFC's payment gateway. For courier services, CaratLane partnered with Blue Dart, renowned for its reliability in delivery services.

The team promoted CaratLane through available digital marketing methods, online marketplaces and strategic collaborations with other brands. However, generating business was so challenging that they would pursue friends and family members, urging them to purchase jewellery from CaratLane and recommend the brand to their networks. Additionally, if there was an inquiry from Chennai or nearby areas, they personally visited prospects to showcase their jewellery. After experiencing gradual growth over a few years, CaratLane secured venture capital funding from Tiger Global in 2011. With the additional funds, the team expanded manufacturing and recruited talent. They also onboarded a few minor celebrities and invested in traditional advertising methods, including TV and billboards. Unfortunately, many of these strategies did not yield the expected results. Avnish commented, 'This was a learning phase for us. The marketing solutions available for digital businesses were also evolving at that time. We had to experiment with everything to understand what worked and what didn't.'

Meanwhile, CaratLane mirrored Blue Nile's unique store format, known as 'web rooms', where customers could explore jewellery online in a physical, store-like environment. CaratLane's first store in Delhi, utilizing the web room concept, didn't stock actual jewellery for immediate purchase. This approach didn't resonate with Indian customers who preferred to physically examine the jewellery before buying. Avnish stated, 'That store was a disaster. We realized that we couldn't merely imitate others; we needed to carve our own path.'

As time passed, the CaratLane team recognized many distinctive characteristics of jewellery e-commerce. For example, presenting the correct image size of jewellery on the website was a significant challenge. Customers desired details, perspective and a sense of how the jewellery would look on them. Striking the right balance was crucial—an image too large might mislead about the item's size, while one too small risked overlooking important details. To address this issue, around 2015, with the assistance of a US-based company, CaratLane created Perfect Look, the world's first virtual jewellery try-on app, providing customers with a more realistic view of their chosen pieces. Thanks to this app, the smartphone became a handy mirror, showing how the jewellery would look on a person from all sides.

Moreover, unlike other e-commerce companies, CaratLane delivery personnel do not wear branded t-shirts. Avnish explained, 'The reason is simple yet significant—safety. If our delivery staff are easily identifiable as jewellery couriers, they could become targets for theft or even abduction. We have heard of such incidents happening with other brands.'

Furthermore, CaratLane cannot process returns instantly upon pick up, as companies such as Myntra might. 'The risk of fraud is considerably higher in the jewellery sector due to the nature of the products. We need to check each returned piece of jewellery thoroughly, though we have streamlined this process to make it as quick as possible,' Avnish explained.

Avnish said, 'Building trust in a new jewellery brand takes decades. This isn't a problem that can be solved by spending big on marketing. To achieve growth, CaratLane needed an association that could instantly gain customers' trust across the country.' Since CaratLane was a solitaire supplier to Titan, Mithun consistently kept in touch with Titan's leadership, updating them about the progress of CaratLane.

Titan already owned Tanishq, India's largest jewellery retail brand. However, CaratLane's strengths were different from those of Tanishq. CaratLane was primarily an online brand targeting a younger audience with a focus on jewellery at a lower price point. In contrast, Tanishq was an offline brand focused on a higher price point. Over a period of time, Titan became interested in CaratLane because of its complementary characteristics.

After much discussion, in 2016, Titan acquired a 62 per cent stake in CaratLane. Since then, the CaratLane branding has always been prefixed with 'A Tanishq Partnership'. This endorsement has significantly boosted CaratLane's trust among customers.

Prior to Tanishq's acquisition, CaratLane experienced slow store growth. However, the pace significantly accelerated post-acquisition. Avnish explained, 'Our offline growth was slow as we navigated various aspects such as store location and design, customer experience, achieving profitability and defining models for partners. We received significant assistance from Tanishq to refine our approach to opening and operating stores.' While receiving support from Tanishq, CaratLane developed its own omnichannel strategy, seamlessly integrating offline stores with its digital approach. Subsequently, retail expansion took off.

Understanding the likings of potential customers in a specific location is critical to creating demand and stocking relevant items. For example, while CaratLane's catalogue boasts 8000 unique products, a typical store stocks only around 1400 products. Avnish said, 'Digital technology plays a vital role in providing essential data for informed decision-making. We strategically position stores in areas with high online order volumes and keep designs that are popular online. This method not only draws our existing online customers to our physical stores but also encourages them to recommend our stores to their friends, family or acquaintances.'

Around 2019, Avnish came across Harvard Professor Clayton Christensen's book, *Competing Against Luck*. The book introduced him to the Jobs To Be Done (JTBD) framework, which suggests that people 'hire' products not just to meet functional needs but also to facilitate emotional or social progress in their lives. Intrigued by this concept, Avnish frequently asked Mithun, 'What business are we in? And what role does jewellery play in the life of a customer?' Initially, Mithun used to get irritated by this question, saying that our business is to provide great design and excellent service to our customers. Avnish recalled, 'Despite his initial reluctance, I persuaded Mithun to read Christensen's book, which he eventually did.'

One particular event that left a deep impression on Mithun was when CaratLane received approximately 90,000 orders, all marked as gifts. Interestingly, of these orders, about 80,000 included personalized gift cards. These cards made it clear that people were not merely purchasing jewellery as expensive gifts; they were keen to add a heartfelt message to amplify the value of the gift. Furthermore, the messages on the cards were not generic. Customers penned long, heartfelt notes, adding an additional layer of emotion, sentiment and meaning to their gifts.

Once, Mithun encountered customers who sought a specific experience for their loved ones, and he observed the extent to which they were willing to go for that. 'These incidents and learnings from the book transformed his approach. He realized that our business wasn't just about selling jewellery; it was about fostering an emotional connection between the giver and the recipient,' Avnish recalled. After gaining this understanding, their mission became helping customers express their emotions through jewellery. In line with this, CaratLane launched a unique feature called 'Postcards'. This allows users to record heartfelt video messages and embed them into any CaratLane ring. The recipient can then scan the ring and relive the message forever. As Avnish stated, 'Although we operate as a technology-driven company, we fully understand the necessity of the human touch.'

In 2023, CaratLane achieved a noteworthy milestone with its complete acquisition by Titan at the valuation of around Rs 17,000 crore. This acquisition serves as a validation of CaratLane's remarkable business success. As of December 2023, CaratLane operates 277 stores across India, solidifying its position as the nation's leading omnichannel jewellery brand.

How Licious Developed Understanding of Consumer Preferences

Contrary to common misconceptions, the majority of Indians are not vegetarians. Approximately 70 per cent of the Indian population consumes meat,[1] leading to a thriving meat industry in India, with an annual revenue exceeding $30 billion.[2] But where do Indians usually buy their meat from? In large cities, you can find special meat stores and supermarket sections with frozen meat. But here is the interesting part—unlike the American market, where frozen meat is accepted, Indians prefer fresh meat.

More than 90 per cent of the meat in India is sourced from local butchers or wet markets, which are often unhygienic.[3] Despite meat being perishable, local sellers often operate without adequate cold storage facilities. Unfortunately, in unorganized markets, neither the sellers nor the customers can be certain whether the meat they are getting originated from a clean and healthy source or was grown in less hygienic environments and then treated with antibiotics.

In India, this food category carries a significant amount of socio-cultural baggage. Unlike vegetables, which are commonly packaged in transparent plastic bags, meat is often wrapped in black plastic bags, similar to packaging used for alcohol, contraceptives and sanitary products. Notably, India is perhaps the only country where meat eaters are uniquely labelled as 'non-vegetarians'. The differentiated attitude towards this category is also evident in supermarkets, where vegetarian items usually take the spotlight, leaving meat products either absent or placed in less visible corners.

Abhay Hanjura, once a rising star in an insurance company, was dissatisfied with the way one of the oldest and largest food categories was treated and consumed in India. His goal was to bring a significant transformation in the meat industry, much like how Amul revolutionized the dairy industry. Recognizing that he could not achieve this change alone, Abhay shared his vision to procure and sell high-quality, hygienically packaged meat online, with his friend, Vivek Gupta, a venture capitalist. Initially, Vivek dismissed the idea, believing that a general grocery e-commerce company would soon address the issue.

However, Abhay had previously attempted to order meat online and had a disappointing experience. To convince Vivek, Abhay set up an experiment. He invited Vivek to lunch and ordered some chicken online. When the delivery arrived, Abhay asked Vivek to collect it. Unfortunately, the packaging was inadequate, some of the fluid leaked onto Vivek's shirt. But what was even worse was the quality; the meat was nearly rotten. Pointing to the chicken, Abhay remarked, 'We have to put life in this dead chicken!'

This incident not only left Vivek upset but also enlightened him on the point Abhay was trying to make. He advised Abhay, 'If it's solely a delivery issue, it's likely to be resolved eventually by e-commerce companies or some food delivery player. What we need to ascertain is the scale of the problem.' The duo decided to delve into the end-to-end meat supply chain in India. To understand how consumers buy meat, Abhay began surveying meat markets and inquiring about people's meat-buying experiences. During these surveys, a doctor friend mentioned he usually sent his driver to make purchases due to the unsanitary conditions in meat markets. Additionally, an NRI friend said he avoided eating meat in India due to hygiene concerns.

On one occasion, Abhay visited Galleria Market in Gurgaon, where he witnessed an intriguing scenario. A woman was berating a street food seller for not wearing gloves, voicing her strong concern about hygiene. However, moments later, the same woman proceeded to buy meat from a nearby butcher's shop, where flies were buzzing around. Abhay was taken aback by the contrast in her hygiene expectations while purchasing different food items.

Intrigued by her behaviour, he approached the woman and asked, 'Do you buy all your groceries from physical stores?' The lady replied that while most of her groceries were conveniently delivered home, she personally visited this particular butcher's shop because she trusted the quality of its meat. Curious to understand her reasoning further, Abhay probed, 'Why not have the meat delivered from the same butcher if you trust him?' The woman responded, 'I want to visually inspect what is being delivered. Due to the rush at the shop, a mistake might occur. Why take that chance?' Abhay then asked, 'So you don't entirely trust the shop?' The woman said, 'I prefer to buy fresh meat.' Abhay then questioned her definition of freshness, explaining that meat remains fresh for about four hours after slaughter, after which it starts to degrade at room temperature. By now the woman had begun to feel offended. Abhay realized that her understanding and articulation of preferences were somewhat disconnected.

Meanwhile, Vivek discovered that meat contributed only a small fraction of revenue to grocery e-commerce platforms, causing him to conclude that they did not give this category the attention it deserved. In 2015, against the wishes of their parents, the duo left their well-paying jobs and founded to provide high-quality meat to consumers.

When it came time to decide which meat category to prioritize, the duo chose to focus on all the popular categories—chicken, mutton and seafood. Abhay explained, 'Many people consume different types of meat for various occasions. For example, chicken is a popular choice for comfort food, mutton carries a sense of prestige and tradition, and fish is a motivating factor for frequent purchases. By offering all these options in one place our goal was to encourage customer retention and repeat purchases.'

In India, culinary preferences change every 100 kilometres, encompassing a wide range, from freshwater to seawater fish, small to large fish, various chicken and mutton cuts and diverse cooking styles. Licious understands these nuances through extensive research. Vivek underscored this point saying, 'Our research doesn't stop at city boundaries; we dive into each area within a city to grasp unique consumer preferences. To truly understand local tastes, our team extensively explores the diverse culinary offerings at neighbourhood restaurants.' The insights gathered by the research team are shared with the product development team at Licious. The company maintains an innovation lab where a team of chefs continuously works on developing new offerings and customizing them for different markets. After internal testing and feedback implementation, the products are shared with a select group of customers for feedback before being launched in the market.

Vivek elaborated, 'We meticulously customize our products to align with the preferences of customers in each region'. For instance, in Delhi, Licious offers a chicken curry cut with two leg pieces, a local favourite. In Chennai, they provide smaller chicken pieces, explicitly for popular curry dishes in that area. Recognizing the preference of Bengalis, when they entered the Kolkata market, Licious introduced bhetki fish fingers.

As a D2C brand, approximately 90 per cent of Licious sales occur through its app. Consequently, the company has access to minute levels of customer data. Vivek pointed out, 'Licious is an extremely data-driven company. We examine conversion and retention data for different customer segments, including those who exclusively purchase chicken, others who opt for both chicken and fish, and some who choose a combination of chicken, fish and mutton, among others.' He further added, 'Whether customers shop with us regularly, take breaks, or haven't returned for an extended period, we are always eager to understand the reasons behind their behaviour.'

The Licious team believes that when a brand is willing to listen, customers are happy to share. Their call centre team is known as the Customer Happiness Team. Vivek said, 'This team isn't reliant on bots; rather, it comprises individuals who engage with customers on an emotional level. They skilfully handle diverse queries about meat purchases and cooking methods and eagerly listen to customer input.'

Based on feedback from customers, Licious has introduced numerous new products. For example, one mother, who is a Licious customer, mentioned that her son was tired of having bread with butter and jam. In response, Licious created the first-of-its-kind meat spread, which has achieved tremendous success. Additionally, some customers expressed a wistful desire for meat that they couldn't consume due to various reasons such as festivals or cultural norms. Consequently, the Licious team developed plant-based meat products, which were launched under the brand UnCrave.

To accommodate diverse requirements, Licious has introduced a range of options. Traditionally, meat consumption in India has been reserved for lunch or dinner, with breakfast and snack options often revolving around potato-based items like samosas, pakodas and patties. To make meat a part of daily meal moments, Licious introduced ready-to-cook and ready-to-eat products like kebabs, crispy snacks, burger patties, wings and more. As of October 2023, Licious offers over 300 SKUs to cater to a wide range of customer preferences.

Abhay emphasized, 'Our goal is to create the most-loved global food brand originating from India. Our greatest accomplishment will be the day when the black polythene bag is entirely eliminated from the meat industry. Until then we remain dedicated to elevating the status of this food category.'

5

Category Creation and Selection

If we don't create the market, it doesn't exist.

—Dietrich Mateschitz, co-founder of Red Bull

The first thing people think of when they encounter a problem is a category of products that offer a solution. Then, they consider specific brands within that category to choose from. For instance, if you have dirty clothes at home, the category that would come to mind as a solution is a washing machine, and after that, you will think about the brands of washing machines to choose from.

I had the privilege of discussing this topic with one of India's most respected experts in consumer knowledge, **Dr Vispy Doctor, chairman of the Ormax Group of Companies**.

Here are some lessons I learned from him:

Before choosing a category, analyse its longevity

'Assessing the longevity of a customer need is indeed crucial to determining the sustainability of a category. Operating in a long-lasting category allows businesses to build solid and enduring brands,' Vispy explained.

For example, as long as construction, urban development and infrastructure projects continue, the demand for cement will remain constant. Therefore, brands like Ambuja Cement belong to a perennial category.

Conversely, needs such as the preference for electronic gadgets and fashion trends are susceptible to change, potentially resulting in the decline of a category over time. For example, pagers were once widely used for communication but sharply declined in popularity with the emergence of more advanced and accessible mobile phone technology.

Launching products in established and new categories presents distinct challenges

Vispy said, 'Launching a product carries a considerable cost, but introducing an entirely new category incurs even higher expenses due to the need for educating customers and altering their perceptions.'

An existing category offers a predefined audience, established distribution channels and established consumer behaviour to leverage. Hence, a new brand entering an established category benefits from many ready-made elements. However, new brands must devise unique value propositions, innovative product features, or exceptional marketing strategies to differentiate themselves from existing players. For example, when the iPhone was released in 2007, most smartphones featured traditional keypads with physical buttons, while the iPhone introduced a touchscreen interface without any physical buttons.

Entering an untapped category without competition offers a significant opportunity for potential market leadership. However, it necessitates educating consumers about a problem they might not even recognize, requiring extra investment in terms of both money and effort. For example, the energy drink category was relatively unknown before the introduction of Red Bull. The brand invested extensively in marketing campaigns, sponsorships and events, building significant awareness and positioning itself as synonymous with energy and extreme sports.

A new category demands both risk-taking capabilities and patience

Entering an entirely new and untested category involves inherent risks and uncertainties. While initial sales might occur due to the product's novelty or customer curiosity, the crucial question remains whether the market will grow steadily over time, and will a new company survive until the market becomes receptive to the new category? Markets often take time to evolve while customers need time to adopt and fully embrace a new product or concept.

An example of a new category that required considerable time to establish itself is the electric vehicle. Although the concept of electric vehicles is not entirely novel, achieving widespread adoption and acceptance took many years. Electric vehicles encountered various challenges, including technological limitations, high costs and inadequate on-the-ground infrastructure such as charging stations. Additionally, customer concerns about battery life and vehicle pricing acted as barriers to mass adoption.

Over time, advancements in battery technology, government incentives, increased environmental awareness and improvements in charging infrastructure have slowly shifted perceptions.

Being a first mover does not guarantee market dominance

Being the first mover in a category can grant a brand a unique positioning as an innovator and trendsetter. It allows the brand to establish a customer base and foster brand loyalty that later entrants find challenging to disrupt. For example, Epigamia's early entry into the Greek yogurt category most likely enabled it to popularize the product, capture consumer attention, and build a loyal customer base before significant competition emerged.

However, being a second mover also has certain advantages. The first mover often has to invest resources towards educating the market and creating awareness for the category. A second mover can learn from the successes and failures of the first mover, fine-tune their product, and potentially capture market share more efficiently. An example of this is Moov, which entered the pain relief market with a formulation that addressed some of the drawbacks of Iodex, such as stickiness and odour. The improved product made Moov more appealing to customers.

Even late entrants in any category can stand out by changing the proposition. A product is the tangible item that a company offers to its customers. However, a proposition represents unique value, benefits and positioning a customer can expect from a product. For example, Crocs' proposition is its comfort, versatility and durability, coupled with a unique design and customizable options that make them stand out in a crowded shoe market.

New propositions should enhance, not overshadow, the primary benefit

While it is crucial to innovate and present unique value propositions, it is equally important not to overshadow the core benefits that hold priority for customers. As Vispy said, 'The primary motive for people to buy a product is to address their core needs. While additional propositions may enhance the feel-good factor, they cannot replace the essential expectation of meeting the core need.'

Let's take pani puri as an example. The key attraction for customers lies in its mouthwatering taste. While a vendor might explore introducing new propositions such as organic ingredients or mineral water to elevate the brand image, it remains crucial to acknowledge that customers primarily consume pani puri for its delicious flavour, which cannot be compromised.

Case Studies

How Zerodha Created the Discount Brokerage Category in India

By 2010, Nithin and Nikhil Kamath, co-founders of Zerodha, had gathered extensive trading knowledge and experience. While trading with multiple traditional brokerage firms, they had observed that these firms charged a fixed percentage-based brokerage fee, ranging between 0.05 to 1 per cent per transaction. This meant that smaller trades incurred lower fees, while larger trades incurred disproportionately higher fees. Nithin remarked, 'The irony is that the trade cost does not increase with the size of the trade; in fact, it only drops as the size grows. But in India, everybody was charging by percentage of the trade size.'

Furthermore, major brokerage firms in India were using legacy systems with cluttered interfaces. In 2008, the NSE (National Stock Exchange) introduced a free trading platform called NOW. While analysing it, Nithin thought, 'If tech is free, can pricing be disrupted?' Nithin and Nikhil were aware of Charles Schwab Corporation, a pioneer in discount brokerage in the US. They believed they could introduce a discount brokerage model in India too. They aimed to replace the traditional percentage-based commission structure with a flat fee system for trading, making it more affordable as well as efficient, for traders.

In August 2010, the duo launched India's first discount brokerage firm—Zerodha. Their pricing structure was straightforward—a flat fee of Rs 20 per trade, regardless of size, and an annual maintenance fee of Rs 300. Nithin explained,

'We believed that this pricing structure could help traders save up to 90 per cent on brokerage charges. Additionally, we offered this single pricing plan to all our customers, in contrast to traditional players who had varying pricing structures for different customer segments. Our hypothesis was that reduced pricing would attract more customers and expand the market.'

Zerodha had an innovative idea, but as a start-up it lacked the reputation necessary to run a brokerage firm. Nithin recalled, 'We were not an e-commerce start-up selling discounted products; people had to invest real money in their trading accounts with us. Moreover, since we were offering discounted brokerage fees, people had additional concerns as low cost is often associated with low quality.' However, believing in the founders, friends and family opened the initial 200 accounts.

Having been an active trader for over a decade, Nithin was a member of many online trading communities. He began promoting Zerodha using a different name, to avoid the perception of self-promotion by the founder. He had also worked in a call centre for an extended period, giving him solid telemarketing experience. Nithin said, 'I had sold anything and everything over the phone by then. I had that experience of cold calling.' So, he began calling traders, portraying himself as a Zerodha employee. Within a year, Zerodha had gained about 1000 customers.

In 2011, something interesting happened. The *Economic Times* published an article on discount brokerage and mentioned Zerodha as a pioneer in the space. Recalling the event Nithin said, 'The journalist was a friend of a friend who was also using Zerodha. Once that article came out, it brought a certain level of credibility as well. Before that, we were opening 100–150 accounts a month, and suddenly the number became 300 accounts a month.'

To improve Zerodha's presence in search engine results, Nithin started a blog to answer people's questions about trading and to promote discount brokerage. 'It's hard to measure how many customers the blog brought in, but we ranked 250th in the popularity index in India according to Alexa back then,' Nithin said with a smile. What made this blog popular was the fact that, at the time, leaders of financial companies were not blogging, and here was a CEO sharing his knowledge and answering people's questions.

For a few years, large brokerage houses either ignored Zerodha or did not respond by initiating their own discount brokerages as they already had huge infrastructure costs—numerous branches for relationship management, corporate offices in prime areas like Nariman Point in Mumbai, add-on services for customers like research and advisory, and so on. Zerodha had none of these overheads as it was totally online.

However, there was a limitation. NOW was confined to trading exclusively on the NSE. What if someone desired to trade on the BSE or MCX? Responding to this challenge, Zerodha established a vendor relationship with a white-labelled platform for online trading. As a result, Zerodha's customers gained the ability to trade on any exchange.

In late 2012, competition began to emerge, emphasizing a similar low-cost approach to trading. Nithin stated, 'That's when it became clear that being low-cost would not remain a sustainable advantage. It had to be technology. So, I began scouting for ways to advance our business by developing a better platform and improving the user experience.'

In 2013, Nithin crossed paths with Kailash Nadh, a PhD in Computer Science from the UK, who had returned to India with an aspiration of creating something in capital markets, along with a group of friends. Unfortunately, their idea had to be abandoned due to a lack of the necessary exchange approvals. But Nithin successfully persuaded Kailash to join Zerodha. With Kailash's arrival, Zerodha embarked on the journey of building its tech team.

In 2014, Zerodha introduced its free financial education initiative—Varsity. It covered a wide range of topics and was dedicated to addressing every question posted in the comments section. Notably, Varsity did not advertise Zerodha in any of its advice or articles. However, it did include a discreet 'open a Zerodha account' link at the bottom of the page, which directed visitors to the account opening page. As of November 2023, Varsity stands as one of the world's largest educational initiatives, consistently receiving approximately 70,000–80,000 daily page views, while its app has been downloaded over two million times. Nithin emphasized, 'Varsity has played a significant role in building trust with our customers.'

In 2015, Zerodha launched its technology platform—Kite—with a robust backend and user-friendly interface. This milestone marked the company's expansion, catering not only to active traders but anyone interested in stock market investing. Typically, traders engage in intra-day trading, which involves buying and selling within the same day. To attract new users, Zerodha removed the fee for equity delivery, which involves buying and holding shares of a company in a demat account for more than a day. Nithin elaborated, 'All in all, I would estimate that the elimination of fees on longer-term holdings impacted approximately 10 per cent of our total revenues. However, the benefits were far more substantial. Within a month our customers increased from 60,000–90,000, all through word of mouth. As we didn't invest in Google Ads or any form of paid marketing, our customer acquisition cost remained at zero.'

Towards the end of 2015, due to Zerodha's pioneering 'zero brokerage' structure, Nithin gained recognition in the *Economic Times* article '10 Businessmen to Watch in 2016',[1] alongside industry stalwarts like Mukesh Ambani and Gautam Adani. This elevated Nithin's credibility and drew a surge of new investors to Zerodha.

The combined impact of Aadhaar-enabled verification and Jio's aggressive data plans marked a turning point in 2016. Nithin explained, 'It took us six years to acquire our first 60,000 customers, each of whom had to sign and mail over forty pages of forms and wait for days. However, we reached one crore customers in the following six years. This was made possible through eKYC, digital signatures (eSign) and digital documents (Digilocker) that facilitated account opening in a few minutes.' Meanwhile, the advent of affordable smartphones also contributed to the growth of online trading.

In 2016, Nithin and Nikhil recognized that they needed to establish an ecosystem comprising like-minded organizations with shared goals to expand their market. Consequently, Rainmatter Fintech was born to support start-ups that could contribute to the growth of capital markets by empowering people to make more informed investment and trading decisions. As of November 2023, *Rainmatter* has invested in forty-five fintech start-ups.

It is not just the product or business strategy that has contributed to Zerodha's reputation. Their principles have played a pivotal role in fostering strong relationships with their customers. Zerodha has always refrained from providing stock recommendations or bombarding customers with offers and updates. They prioritize investor safety by issuing warnings before the purchase of penny stocks and promptly disable trading for those investors experiencing consistent losses. Similarly, the company implements various other customer-centric policies. As Nithin put it, 'Our priority is to minimize customer losses rather than focusing solely on maximizing our profits. As we don't invest in paid marketing for customer acquisition, we don't have the pressure of recovering the acquisition cost from the customers.'

Zerodha's remarkable growth since 2010, has sparked the emergence of numerous competitors in the market. As of November 2023, the company faces formidable competition from over fifteen discount brokerage firms. Nevertheless, Zerodha has maintained its status as India's largest brokerage firm in terms of revenue and profitability. With a customer base surpassing one crore and millions of daily orders, it continues to dominate the market.

How Epigamia Expanded Its Portfolio of Dairy Products

Dairy products such as milk, butter, curd and cheese have been integral to the Indian diet and culinary traditions from the earliest times. However, in the modern era, we are witnessing the emergence of a rapidly expanding market for value-added dairy products in India. Several factors have contributed to the growth of this market.

First, many people find it hard to digest lactose, the natural sugar in milk, due to lactose intolerance. Also, many people have allergies to the natural proteins present in milk. This has increased demand for lactose-free dairy and plant-based options like almond, oat and soy milk.

Second, people are becoming more health conscious and seeking dairy products with higher nutritional value. Greek yogurt, protein shakes and smoothies are examples of value-added dairy products that provide added protein and other nutrients, appealing to health-conscious customers.

Third, the increasing purchasing power amongst Indians has increased demand for unique flavours and premium offerings. Products like artisanal (handmade) cheeses and flavoured butter are gaining popularity among customers willing to pay a premium for superior quality and taste experiences.

In this evolving market for value-added dairy products, Epigamia has successfully made its mark. Epigamia began its journey in 2015 as a pioneer of Greek yogurt in India. Trying samples is a risk-free way for shoppers to explore new products without committing to buy. Epigamia's team visited hundreds of modern trade and *kirana* stores in Mumbai to get space for the products and put up sampling counters. Initially, retailers were hesitant about allocating space to a new brand and unfamiliar product. However, through persistence and encouraging shopkeepers to taste their products, the Epigamia team gained the approval of many retailers. Approximately 200 big and small stores in Mumbai's prime locations agreed to provide space.

The brand saw sales of 10,000 cups within the first month of launch. Over time, Epigamia launched multiple variants of Greek yogurt with flavours like mango, vanilla and blueberry. Within a short span of four years Epigamia was selling over three million cups of Greek yogurt monthly, through e-commerce websites like BigBasket and Amazon, retail chains like Godrej Natures Basket, Reliance Retail and D-Mart, numerous kirana stores and hotel chains such as the Taj Group, Marriott and Westin.

Through market research, the Epigamia team identified that the brand had garnered significant awareness but had not penetrated a broader customer base. Rohan Mirchandani, co-founder at Epigamia explained, 'While many people were aware of Epigamia's commitment to natural taste without preservatives or artificial flavours, there was a gap in actual product trial, possibly because Greek yogurt didn't align with their consumption habits. The pivotal question for us became: what products could we introduce to broaden our customer base and integrate Epigamia into the daily lifestyle?'

The customer insights team at Epigamia actively gathered feedback from both current and potential customers, concurrently analysing global and domestic trends. Having done the due diligence, the Epigamia food innovation laboratory filtered product opportunities, adhering to the brand's commitment of utilizing all-natural ingredients without preservatives.

Rohan outlined the product development process at Epigamia, which mirrors practices in technology companies. In the laboratory, a team of chefs conducts bench trials to refine each recipe. Then, all new products undergo thorough alpha and beta testing phases. During the alpha testing phase, internal stakeholders, including management, marketing, the sales team and select existing customers, evaluate new products. If a product receives positive feedback, it progresses to the beta testing phase.

In the next phase, the product is produced on a small scale and distributed to 300 carefully selected stores in Mumbai, including both high-end supermarkets and kirana stores. Sales data received for new products is meticulously collected during this phase. Additionally, a select group of food influencers is invited to try the product. Positive responses from influencers and repeat purchases from stores signify a successful passage through the beta testing phase, allowing the new product to proceed to full-scale production.

Over the years, Epigamia has conducted various product experiments. Guided by market feedback, it has gone on to selectively launch a few. Products such as smoothies and artisanal curd have gained considerable customer appreciation, while others like ghee have faced challenges. Failures provide valuable lessons, hence it is worth looking at some of the reasons behind Epigamia's entry into the ghee category and the subsequent difficulties that led to failure.

Ghee has been an integral part of Indian households for centuries. Rohan noted, 'It's interesting to see the evolution of perceptions around ghee over time. For a long time, the western world perceived ghee as not being heart-healthy. However, there has been a shift in perspective in recent years, with ghee being recognized as a beneficial and nutritious superfood.' Epigamia, recognizing the changing narrative around ghee, aimed to introduce healthier and more versatile ghee for daily use, such as a spread for bread or chapatis. Thinking to further enhance the appeal, Epigamia introduced it in flavours like mango and blueberry.

Rohan explained, 'While many retailers appreciated the product and recognized its quality, the ultimate decision-maker in the market is the customer.' Unfortunately, the product did not perform well in the market, and the sales numbers fell way below expectations. Eventually, the product was removed from the market. The team believes that one of the key reasons for this failure was the lack of customer understanding of the product. Significant advertising efforts were required to educate customers about the usage and advantages of the Epigamia ghee.

Another factor that contributed to the failure was the timing of the product launch. Epigamia introduced the ghee during the Covid-19 pandemic. Due to the restrictions imposed by the pandemic, the team was unable to conduct traditional testing, such as placing the product in physical stores and capturing consumer feedback in real-life settings. Instead, the company relied solely on digital advertisements and D2C sales, which did not yield the desired feedback. When the markets opened up, retailers hesitated to stock Epigamia ghee as they had to focus on economic recovery by selling popular brands and products. Rohan noted, 'As a start-up, we had limited resources and bandwidth. We decided to stop the production and focus on other promising products. We may relaunch ghee in the future.'

Meanwhile, Epigamia developed many products that have helped expand its customer base. 'Customer feedback plays a crucial role in shaping Epigamia's product development and launches. For instance, some customers appreciated our Greek yogurt and its integration into their daily routines. However, following gym sessions, they desired a convenient option without the need for a spoon or cup. In direct response to this valuable feedback, Epigamia introduced its line of drinkables, starting with Greek yogurt smoothies and subsequently adding protein shakes to the range,' Rohan explained.

Epigamia also ventured into the pudding market, offering a dessert alternative that appealed to those seeking indulgent yet healthier treats. Additionally, the brand tapped into the growing popularity of almond and oat milk, providing a plant-based milk option for individuals with dietary preferences or restrictions.

Value-added dairy products have a limited buyer base in India. To expand into the mass market, Epigamia saw milkshakes as a potential category to explore. Rohan pointed out, 'Despite the competitive nature of the milkshake category, our entry was relatively effortless. Indian consumers have a strong affinity for milkshakes, and many quickly recognized our brand, associating it with high quality, thanks to the perception created by our previous products. To differentiate, we introduced thicker milkshakes with unique flavours, natural ingredients and no preservatives.'

Additionally, Epigamia ventured into the buttermilk category, introducing a distinctive product that was absent from the market—a mint-based buttermilk made with high-quality and all-natural ingredients that was free of preservatives. Rohan noted, 'Through surveys we discovered that many customers who initially began their Epigamia experience with standard products like milkshake and buttermilk, subsequently explored our value-added dairy products as well.'

Since Epigamia entered the crowded dairy market with numerous new products that people were not always aware of, it became crucial to educate both retailers and customers about the product benefits. Rohan smiled as he said, 'Being a start-up we are poor in our advertising budget, but we behave like we are rich while sampling our products.' Every month, the Epigamia team strategically selects fitness events like marathons, as well as college festivals and corporate offices, to distribute samples of their products. 'The exceptional quality of our products not only captivates customers during sampling but also plays a pivotal role in fostering repeat purchases,' Rohan said.

In India's highly competitive dairy market, marked by the presence of national giants like Amul as well as many regional and local players, newcomer Epigamia has successfully carved out a distinctive identity. As Rohan emphasized, 'To distinguish ourselves in the market we consistently push boundaries by introducing new categories, unique flavours and unparalleled quality not experienced before in India. Additionally, we aim to revolutionize existing dairy products through a fresh approach, utilizing high-quality ingredients while avoiding preservatives.'

With numerous groundbreaking products in the pipeline, Epigamia holds the potential to reshape the landscape of dairy products in India.

How Atomberg Identified Categories for Disruption

In 2012, Atomberg was founded at SINE, IIT Bombay. For the first three years the company faced challenges with product–market fit. However, a turning point arrived in 2015, when co-founders Manoj Meena and Shibam Das noticed the potential of the Brushless Direct Current (BLDC) motor, while experimenting with an electric fan.

Electric fans are ubiquitous in Indian homes and offices. They predominantly use cost-effective but energy-inefficient induction motors. Manoj highlighted the issue: 'A typical ceiling fan with an induction motor consumes 75–85 watts of electrical power, yielding a mere 22 watts of mechanical output. This results in over 50 watts being lost. Moreover, these fans become even less efficient over time due to winding damage.'

In response to this challenge, the duo conducted a test, replacing the induction motor with a BLDC motor. The results were astonishing. The BLDC fan consumed just 30 watts, starkly contrasting with the traditional fan's 80 watts. This translated to substantial savings of approximately Rs 1500 per fan annually. Recognizing the challenges of limited electricity access for many in India, soaring electricity bills and the urgent threat of global warming, the founders felt compelled to address the significant energy wastage caused by millions of fans in the country.

Since entering the market in 2015, Atomberg has introduced over 100 SKUs* of smart fans across various categories, including ceiling, wall, exhaust and pedestal fans. Shibam noted, 'We became pioneers in India by developing the most energy-efficient fans that can be operated using a remote. We also introduced design innovations and compacted products, while infusing them with a luxurious aesthetic, completely transforming the conventional appearance of ceiling fans.'

To set its products apart from the competition, Atomberg strategically brought in professionals from various industries to infuse best practices into their products and operations. For instance, they give priority to individuals with automotive backgrounds for roles associated with quality, benefitting from the automotive industry's commitment to quality control. Similarly, for design aspects, they have engaged experts from the mobile and healthcare sectors, renowned for their emphasis on minimalism and safety respectively. In order to ensure consistent product quality and design as they expand, Atomberg has instituted comprehensive design guidelines that their teams rigorously follow.

Over time, Atomberg has entered other categories of small home appliances like mixer grinders and smart locks. Shibam said, 'We look for three things while choosing a category. First, how large can we become in that category? Second, how efficiently can we solve problems? Meaning, do we need to rebuild everything from scratch, or can we use previous capabilities and distribution? Third, we ask ourselves if we are solving a real customer problem? We are okay if the first two are not always 100 per cent yes, but the third is non-negotiable.'

_____

* Products in different colours, sizes, styles and other attributes.

Atomberg's team follows a systematic approach to gathering consumer feedback and insights. First, they conduct an online scan of competing products, analysing customer feedback to understand preferences, dislikes, critical reviews and the consistency of reviews. The second part of their research involves direct engagement with distributors, retailers and customers, to gather opinions and gauge consistency between their feedback and the online reviews. This information is then mapped to identify patterns and define the problem statement. Additionally, the team regularly visits at least ten existing customers every month to gain deeper insights into their hidden needs through scenario-based questions. The combination of these research methods ensures for Atomberg a comprehensive understanding of customer preferences and requirements.

Mixer grinders, the second largest category of small home appliance after fans, presented a unique challenge for the Atomberg team. They discovered that many customers were unable to create orange juice and hummus in their mixer grinders due to the high speed of the motors. This resulted in issues such as the mixing of orange seeds in the juice, adding bitterness, or making hummus too thin, leading to the loss of texture. To address this challenge, Atomberg developed India's first BLDC mixer grinder, offering a range of speeds suitable for various items.

Now let's shift our attention to another of Atomberg's innovative endeavours—digital locks. Shibam shared the story behind their decision to explore this category, which is currently small but has the potential to become huge in the future. In October 2022, Shibam found himself locked out of his own house, leading to a frustrating wait that lasted hours until he managed to find someone to break the lock. When he shared this experience with Manoj, it began a discussion on the numerous inconveniences associated with traditional locks, especially due to their reliance on physical keys. It became quickly evident to both that a smart lock offering multiple access methods was the logical solution.

However, during conversations with current smart lock users, they were disheartened to learn that while a few smart lock options were available in India, the overall user experience was not satisfactory. Additionally, there were concerns regarding data security, particularly since many of these digital locks, primarily manufactured in China, stored user data on servers in China. This realization prompted them to embark on a mission to create user friendly 'Made in India' smart locks, ensuring that the data remained in India.

Atomberg typically adopts a strategic approach when launching new products. Initially, they exclusively release products on their website, selling them to a targeted group of customers. This allows them to closely monitor initial responses, engage with consumers directly and gather valuable feedback on the product's performance and reception. After making necessary improvements, they approach e-commerce platforms like Amazon and Flipkart, followed by offline retail stores. This meticulous process allows Atomberg to maintain high customer satisfaction and ensure the best possible product experience.

With a focus on quality, design and a systematic approach to understanding customer needs, Atomberg has poised itself to continue reshaping the small home appliances industry in India.

6

The Importance of Segmentation

Your brand's power lies in dominance. It is better to have
50% of one market, instead of 10% of five markets.

—Al Ries, marketing strategist and author

Market segmentation is a strategic approach that divides a larger
market into smaller, distinct groups. This allows companies to
tailor their offerings and marketing messages for each group,
leading to increased customer satisfaction, higher sales and
stronger customer loyalty.

Here are some lessons I learned about market segmentation
from **Dr Vispy Doctor, chairman of the Ormax Group of
Companies:**

Don't halt at surface-level segmentation; dive into deeper analysis

Vispy said, 'Entrepreneurs often limit their segmentation to
broad groups like men or women. However, matching a suitable

value proposition with the right audience requires a deeper dive.' Take Livon, for example—its target audience wasn't just females but specifically 'females with shoulder-length hair'.

Hair breakage is a common issue for women, particularly when wet hair becomes tangled and consequently, more prone to damage. Darshan Patel, co-founder of Paras Pharma at the time, recognized this concern while observing women untangling their hair after washing them. Following two years of research and formulation, Paras Pharma introduced Livon as a solution for wet, tangled hair, specifically addressing the problem of hair breakage in women with shoulder-length hair.

Look beyond external traits and delve deeper into consumer mindset

Segmentation isn't just about external characteristics like gender, city, education and economic status. It also delves into the psychological aspects of customer behaviour, identifying distinct groups based on attitudes, preferences, motivations and purchasing behaviours. Brands often fail because they don't correctly segment their target market or appropriately match offerings with their mindset.

For instance, one of the key reasons behind the failure of Tata Nano was the stigma attached to buying a 'cheap' car. The Tata Nano was primarily marketed as a low-cost alternative to motorcycles and scooters for middle-class families who wanted to upgrade to a four-wheeler. Many buyers in the target segment aspired to own a car as a symbol of social status and prestige. The emphasis on price and the imagery of a 'cheap' car instead of an 'affordable' car undermined the Nano's value proposition and failed to attract customers looking for status upliftment.

Clear segmentation guides brand positioning and messaging

Vispy said, 'If the segment isn't accurately defined, the branding process suffers as it becomes uncertain for whom the brand is being developed. Clarity in the segment directs brand positioning, messaging, and the overall brand identity.'

For instance, Fevicol and Fevikwik are adhesive brands offered by Pidilite. Fevicol targets woodworking professionals, including furniture makers and carpenters. In contrast, Fevikwik is popular among individuals seeking DIY (Do it Yourself) solutions to repair household items such as toys and sunglasses. Fevikol is synonymous with creating a strong bond, popularized by its messaging *'Fevicol ka mazboot jod hai tootega nahi!'* Meanwhile, Fevikwik is known as an instant adhesive solution popularized by its messaging *'chutki mein chipkaye'*.

Change in segment can change a company's fortune

Vispy said, 'Effective segmentation happens when a founder can foresee how people will behave and how revenue will progressively grow in the future.'

For instance, Moov initially focused on providing relief for knee pain, which is commonly associated with aging or older individuals, limiting the potential customer base. On the other hand, back pain can affect people of all ages, making it a larger and more diverse market.

Back pain is on the rise in India, fuelled by factors like insufficient physical activity, poor posture and prolonged periods of sitting or standing. According to various reports, lifestyle elements such as stress, inadequate rest and monotonous daily routines further contribute to this prevalent issue. Recognizing the opportunity to tap into a broader customer base, Paras Pharma repositioned Moov as a specialist in back pain relief.

Target a segment that's overlooked by competitors

Targeting segments already pursued by major players might seem apparent and suitable. However, entering an untapped segment offers a new company the opportunity to gain a competitive edge and position itself as a frontrunner in a fresh market space. For instance, in the 1960s, multinational detergent brands predominantly targeted the premium market segment. Meanwhile, middle-class households in India depended on laundry soap bars or traditional detergent powders to wash clothes. However, these options demanded considerable time and effort, especially to deal with tough stains.

In contrast to multinational companies, Karsanbhai Patel recognized the potential of the mass market and introduced Nirma, a low-cost detergent powder. Thanks to its focus on high-quality products at an affordable price, Nirma quickly gained popularity among price-conscious customers whom larger brands had overlooked.

As consumer preferences shifted towards seeking value for money, Nirma experienced significant growth in market share. Nirma's success prompted multinational brands to reevaluate their strategies and introduce more affordable alternatives to compete in the mass market segment.

Case Studies

The Evolution of CaratLane's Market Segments

In 2008, when CaratLane began selling jewellery online, India's e-commerce was still in its early days. Identifying the right customer base for online jewellery sales was difficult. So, the team decided to observe how users shopped on their website and then define specific market segments.

Utilizing platforms like Google and later Facebook, the team targeted people actively looking for jewellery online. Given that the cost per click (CPC) was relatively low at the time and competition was limited, CaratLane was able to generate a lot of impressions and clicks at a cost-effective rate. The website prominently displayed a contact number, encouraging interested individuals to get in touch. While CaratLane had a customer service team, the leadership team, including Mithun Sacheti, Kalaivani Sadagopan and Avnish Anand, personally took these calls to understand people's expectations, how they discovered the brand, and what it would take to convince them to buy from CaratLane. However, no orders were received in the first week.

Then, one morning, the team received a significant order worth Rs 7 lakh from Japan. An Indian resident residing there wanted to gift solitaire jewellery to his wife in India. However, he encountered payment challenges, hindering the completion of the order. In a conversation with Avnish, the customer expressed his frustration. Avnish assured him that the issue would be addressed and requested a day to resolve the matter with the bank.

Avnish explained, 'We had chosen HDFC's payment gateway. Due to security reasons, the bank had implemented a transaction limit of only Rs 50,000. An international transaction of such a high amount for an online jewellery purchase surprised the bank, and they considered it could be potential fraud. Luckily, we were able to convince HDFC to make an exception and increase the limit for a four-hour window.' Avnish informed the customer, and thus, the first order was placed!

The next few months were challenging for the company as inquiries and orders were scarce. Then, one day, after receiving a referral from Mithun's family business, Jaipur Gems, a seventy-five-year-old affluent lady from Chennai called CaratLane to inquire about purchasing a pair of solitaire earrings for her daughter, who lived in Australia. Avnish answered all her queries, took her to three or four stores in Chennai to compare prices and assess quality, and even spoke to her daughter in Australia. Eventually, the woman made a purchase. This example illustrates the extent to which the team went to secure just one order.

CaratLane did not maintain a substantial inventory. It had established relationships with various suppliers and reached out to them upon receiving orders. However, due to the lack of volume, suppliers did not take CaratLane seriously and were unwilling to provide the desired margin. One day, a Delhi-based jeweller called CaratLane's office and inquired about a solitaire listed on the website. He asked for a lot of details and eventually purchased the diamond without seeing it. This marked CaratLane's first B2B order. Avnish said, 'There wasn't enough traction in the B2C business. This B2B order showed us a new source of revenue.' He explained, 'In B2B, we didn't have to wait for customers to come to us. We could go to jewellers and sell one-on-one. Moreover, we felt that B2B would give us the volume to negotiate better pricing with suppliers.'

To expand their B2B business, the team implemented various strategies, including online ads, cold calling, visits to jewellers and SMS campaigns targeting jeweller databases. They also organized jeweller meets in hotels to showcase their products. Gradually, B2B revenue began to grow, albeit at a lower margin. Simultaneously, after numerous discussions and negotiations, the CaratLane team succeeded in persuading Tanishq to become a B2B customer. Avnish recalled, 'While we were just another vendor for them, this association brought us a lot of credibility and sales.' The cash flow generated from the B2B business proved instrumental in supporting the B2C side of their operations.

Initially, the team employed traditional segmentation methods, such as demographic. However, as CaratLane was an online business, they did not make significant progress with this approach. A significant insight emerged when the team observed considerable self-purchase and gifting activity on their platform. Avnish told me, 'We realized that more than customer demographics, occasions matter.'

Many women in the age group of twenty-five to forty-five celebrate personal milestones and special occasions by buying jewellery for themselves. There are also other motivations for buying jewellery. For instance, some women buy unique pieces to stand out at social events. They seek out jewellery that makes a statement, prompting compliments and inquiries about where they bought it. Avnish added, 'At times it might seem that a man is making the purchase when in reality he's only providing his credit card details while the woman selects what she wants, blurring the line between gifting and self-purchasing.'

While weddings are a major occasion for jewellery gifting, numerous micro-occasions, such as birthdays and anniversaries, play a crucial role in people's lives. For instance, many individuals purchase something special for their mothers upon receiving their first substantial salary. Another instance is the tradition of gifting jewellery to children by parents and relatives. This inspired CaratLane to develop an extensive children's collection. Also, men buy jewellery for their wives on birthdays and marriage anniversaries, and for sisters on Rakhi.

The team also realized that younger women, such as twenty-three-year-olds, often allocated their funds to items like watches, handbags, clothes, phones, parties or travel. However, this didn't diminish their aspiration for quality jewellery; instead, they preferred to have their parents buy it for them. Additionally, in traditional Indian households, women often desire a piece of jewellery but lack the financial independence to make the purchase themselves, leading them to ask their husbands to buy it for them.

The team acknowledged that many individuals, although not direct purchasers, served as influencers within their households. Avnish explained, 'Through conversations with our customers, we discovered that even independent and successful women often seek advice from their mothers or mothers-in-law when making jewellery purchases, considering the elders' knowledge of jewellery quality.' Recognizing the influential role of elders in the family, their smartphone access and their activity on platforms like Facebook, CaratLane began targeting them with engaging content. As Avnish said, 'The strategy worked, and we noticed that many references to our brand among younger women came from their mothers or mothers-in-law.'

Furthermore, because of its emotional significance and enduring nature, the older consumer segment often purchases jewellery as gifts for their daughters, daughters-in-law and grandchildren. Avnish said, 'We refer to affluent older individuals as the "platinum class". With completed commitments, no liabilities, substantial financial resources and a motivation to gift, they constitute a valuable demographic with significant purchasing power in the realm of jewellery.'

The CaratLane team then started to understand where to find customers for various micro-occasions. They knew that there was a certain type of customer, like urban migrants, who would buy from them. Avnish added, 'People who relocate from their hometowns to larger cities for job opportunities are unable to access their family jewellers. However, it was difficult to reach out to such customers through traditional segmentation. Therefore, we devised proxies to identify and reach out to these potential customers.'

Google and Facebook allow targeting based on pin codes. The team aimed to reach audiences in diverse micro-markets with a significant population of urban migrants. 'Gradually, we began segmenting our audience based on areas. Our hypothesis was that individuals in the same vicinity share similar attributes, like income levels and preferences,' Avnish explained. To enhance service in specific pin codes, CaratLane opened physical stores for a touch-and-feel experience before purchase and partnered with Blue Dart for expedited online order deliveries.

Avnish elaborated, 'Our strategy has evolved over time to identify micro-markets and the specific micro-occasions within them.' He added, 'As our target audience is on Google and Facebook, the challenge doesn't lie in reaching out to people; it's about identifying when they intend to make a purchase. We focus on occasions where emotional considerations outweigh rational ones, such as price comparisons. In our messages, we aim for specificity, whether it's targeting someone seeking a retirement gift for their mother or a birthday present for their daughter.'

In the context of emotional purchases like jewellery, people often seek recommendations from colleagues, neighbours or family members. Even though measuring word-of-mouth through data can be challenging, the CaratLane team observed during customer interactions that many new customers were referred to them by the existing ones. Avnish stated, 'Authentic endorsements from satisfied customers carry more weight than celebrity endorsements, as customers have invested their own money, unlike celebrities who haven't made personal purchases. Hence, our most significant brand ambassadors are our customers.'

He further underscored this phenomenon, stating, 'As more people become our customers, the likelihood of them discussing CaratLane in their conversations increases. This contributes to word-of-mouth marketing, leading to increased trust and affinity for the brand within social circles.' Consequently, CaratLane's strategy is focused on achieving a critical mass of customers in micro-markets, including families and localities.

While many customers naturally advocate for the brand, CaratLane has recently implemented referral programmes. Additionally, they showcase customer testimonials on their website and adorn their stores with a dedicated wall featuring pictures and accolades from satisfied customers. Moreover, CaratLane invites its top customers to inaugurate store openings, solidifying their status as brand ambassadors.

In its commitment to provide a seamless and positive customer experience, CaratLane ensures excellence across all touchpoints. This includes online interactions through their website or app, in-store engagements, call centre communications and sales and post-sales experiences, including repairs and refunds. The company's dedication to delivering an exceptional customer experience is so deeply ingrained that the sales team's incentive component is tied to customer experience metrics instead of just revenue targets. Avnish elaborated, 'We firmly believe that a meticulously curated experience at every touchpoint contributes significantly to our reputation as a professional and trustworthy brand, increasing our customer repeat rate and positive word of mouth.'

Moreover, since jewellery is not typically a high-frequency purchase category, prompting CaratLane to devise unique methods for customer retention, even if they don't generate immediate revenue. Every month, CaratLane launches new designs to encourage regular browsing. They celebrate customers' birthdays and anniversaries, fostering a sense of community and connection. CaratLane has also developed an app where customers can check the current value of their jewellery every day, much like monitoring stocks. They offer complimentary cleaning services for jewellery, even if it wasn't purchased from CaratLane. Additionally, they offer savings schemes for gradual gold investment and allow customers to exchange old gold for new pieces. Further services, such as ear-piercing and instant engraving for personalization and unique packaging options for different occasions, enhance the overall customer experience.

One feature that significantly enhances customer satisfaction is CaratLane Live. Recognizing the common preference among women to shop in groups, CaratLane introduced this assisted selling service. It allows customers to explore jewellery options through live video calls, providing them with the opportunity to virtually include their friends in the shopping experience. This innovation gained significant traction, particularly during the Covid-19 pandemic, inspiring numerous other brands to implement a similar approach.

CaratLane's successful customer segmentation and retention strategy has propelled it to the position of India's foremost omnichannel jeweller. In FY23, the company recorded sales of Rs 2169 crore through its e-commerce platform, encompassing both its website and mobile app, as well as its offline channels.

How Epigamia Segmented the Market with Its New-Age Dairy Products

With a population of over 1.4 billion (140 crore),[1] India presents a tremendous opportunity for start-ups. Targeting even a tiny percentage of this population can lead to the creation of billion-dollar brands. For instance, 0.5 per cent of India's population would be approximately 7 million (70 lakh). Selling a Rs 40 product to each of them, once a year, would generate a revenue of about Rs 28 crore. However, if a Rs 40 product was sold daily for 365 days to this 0.5 per cent of the population, the potential annual revenue could reach an impressive Rs 10,220 crore.

There are various categories such as snacks, dairy and bottled water where daily purchases occur. Epigamia is a prime example of a start-up excelling in this strategic direction. It has carved out a distinctive niche in a crowded dairy products market by launching multiple value-added products. Through market segmentation, the company seeks out customers who can be transformed into loyal and regular patrons.

Epigamia's first offering was Greek yogurt. Its high protein content and ability to make people feel fuller make it an excellent substitute for unhealthy snacks. Additionally, Greek yogurt could be offered in multiple flavours, making it a healthier alternative to sugary desserts like ice cream. Given these benefits, Epigamia could have targeted multiple customer segments. However, due to limited resources, start-ups usually target a segment that is most receptive to trying their products. Let us look at how Epigamia identified its initial core segment.

In 2015, Greek yogurt was a novel category in India, characterized by premium pricing. As a result, its ideal target segment consisted of upper-middle-class individuals. Typically, residents of metro cities are more inclined to embrace new trends and products, especially those popular in western countries. Consequently, Epigamia directed its efforts towards establishing a customer segment of older millennials, between twenty-eight to thirty-five years old, who possessed reasonable disposable incomes and resided in metro cities.

People have diverse food preferences and health priorities. To gain a deeper understanding of their choices, let's explore how individuals approach their dietary decisions on a spectrum of health awareness. On the one hand, there are those who emphasize the nutritional aspects of their food, carefully monitoring their dietary intake. We could term them the 'health-focused group'. On the other hand, there are those who prioritize the taste of their food, giving less importance to factors like calories or sugar content. We could identify them as the 'taste-focused group'. In the middle is a group that values both taste and some degree of healthiness in their food. We could call them the balance-seekers. For its Greek yogurt, Epigamia focused on the balance-seekers.

Balance-seekers

← — →

Taste-focused   **Health-focused**

In regular eating habits, full meals are generally consumed to satisfy big hunger, while snacks address small hunger. However, people also eat to celebrate, to relieve stress or reward themselves, to enjoy the visual appeal of dishes and to incorporate dietary supplements for nourishment. Although Greek yogurt can be enjoyed for various reasons, Epigamia initially focused on positioning it as a solution for satisfying small hunger.

As we all know, small hunger can strike at various times throughout the day. Thus, Epigamia needed to identify the most suitable occasion to capture the market. After careful analysis they determined that most people encountered small hunger between 4 p.m. and 6 p.m. It is the reason why many office cafeterias serve snacks during this period. It is also worth noting that most evening snacking options like bread pakoda, samosa and vada pav, while tasty, are not healthy because they are fried. In contrast, Greek yogurt presented a healthier, more delicious alternative. Thus, Epigamia strategically targeted the vast potential of Greek yogurt in office settings between 4 p.m. and 6 p.m.

Subsequently, the Epigamia team expanded its focus to include additional segments for Greek yogurt. These included fitness enthusiasts in search of post-activity snacks after yoga, marathons, gym sessions, as well as individuals seeking healthy breakfast additions, convenient on-the-go snack options and healthier dessert alternatives.

Following the success of its Greek yogurt, Epigamia has consistently expanded its product line to a wide array of consumers. For those seeking taste and nutritional balance, Epigamia has introduced products such as almond milk, oat milk and smoothies. To meet the demands of exceptionally health-conscious customers, Epigamia has rolled out high-protein, zero-sugar options like the Turbo milkshake and yogurt. For those with a pronounced focus on taste, Epigamia has crafted indulgent yet healthier alternatives like puddings and milkshakes. These treats stand out due to their low sugar content and lack of preservatives, providing a healthier spin on flavourful indulgences.

Young adults, including students, daily commuters and working professionals, often consume a large quantity of beverages. However, most affordable options in the market are laden with sugar and preservatives. To address this lacuna, Epigamia has introduced an affordable, healthier option— Refresh, a mango lassi made with milk, rich in calcium and free of preservatives.

While segmenting its audience for various offerings, Epigamia systematically gathers valuable feedback from potential customers through its sampling initiatives. Equipped with product samples, the team strategically travels to diverse locations. Their objective is not only to encourage people to try the product but also to engage in meaningful conversations. During these interactions, the Epigamia team poses targeted questions to understand customer perspectives and preferences at a deeper level. The collected data, encompassing variables such as location, age group, gender and focus on health and nutrition, undergoes meticulous analysis to extract valuable insights. This comprehensive analysis aids the team in evaluating how well customers grasp the core proposition of the product while identifying any additional expectations.

Furthermore, the Epigamia team strives to pinpoint the age group, gender and income brackets that would resonate best with a particular offering. They also evaluate the effectiveness of sales channels, including e-commerce, general trade and modern trade, while assessing the suitability of cities for specific product offerings.

To make its communication effective and targeted, Epigamia identifies the core audience for every offering. For instance, when it introduced Everyday Yogurt, it focused on mothers aged twenty-seven to thirty-five. 'Mothers play a crucial role in ensuring nutritious meals for their families. We named the product Everyday Yogurt to underscore its appropriateness for daily consumption, similar to providing a child with a glass of milk every day,' Rohan Mirchandani, co-founder of Epigamia, explained.

Similarly, during its survey and sampling in various gyms and fitness-related events, the Epigamia team observed that when it came to fitness-related food items, men generally have more exposure than women. As a result, when the brand introduced its Turbo range, featuring performance-oriented, high-protein Greek yogurt and milkshake, Epigamia primarily targeted men in the age group of twenty-four to twenty-eight.

Once segments are identified, it is crucial to communicate the most effective message in the most engaging format. As Epigamia's core target audiences are Gen Z and millennials, who consume a lot of content on the internet in comparison to TV, the team took the digital content creation route to reach them. Epigamia partnered with Pocket Aces, a digital entertainment company, for the web series *What the Folks*. In August 2017, Season 1 was released with Epigamia as the title partner. It was a massive hit, with over thirty million views. This web series gave Epigamia a high ROI in terms of brand awareness and Greek yogurt trials among customers. Later, Season 2 became the perfect platform for Epigamia to launch new products such as smoothies, lactose-free curd and mishti doi.

Food bloggers and nutritionists play a significant role in influencing food habits. Collaborating with them, the team ran multiple campaigns in which food bloggers and nutritionists talked about the benefits of Greek yogurt and the many exciting ways in which it could be used in day-to-day meals. The pictures of exciting dishes created using Epigamia yogurt started going viral on Instagram, and the brand's popularity shot up.

To make Epigamia part of the breakfast menu at popular high-end restaurants, the team shared products with chefs in those restaurants, who eventually shared their positive views with purchase managers. To capture the target audience at airports, Epigamia did six months of sample promotions at metro airports. In 2019, Bollywood actress Deepika Padukone invested in Epigamia and became its brand ambassador. The brand launched multiple advertisements featuring her.

In 2023, Epigamia collaborated with MTV for its Question Marks campaign, aimed at redefining success for youth beyond exam marks. Rohan highlighted the widely practised tradition in India of consuming dahi shakkar before significant occasions, as a symbol of good luck. As a gesture of support for parents and students during the stressful exam season, Epigamia launched a limited-edition product called *Naye Zamaane Ka Dahi Shakkar.*

In the near future, Epigamia aims to expand its presence in the top fifty cities in India, offering products at various price points. The brand also envisions tapping into broader South Asian markets, including Bangladesh, Sri Lanka, and eventually the Middle East and Southeast Asia.

Epigamia's journey serves as a testament to the remarkable opportunities India provides to innovative start-ups, particularly those catering to a health-oriented yet taste-conscious customer base. The brand's strategic focus on segmentation has allowed it to find customers for its various offerings within the competitive dairy market. And if Epigamia can successfully integrate its products into the regular diet of its customers, the potential for revenue growth could be truly spectacular.

How Kraftshala Approached Market Segmentation

Having completed his MBA from FMS Delhi in 2011, Varun Satia worked with Nestle as a brand manager for their Maggi brand. His business school background had helped him network with intelligent individuals and secure a good job, but he soon realized that practical experience in the field differed vastly from academic learning. In 2016, Varun started Kraftshala to help students learn contextually and achieve mastery in their chosen field through practical guidance from experienced professionals.

Although practical guidance is beneficial across various fields such as finance and operations, Varun made the deliberate decision to focus solely on marketing, given his own expertise. To aid him in this endeavour, he brought on board Eshu Sharma, an FMS alum, then working with Hindustan Unilever (HUL), and Nishtha Jain, an IIM Lucknow alum, then employed with Nestle, as his co-founders.

Having gained insights into segmentation strategies while working at Nestle, Varun felt that start-ups, given their limited resources, ought to approach segmentation differently from larger brands. He stated, 'Instead of pursuing the largest market right away, start-ups should concentrate on a smaller market that offers the highest likelihood of success. Once you establish your position as a prominent player in the small market, you can gradually expand into progressively larger markets and repeat the process. To be clear, it's not always possible to expand your products into new markets, which is why so many start-ups need to pivot their product and business model in order to achieve scale.'

Kraftshala could indeed have offered marketing courses to multiple segments, but they chose to target the one with the highest probability of success. In its early days, Kraftshala focused on business school audiences since the co-founders were former MBA students themselves and were familiar with the mindset and needs of that cohort.

Varun explained that attitudinal differences exist among students participating in placements. Additionally, dynamics like career aspirations and response to academic challenges differ between students from top-tier and lower-tier business schools. In light of these differences, Kraftshala created a further sub-segment of top-tier MBA colleges. Kraftshala initially targeted students from twelve top-tier campuses, including a few IIMs, ISB, FMS, SP Jain, XLRI, MDI, IIFT and JBIMS. This strategic selection allowed Kraftshala to create a homogeneous market and tailor their training programmes for specific audiences.

Contrary to common perception, students in top MBA programmes have their fears and insecurities too. They are required to consistently compete against their peers, most of whom are equally intelligent and ambitious. Hence, the desire to stay ahead and enhance their learning experiences drives their motivation. Varun also noted that the competitive spirit among these students made them more receptive to learning.

Varun explained, 'All students at top business schools were not our target audience. We specifically targeted those who considered marketing a significant aspect of their career aspirations. These students believed that by engaging in a programme that was not widely pursued by their peers on campus, they could gain an advantage in their placement opportunities.'

Students pursuing prestigious MBA programmes are highly selective when it comes to learning, choosing carefully what and whom they learn from. Varun noted, 'When we started Kraftshala, nobody had heard of me or my co-founders. Therefore, we needed to build credibility to attract these top students.'

To establish such credibility, Varun decided to partner for projects and expert guidance with companies that students admired. These companies believed that driving learning on campus was an excellent way to provide additional education to students and build an attractive employer brand. Consequently, Kraftshala partnered with several well-known FMCG companies, such as Nestle and HUL, to launch its first programme in 2017.

Eshu and Varun, both FMS alumni, believed that their alma mater would be the perfect place to launch their programme. They were confident that FMS students would appreciate this unique offering created in collaboration with top companies. However, the launch proved to be a failure and Varun and Eshu were left questioning themselves, wondering what had gone wrong. They had made sure everything was in place, so why hadn't things worked out? Was it the pricing or something else? After gathering feedback from students, they realized the issue was not the proposition itself but the co-founders' inability to clearly explain the value proposition the programme offered. Since the students did not understand the benefits in simple and clear terms, Kraftshala failed to capture their interest.

This experience taught the founders what effective communication should ideally be in this category. Varun said, 'When it came to FMCG, articulating benefits was enough, but when it came to education, a more immersive understanding of benefits was required.' Varun changed his approach for the next launch at IIM Bangalore. Instead of simply mentioning the programme benefits, he first conducted a marketing session, training students on some foundational ideas in marketing in a way that students had not seen before. Post this session, when he introduced Kraftshala's programme, the students could clearly perceive the benefits of the programme and how it differed from anything they had experienced thus far on campus. Many enrolled in the programme.

Varun explained, 'We didn't have a substantial marketing budget, and to be honest, even if we did, it would not have worked as well as the strategy we employed—conducting live sessions at college campuses. This zero-cost activity garnered significant attention from students. Even a single live session per college proved sufficient to attract multiple batches of students.'

After targeting the top twelve MBA colleges in the first year, Kraftshala expanded its reach to an additional thirty business schools the next year. In the second year, when they launched their programme in the initial set of twelve colleges, they received a great response from students due to the positive word-of-mouth from senior students who had previously participated in the programme. However, on one particular campus, the story was different and Kraftshala faced detractors who did not perceive sufficient value in the programme. Varun acknowledged that encountering both supporters and detractors is an inherent part of any journey.

While the business school segment thrived, Kraftshala had to maintain affordable pricing for students who were not yet earning. To ensure profitable growth, Kraftshala decided to target another segment—working professionals aspiring to advance their marketing careers or transition into marketing from other fields. However, to execute this strategy successfully, Kraftshala needed a reliable pool of experienced practitioners, particularly senior marketers. Varun explained that many senior marketers are passionate about teaching but often struggle to find time due to their busy schedules. To address this challenge, Kraftshala's online programme offers flexible scheduling for coaching sessions, ensuring convenience for both trainers and students. The programmes have successfully attracted experienced professionals to join as trainers and working professionals to enrol as students. As Varun noted, 'Senior marketers bring multiple perspectives to the same problem, which helps us sharpen students' thought processes.'

Kraftshala charges premium fees from working professionals enrolling as students, due to the highly valuable time commitment required from senior marketers who serve as trainers. This approach enables Kraftshala to establish a sustainable business model for their comprehensive programme, ensuring fair compensation for trainers' time and expertise, while maintaining high-quality instruction for students. Varun expanded on this saying, 'For this segment, social media—both organic and paid ads—served as the primary discovery channel for students. Then their trial journey with us typically began by attending one of our free online sessions, led by senior marketers. Through these sessions, the audience became more engaged and enrolled in our programmes.'

Kraftshala's programme, *Brand Management in the Digital Age*, designed specifically for this segment, became their most significant revenue generator in both 2019 and 2020.

While Kraftshala excelled in its established segments, the company identified a significant market opportunity in a new segment—entry-level employees focused on digital marketing opportunities. So Kraftshala launched the *Marketing Launchpad* programme, which helps students from various backgrounds start their marketing careers in top companies like Google, Tata Cliq, Publicis, Group M, etc. Unlike Kraftshala's other programmes, the Marketing Launchpad has a clear job-linked outcome. Students pay only if they land a job. To accomplish this, Kraftshala's selection process is highly selective. The team then equips the chosen cohort with the most relevant and in-demand skills. Varun explained, 'Our approach to reaching this particular segment involved a combination of paid social media ads and organic social media posts, including educational videos on our YouTube channel.'

Varun emphasized that just as large brands show interest in business school students, marketing agencies and start-ups are eager to hire fresh digital marketing talent and are willing to offer competitive salaries. However, in the first batch, the challenge lay in convincing recruiters to pay Kraftshala students higher salaries than other entry-level employees. To address this, Kraftshala had to demonstrate the value and potential of their trained students. Initially, companies offered internships to Kraftshala students, allowing them to demonstrate their capabilities as compared to other candidates. The students showed deeper marketing knowledge and a genuine passion for the field. As a result, recruiters began recognizing the significant value that Kraftshala students brought to the table and started offering full-time roles with competitive salaries. Remarkably, the placement rate for this programme exceeds 94 per cent.[2] By 2022, Marketing Launchpad emerged as Kraftshala's largest revenue source, reflecting the effectiveness and impact of the programme. Given the high demand for this programme, Kraftshala has created an in-house team of trainers alongside the external experienced practitioners, to guide their students.

Varun said, 'This programme is our biggest differentiator since we own the life cycle of a student from joining us to getting a job. This end-to-end approach is unique in the market and allows us to generate a lot of applications from very ambitious students that are otherwise being ignored. By taking responsibility for the entire process, we are able to provide our students with the necessary skills and support to succeed in their careers and meet the needs of employers seeking top talent.'

In a highly crowded EdTech market, Kraftshala may not be the most visible start-up brand in the media, but it stands out in terms of consumer love and sustainable growth. Varun explained that most reputable education providers usually aim for a Net Promoter Score (NPS) of between 50–65. However, Kraftshala set a higher goal for itself, seeking an NPS of 70 and even striving for 80.

Kraftshala also introduced a referral programme called 'Propel', to encourage existing students to recommend its programmes. Through 'Propel', students can earn credits that can be utilized not just for paying their Kraftshala course fees, but also for courses offered by other EdTech platforms, or purchasing books, or using tools like Canva, as well as much more. This incentive structure has motivated students to actively engage in the referral programme, leading to the growth and success of Kraftshala.

Varun explained their approach saying, 'Every student we enrol represents both an opportunity to establish our brand and a potential liability if we fail to provide them with a satisfying experience. Therefore, when we launch a programme, we wholeheartedly commit to it. There is no room for complacency, and our focus remains unwavering.'

Kraftshala has established a strong name in marketing and branding education within a short period. As it pursues further growth, Kraftshala plans to expand into other domains and provide support to students in their career growth journey. For example, akin to Marketing Launchpad, Kraftshala has introduced the Business and Sales Leadership Launchpad, a programme that empowers candidates, including freshers, to secure sales jobs with competitive salaries in leading companies.

7

Achieving Product–Market Fit

Don't find customers for your products, find products for
your customers.

—Seth Godin, author and entrepreneur

Product–market fit is a pivotal stage in a business journey.
It signifies alignment between what the company offers and
what customers genuinely desire, leading to a competitive
advantage, customer attraction and retention and sustainable
revenue generation.

Here are some lessons I learned to the topic from **Dr Vispy
Doctor, chairman of the Ormax Group of Companies:**

Attaining product–market fit is not a singular event; it's an ongoing process

Vispy highlighted that achieving a perfect fit between a product
and its target market is an ongoing process rather than a static

achievement. This is because customer needs, preferences and expectations are not fixed; they evolve over time because of factors such as changing lifestyles, technological advancements and cultural shifts. As a result, companies must continuously adapt their products to meet evolving customer demands.

Take Nokia, for instance. It was once the dominant player in the market, renowned for its sturdy and reliable mobile phones. However, it underestimated the impact of changing customer preferences and the importance of evolving technology. Consequently, Nokia lost significant market share to competitors like Apple and Android-based smartphones from other companies.

Vispy further emphasized that successful companies understand the need to stay attuned to market trends, conduct market research, gather customer feedback, and invest in research and development to keep their products relevant.

Industry and category dynamics impact product–market fit evolution

The rate of evolution in achieving product–market fit varies significantly across industries, and within each industry, it further diverges based on specific categories. For instance, certain industries such as stationery and steel plants often undergo slower rates of change. While incremental improvements in processes or materials do occur over time, these industries typically do not experience frequent or rapid transformations.

Conversely, industries such as finance and technology witness faster rates of overall change. However, even within these, different categories may exhibit varying rates of change. For example, fintech may undergo rapid innovation and transformation due to emerging technologies and shifts in customer behaviour, whereas other financial services categories may evolve at a comparatively slower pace. Recognizing this pace of change is crucial for companies as it helps them determine the appropriate speed and intensity of their product evolution efforts.

Customize product–market fit for each segment

Different customer segments have unique needs, preferences and behaviours. This necessitates tailored approaches to achieve a strong product–market fit for every segment. For example, Spotify offers a music streaming service catering to various customer segments, each of which has different requirements.

For their free-tier users, Spotify's product–market fit revolves around providing access to a wide range of music while occasionally displaying ads. The monetization model relies on generating revenue through targeted advertisements aimed at these users.

Conversely, the product–market fit for Spotify's premium-tier subscribers involves providing music alongside an enhanced, uninterrupted, ad-free listening experience, with additional features. The monetization model relies on subscription fees paid by these users.

Spotify's success in retaining and satisfying a diverse user base can be attributed to its ability to tailor product–market fit, monetization models and user experiences to suit distinct customer segments.

Listen to your customers and keep them close

Vispy emphasized that failing to understand customers is a critical misstep for any company. Successful companies prioritize continuous customer engagement, making it a core aspect of their operations. This involves actively seeking feedback, promptly addressing concerns and utilizing user data to comprehend evolving needs and market trends.

Start-ups can implement various strategies to bolster customer engagement.

- They can regularly seek customer feedback through reviews, ratings and surveys. This can help them to gain insights, pinpoint areas for improvement and tailor offerings to meet customer expectations better.
- Active engagement on social media platforms not only fosters a sense of community but also provides valuable insights through the analysis of customer conversations.
- Involving customers in product development by offering beta versions or early access for feedback is another effective approach. This can enable start-ups to gather valuable insights for refining features, resolving issues, and ensuring products align with user needs.

Vispy also added, 'By staying connected and engaging with customers, companies can cultivate robust relationships and adapt products and services to meet ever-changing market demands. This comprehensive approach can strengthen bonding with customers and fuel continuous innovation within the company.'

Be mindful of the metrics you track and the advice you seek

When measuring success and making informed decisions around product–market fit, it is essential to be aware of what metrics to focus on and whose opinions to value. Vanity metrics, such as raw numbers of app downloads or social media followers, may appear impressive but often lacks any meaningful association with actual user engagement or business growth.

Vispy cautioned against mindlessly pursuing vanity metrics as a measure of product–market fit. Instead, he advocated identifying metrics that truly gauge the value users actually gain from a product or service. He said, 'By understanding and measuring what truly matters to users, start-ups can move closer to achieving true product–market fit.'

Further, Vispy emphasized, 'Entrepreneurs should also exercise caution in seeking strategic advice. While consultants may excel at making compelling presentations and conveying ideas, they may not possess expertise in every field.' Vispy suggested that entrepreneurs should not seek guidance from consultants or agencies whose core competencies do not align with the specific areas where advice is needed. For instance, depending on an advertising agency for business strategy guidance may not produce the desired results, as their expertise lies in creative work and marketing campaigns. Similarly, seeking assistance from a design agency for social media can lead to unfavourable outcomes.

Case Studies

How Hector Beverages Achieved Product–Market Fit with Paper Boat

Hector Beverages was founded in 2009. Neeraj Kakkar and Suhas Misra, two of the co-founders, wanted to develop a beverage that would be perceived as healthy. They believed that the soy protein market was promising, especially when they considered its rapid adoption in the USA. Moreover, Indians who were vegetarian and interested in fitness, seemed a perfect target audience for this protein-filled beverage. The founders began by selling soy protein beverages in Delhi, frequently offering free samples in the city's gyms to build customer interest.

However, creating a new category while educating customers about the health benefits of soy protein was challenging. Some of those who tried the samples complained that they did not see immediate health benefits, while others worried that consuming soy protein could lead to impotence. The feedback made it clear; the founders had overlooked local market research and were mistakenly trying to mimic the American growth story. So, they decided to change course and explore other beverages with a stronger appeal among Indian consumers. Following further research they settled on energy drinks.

By this time, James Nuttal and Neeraj Biyani had also joined the company as co-founders. Due to Red Bull's success, the energy drinks market seemed attractive from all angles. At the time, a Red Bull can of 250 ml was priced at about Rs 80 and a can of Coke sold for Rs 20. The team figured that if they could provide a tasty energy drink at no more than a 30 per cent premium to a regular soft drink, they could capture a large share of the energy drink market. They then launched the brand, Tzinga, with three flavours. Focusing on the younger generation, the team conducted sampling at many locations, primarily at office cafeterias, colleges and schools. The market response was better than the previous soy-based beverage.

During the summer, Suhas had brought some aam panna to the office and shared it with the other co-founders during lunch. The team liked the drink so much they wanted more, but it was unavailable in the market. The founders felt they could make this drink. But to focus on Tzinga, they shelved the aam panna idea.

Almost two years after the launch of Tzinga in early 2012, the team realized that maintaining customer excitement for the product was proving to be a challenge. While there was some growth following advertising campaigns, sales numbers usually fell back within a few weeks.

Perhaps, the time to revisit the idea of working on traditional drinks like aam panna had arrived. The team discovered that young adults, particularly those starting their careers in major Indian cities, cherished the authenticity of traditional drinks. However, recreating these drinks outside the home proved challenging due to time constraints, the inability to source the right ingredients, and the absence of parental recipes. Furthermore, they observed that there was no major competition in the market for packaged traditional drinks. Recognizing this gap in the market, Hector Beverages targeted a unique niche—Indian ethnic beverages. Their goal was to combine traditional Indian drinks with modern packaging, ensuring easy availability at retail outlets while preserving the authenticity of homemade recipes.

Maintaining the authentic taste of their products became the team's top priority. They went into the kitchens of families who still made these traditional drinks and learned the recipes. However, finding ingredients in bulk was not easy. For example, aam panna required unripe green mangoes, which had to be boiled, peeled and pulped. This posed the challenge of finding a processor that could handle green mangoes.

While searching for ripe mangoes to make aamras (sweet mango pulp), the team discovered that the larger food processors generally use ethylene chambers to speed up the ripening, which compromised the mango's colour and taste. However, one of Hector Beverages' core practices was avoiding the use of artificial flavouring agents and colours. They wanted to let the mangoes ripen naturally, which is why, in the first year of production, the team ripened 200 tonnes of mangoes for the drink, using a natural and labour-intensive process. The mangoes were placed in a large field and covered with grass, with each mango being individually turned every two days to ensure uniform ripening.

The team wanted to position their product as a premium drink, so they priced Paper Boat in the Rs 20–30 range, a little more than the average price of a soft drink. Their initial product, Aamras, launched in August 2013, garnered an excellent response. Subsequently, in October 2013, Aam Panna was introduced. Initially, instead of following the regular route, Hector Beverages approached Indigo Airlines for a distribution partnership. Indigo liked the products and felt they could offer their customers something new and different. Through this partnership, Paper Boat captured the attention of travellers. Many influencers discovered the brand while travelling with Indigo and talked about it on social media.

The product–market fit had been achieved. Within six months, Paper Boat's sales surpassed those of Tzinga. As a result, the team shifted its focus solely to the Paper Boat brand, gradually phasing out Tzinga. To expand further, the company introduced several other ethnic drinks and formed partnerships with modern retail stores such as Reliance Fresh, coffee chains like Barista Lavazza, hotels like Westin and Trident, and companies like Google, Facebook and others.

In 2016, Paper Boat generated revenue of about Rs 70 crore, with over 80 per cent of the brand's sales coming from the top six metros.[1] Despite the brand's popularity, the sustained revenue growth fell short of the team's expectations. The primary reason for this was the limited market for premium drinks and a lack of distribution in tier-2 and tier-3 cities. In the chapter on brand extension, we will delve into how Paper Boat navigated these challenges.

Kuku FM's Journey to Achieving Optimum Product–Market Fit

Before 2017, Lal Chand Bisu associated audio mainly with music. But that year he discovered a podcast featuring Naval Ravikant, an American entrepreneur-investor. The wisdom he gained from that podcast changed his viewpoint, and instead of music he began listening to podcasts during his daily commute, lunch breaks and morning jogs. Bisu introduced podcasts to his friends, Vinod Meena and Vikas Goyal. It did not take long for them to become equally enamoured with this medium. They all recognized almost immediately that while reading books and watching videos demanded undivided attention and dedicated time, audio content could be consumed seamlessly while travelling or working.

About the same time, Jio was revolutionizing internet access in India, extending its reach to even remote and smaller towns. However, it is worth noting that the majority of Indians remain non-proficient in English. Despite this, their smartphones—the primary gateway to internet in India—often came equipped with English keyboards. Consequently, there was a surge in WhatsApp voice message usage as an alternative to typing in English. Additionally, radio has always been a prominent medium of communication in India. Recognizing people's preference for audio, the trio saw a promising opportunity for podcasts to gain popularity in India, mirroring their success in the USA.

In their quest to understand India's content landscape, the trio engaged in extensive discussions with content creators and companies. During these conversations they uncovered a striking fact—despite only 10 per cent of the Indian population being proficient in English, the majority of digital content was primarily in that language. Furthermore, around 1 per cent of Indians were actively engaging with podcasts in English that were primarily of American origin.[2] This realization prompted them to establish Kuku FM, a non-English audio platform for the Indian audience. They chose this name since 'Kuku' is associated with the melodious song of the koel bird, and 'FM' gave it a radio-like connect. Bisu explained, 'We liked the name because it was short, catchy and unforgettable.'

The trio decided to focus on non-music content since numerous platforms already existed that catered to music. However, they encountered a significant challenge—India lacked an existing ecosystem for non-music audio content, unlike the thriving podcast archive in the United States. This meant that they had to start from scratch. To populate their new app with content, they actively scouted for potential audio content creators. They reached out to radio jockeys, discovered YouTubers specializing in audio content, sent messages to popular Hindi-speaking influencers and found poets and storytellers on Facebook. They invited these creators with a straightforward pitch; just as YouTube did in its early days, creators on Kuku FM needed to build their fanbase before they could start making money. The trio encouraged creators to upload 'podcasts' as in the West.

Once Kuku FM had enough content, the trio used Facebook and Google ads to attract listeners. The results were promising, and it became evident that there was a significant interest in non-music, non-English audio content. Users spent an average of forty minutes a day on the app, surpassing the time spent on music streaming services, which averaged around twenty-two to twenty-four minutes. However, Kuku FM faced a challenge with user retention. Bisu noted, 'Users didn't like the experience where they listened to one episode of a podcast and the next episode was completely different and unrelated to the first. That's why there was a big drop-off.'

To explore the potential of user-generated content, they revamped Kuku FM into a platform akin to 'Twitter for audio', enabling users to upload and share short audio clips lasting three to four minutes. However, this approach did not succeed in retaining users, largely due to poor audio quality. The team discovered that, unlike video or gaming, where multiple senses are engaged, audio relied solely on listening and variations in production quality greatly affected the listening experience. Bisu noted, 'While audio content is relatively easy and cost-effective to create compared to video content, people have little patience for a poor-quality product.'

To understand their audience better, the team initially attempted outbound calls, but many users rejected these calls. They then introduced a prominent 'call' button on the app home screen, allowing users to contact the team directly. Surprisingly, this approach led to many interested individuals calling in, eager to speak in detail and share their feedback, making it a more effective way to gather insights for product development.

After a year of experimentation and ten iterations, the team found success with a long-form episodic series. Bisu noted, 'Indians love soap operas which have multiple episodes in continuation, so we decided to focus on this in audio format.' These series had episodes of ten to fifteen minutes and users typically engage with two to three episodes daily, spending an average of fifty minutes on the app.

The team discovered that the app's greatest engagement and listening times were with non-fiction series, encompassing audiobooks, book summaries, courses, biographies, self-help and personal finance content, all in Hindi. The internet had transformed the aspirations of small-town India, where people now sought knowledge, personal growth and learning, aspiring to become YouTubers, podcasters, stock traders and tech founders. This was because the conventional education system still struggled to adapt to these changing aspirations. Bisu noted, 'We realized that Kuku FM was addressing an education gap rather than an entertainment gap.'

Having finally achieved product–market fit along with content supply, the team turned their attention to increasing demand. Bisu explained, 'Google and Facebook ads are easy to start and are used by everyone, which drives up the cost of customer acquisition through performance marketing over time. So, we decided to explore a relatively new channel at the time— influencer marketing.' Kuku FM sponsored YouTube videos by several influencers. The advantage of influencer marketing was that influencers already had established relationships with their target audiences and their recommendations carried weight, unlike in performance marketing. Bisu added, 'After some initial unsuccessful attempts, we identified influencers whose target audience closely matched ours.'

Like many content businesses, Kuku FM experienced significant growth during the pandemic, tripling its user base. By mid-2020, the app had garnered several million downloads on the app store.

According to Bisu, achieving product–market fit has two distinct aspects. The first revolves around user engagement, ensuring that the product resonates with and effectively meets the needs of the target audience. The second centres around achieving monetization and establishing a sustainable business model that generates revenue from the product's value proposition. Bisu explained, 'Our next challenge was to find sources of monetization.'

The team were faced with a critical choice—should they generate revenue through ads or through subscriptions? Bisu highlighted the challenges of ads, stating, 'Monetization through ads is tough because most ad inventory goes to Google and Facebook, leaving others to compete for the rest.' He also noted, 'In India, people are comfortable with price points of Rs 49 and Rs 99, as they are common in mobile recharge plans.'

In January 2021, Kuku FM introduced its subscription plan with a monthly fee of Rs 49 and an annual fee of Rs 399. They gradually moved a significant portion of their content behind the paywall and used 'free samples' to encourage users to switch to paid plans, allowing them to listen to the first episode of each series for free, with the rest locked. Within six months, their subscription numbers reached five figures. Later, they increased the prices to Rs 99 for the monthly subscription and

Rs 899 for the annual subscription, but the subscriber growth rate remained consistent.

In 2021, Kuku FM successfully converted 2 per cent of their active listeners to paid subscribers—a monumental goal. The following year, they made significant strides by expanding their platform to include six additional regional languages—Tamil, Telugu, Kannada, Malayalam, Bengali and Marathi. By June, they had surpassed the remarkable milestone of having over one million active paid subscribers.

As of August 2023, Kuku FM's conversion rate stands at an impressive 10–11 per cent. With an impressive user base of nearly three million paid subscribers, Kuku FM has emerged as the largest platform for audio content in India. Its user base surpasses that of any other vernacular content platform in the country.

Bisu highlights Kuku FM's new challenge—maintaining a high standard of quality content while efficiently managing content production cost. He further elaborates that the company has diligently built an extensive database of creators spanning various languages and genres. Kuku FM's team of creator-producers keep pitching new show ideas and carefully matching them with creators who are suited to the content. Part of their responsibilities include negotiating deals with publishers and writers to secure audiobook rights aligned with the platform's offerings. Kuku FM takes on the comprehensive responsibility of managing the entire content production process, from production to marketing and distribution. Additionally, the platform appoints Content CEOs responsible for closely monitoring the performance of each content piece.

Bisu emphasized that achieving the ideal balance between the product and the market is an ongoing journey. He said, 'At times we have to optimize the fit for our marketing channels;

other times we have to finetune it for content and features. As our user base expands, new insights and expectations emerge, driving the continuous evolution of our product and enhancing our marketing strategies. Throughout this journey, we have recognized the significance of patience and consistency in attaining the perfect alignment between our offering and the ever-changing landscape.'

How Meesho Achieved Product–Market Fit

In India, the major e-commerce platforms-initiated business with their focus on branded categories such as electronics and fashion, targeting the upper-middle-class and urban customers. As a corollary, the unorganized retail sector selling non-branded products to mid to low-income groups remained predominantly offline for a considerable time.

In 2015, Vidit Aatrey and Sanjeev Barnwal chartered the problem statement: 'How to bring small businesses in India online?' With both co-founders based in Bangalore, they began visiting small shops in the Koramangala and HSR areas to understand the problems shop owners faced. These shops already had a local customer base, so the duo pondered how they could facilitate customer transitions to online transactions while still supporting the local businesses.

They began by developing a mobile application called 'Fashnear', which allowed customers to access nearby fashion shops online. Customers could select up to three products for trial, and a shop representative would personally deliver the chosen items to their homes. The customer could then try on the products and keep what they liked, returning the rest.

However, after four months of trials, the duo realized that this particular model was not effective. They learned that the availability of a diverse selection was paramount for customers shopping for fashion online. However, curating a substantial variety of options locally proved to be a challenge.

The duo decided to get back on the ground to better understand the retailers' pain points. They also sat outside shops to observe retailers' operations. They soon noticed a fascinating behaviour—shopkeepers typically asked customers for their WhatsApp numbers after making a sale. Upon enquiry, they learned that shopkeepers used WhatsApp groups to share photos of new products. This helped them inform customers about the latest items available at the shop.

Delving deeper into this, the duo learned about some of the challenges that shopkeepers faced while using WhatsApp. For instance, when people saw something they wanted to buy, they often found those items had already sold out, which was quite frustrating. Also, collecting money was a problem because back then many people were uncomfortable about making payments online and paying the right amount of cash was tricky.

To tackle these challenges for shopkeepers, the duo developed a new app called 'Meesho', derived from the term *meri shop* (my shop). This app seamlessly integrated with popular social media platforms such as WhatsApp and Facebook, empowering small business owners to list their products, manage orders, monitor inventory and handle payments.

The initial signs of Meesho being adopted motivated the duo to expand their efforts. However, after a few months, they noticed that many users had stopped using the app. The duo then spoke to retailers who had discontinued use of the app and found that they were not interested in using a new tool that would not bring them new customers or cut down costs. After disappointing conversations with many shopkeepers, the duo thought to look at the small subset of users who exhibited consistent and substantial engagement with the app, using it extensively throughout the day. A distinct pattern emerged through this analysis—all these active users were women. To dig deeper, they interviewed these women and found a typical pattern; they used the Meesho app to operate their online boutiques through WhatsApp.

The duo found that many women were keen on launching their own fashion boutiques. However, constrained by limited funds to set up traditional offline stores, these women turned to forming WhatsApp groups and inviting friends, family and neighbours to join. These groups served as a means for women to connect with potential customers. Developing connections with sellers, these women received regular updates on new products and shared curated selections within these WhatsApp groups, allowing interested customers to express their preferences. When a product was chosen, the seller shipped it directly to the customer.

The duo realized that unbranded products often reached customers through the establishment of trust-based connections. For example, these women entrepreneurs (the resellers) had connections within their WhatsApp groups—something the shopkeepers (the main sellers) did not possess.

Vidit explained further, 'Through these interactions, we realized the potential of our platform to make a meaningful impact on the lives of these enterprising women.' The duo decided to enhance their offering to serve this group better. They launched the updated app version in March 2017. To maintain a connection with these women entrepreneurs, they also established a WhatsApp group. To gather insights from different touchpoints, the duo managed the process of collecting orders from sellers and subsequently delivering them to buyers. Since sellers could cut costs on marketing and logistics, they were comfortable paying a commission to Meesho.

Vidit said, 'The common perception is that product–market fit (PMF) exists in a binary state—either you've achieved it, or you haven't. But we realized that it usually starts weak and then strengthens. It's about improving the match between the product and the market over time.'

As the next step, the company aimed to enhance the earning potential of each reseller on a monthly basis. This involved introducing additional categories such as furniture, kitchenware and cosmetics, allowing resellers to diversify their sales offerings. With the expansion of categories, the reseller network also grew. Notably, even retired and unemployed individuals started shops on the platform. Sellers started listing their products on Meesho, enabling resellers to choose from a wider range of items and sell them to customers using social media platforms like Facebook, Instagram and WhatsApp.

The Indian online shopper can be broadly categorized into two groups—those who prioritize convenience over price and those who prioritize price over convenience. Meesho's focus was on catering to the latter group consisting of value-seeking mid-to-low-income households. With the advent of Jio, many individuals from this segment began to access the internet and purchase unbranded products. A majority—80 per cent—of Meesho users come from a range of markets (tier-2, 3 and 4), and many are relatively new to online shopping.[3]

As the customer base of Meesho expanded, it led to increased business for both sellers and resellers. To ensure accessibility for users in small towns and those with limited internet bandwidth, Meesho developed India's lightest e-commerce app on the Google Play Store, weighing only 13.6 MB. This helped the company cater to users with lower-end phones that did not support heavier applications.

In smaller towns, people prefer using vernacular languages. This is why, from 2021 onwards, Meesho introduced languages like Hindi, Bengali, Telugu, Marathi, Tamil, Gujarati, Kannada, Malayalam and Odia on the platform.[4] Additionally, the team simplified the app's user interface. Vidit said, 'The goal we had internally was to build something as easy as WhatsApp. In fact, the first few versions of our app looked very similar to the WhatsApp's interface because everywhere people were familiar with it.'

In mid-2021, Meesho implemented a change in its business model. The company ceased charging sellers a commission on each sale and shifted its focus to generating revenue through fees for order delivery and seller advertisements. This change attracted more sellers to join the platform. With more sellers there were more products and better prices, which brought in many new customers.

By 2021, Meesho had established itself as India's largest social commerce platform, where resellers acted as intermediaries, connecting sellers to customers. Over time, factors like increased awareness of e-commerce and the surge in online shopping during the pandemic, influenced evolution in customer behaviour. Customers began to feel more comfortable purchasing directly from sellers. To meet the evolving needs of its growing customer base, Meesho began transforming from a social commerce platform to an e-commerce player. This transformation entailed establishing a direct link between sellers and customers. Vidit elaborated, 'Our purpose—democratizing e-commerce, and our vision—to enable 100 million small businesses in India to succeed online, remained consistent. However, our approach evolved based on user feedback.'

The transition into e-commerce positioned Meesho as a direct competitor to Amazon and Flipkart. While Meesho's business model may resemble them, its unwavering commitment to catering to non-branded products and serving mid to low-income customers in small towns has remained unchanged. Moreover, Meesho doesn't categorize sellers into different levels, nor does it have private labels or an inventory-led play.

In 2022, Meesho achieved a remarkable milestone by onboarding one million sellers, comprising SME (small and medium enterprises), MSME (micro, small and medium enterprises), to individual entrepreneurs. This achievement solidified Meesho's position as India's fastest-growing e-commerce platform. Notably, nearly 50 per cent of these sellers hailed from tier-2 cities and the regions beyond them, spanning the farthest corners of the nation, including Pulwama in Kashmir, Una in Himachal Pradesh, Jowai in Meghalaya and Mount Abu in Rajasthan.[5]

Meesho has consistently supported sellers in learning how to sell online while maintaining good communication with them and their delivery partners. To make the platform better, the Meesho team actively seeks inputs from both sellers and customers. Vidit made an important point: 'When we assume what users want without asking, we make mistakes.'

Meesho demonstrates its commitment to understanding its users through a practice called 'Listen or Die'. As part of this initiative, Meesho's leadership team actively engages with customers and sellers on a quarterly basis to gather their thoughts and insights. Moreover, this initiative is integrated into Meesho's induction programme, ensuring that every new employee aligns with the company's user-focused approach from the very beginning. Meesho also offers comprehensive support to sellers, including assistance with logistics, payment processing, and dedicated customer care, as well as providing efficient tools for creating online catalogues. Additionally,

Meesho leverages data-driven insights to offer valuable guidance to sellers about understanding market demand to refine their product assortment. This holistic approach empowers sellers to optimize their businesses.

Vidit said, 'We are driving a compelling value proposition—of being the lowest-cost platform with a vast selection of quality unbranded products. This has found instant recognition among value-conscious customers, spurring organic interest through word-of-mouth for Meesho.' As of August 2023, Meesho efficiently handles an average of approximately ninety million orders every month, solidifying its position as India's largest e-commerce platform focused on selling high-quality unbranded products. Notably, Meesho's remarkable achievements have led to its inclusion in *TIME*'s prestigious 2023 list of '100 Most Influential Companies in the World'.

PART IV

Brand Development

8

Dynamics of Brand Positioning and Transformation

We believe in saying no to thousands of projects so that we can really focus on the few that are truly important and meaningful to us.

—Tim Cook, CEO of Apple

Markets are becoming increasingly complex. Over time, every niche becomes crowded with competitors and customer expectations, along with engagement methods, continue to evolve. To succeed in this dynamic landscape, start-ups are required to establish a clear positioning and remain open to brand transformation.

I had the privilege of discussing this topic with one of India's most respected brand experts **Lulu Raghavan, President of APAC at Landor, the world's largest brand consulting firm.** Throughout her career, she has played a pivotal role in crafting brand strategies for many global organizations, including renowned Indian brands such as Tata Group, Mahindra Group, Aditya Birla Group, NSE, Digit Insurance, Zepto and others.

Here are some lessons I learned from her:

Positioning begins with understanding the pain points of customers

Positioning refers to the strategic process of establishing a distinctive place for a brand in the mind of its target audience. Lulu said, 'The crucial starting point of the positioning strategy should be identifying the anxieties and aspirations of those you aim to serve. This understanding allows you to determine what is missing and identify the opportunity space.' She added, 'It's not just about the opportunity. How you pursue it matters significantly. Therefore, start-ups must be very clear on their value proposition. It's also important to analyse competitors and how customers perceive them. Finally, considering the cultural context in which the brand will operate is essential.'

When we put all of that together, building a successful positioning fundamentally comes down to two things:

1. **Differentiation:** It encompasses the unique features or benefits that make a brand stand out in the market. Lulu pointed out, 'Many start-ups don't invest sufficient time in identifying meaningful differentiation, leading to numerous failures.' She emphasized that practices like design thinking and business model canvas can help uncover unexplored territories of differentiation.

2. **Relevance:** Relevance refers to how well a brand resonates with the target customers' needs, desires and preferences. Lulu explained, 'Prioritizing relentless relevance can

unveil more opportunities for start-ups than striving solely to be different.'

Let us look at a specific example. Insurance is often regarded as a complex industry. Kamesh Goyal clearly envisioned making insurance products so easy that even grandparents could buy them. So, he founded Oben, one of India's first online insurance companies. But Oben meant nothing to customers. So, he desired to create a brand identity that emotionally connected with the customers. With the help of Landor, Kamesh rebranded Oben to Digit Insurance. Lulu said, 'When we interviewed customers, simplicity emerged as a key element for positioning. A "digit" embodies the digital world and signifies simplicity, reminiscent of the foundational numbers we learn first. Hence, the brand name "Digit" was born.'

Lulu further explained, 'Every interaction with a brand, at every touchpoint, should consistently reflect what it stands for.' In the case of Digit, the differentiation emerged from the meticulous implementation of simplicity across every touchpoint. Whether through the brand identity and name, or the app's intuitive design, or the operations of the call centre, or the simplified language in product descriptions and claims processing, everywhere the brand demonstrated its commitment to making insurance simple.

Landor owns the world's largest database of brands known as BAV (BrandAsset® Valuator). Lulu explained, 'Over two decades the BAV data has consistently revealed a powerful insight—brands that successfully establish differentiation and relevance early on have a greater likelihood of emerging as leaders.'

Having achieved meaningful differentiation and relevance, a start-up can focus on building its brand stature by focusing on two fundamentals: **Esteem**—the reputation a brand holds in the marketplace, and **Knowledge**—the level of awareness and understanding consumers have about the brand.

Lulu noted, 'If a start-up wants to build equity in the consumer's mind faster, its messaging should be consistent and cohesive with the brand's core idea—what it stands for.' For instance, Digit has consistently emphasized simplicity in its messaging. Also, Virat Kohli's involvement as an investor and brand ambassador has significantly enhanced the brand's reputation.

Understanding business strategy is critical to developing brand positioning

A brand exists to serve a business and its objectives. Therefore, while developing the brand strategy, it is crucial to have a deep understanding of the company's ambitions and where its energy is directed. For example, if a company's business strategy focuses on attracting a younger demographic, the brand strategy may emphasize elements such as vibrant colours and trendy designs to create a visually appealing and modern brand image that resonates with the younger demographic. On the other hand, if the business strategy is centred around cost leadership, the brand strategy may prioritize competitive pricing and value for money to attract price-conscious customers.

As a case in point, Nature's Basket crafted a business strategy focusing on increasing customer frequency. To establish it as an everyday premium grocery store, Landor devised a compelling brand positioning—'Everyday Delights'. It aimed to communicate that the brand offered a wide range of delightful products that catered to customers' daily needs. By presenting Nature's Basket as an everyday destination,

Landor sought to motivate customers to visit the store more frequently, aligning with the overarching business strategy of driving frequency.

The brand name must be suited to both present and future positioning

Dunkin' Donuts prominently featured 'Donuts' in its brand name to emphasize its focus. While this name strongly positioned the brand, it inadvertently limited market perception of its growth opportunities. As the brand expanded its menu beyond donuts to include burgers and more, the name became confusing for consumers, leading them to rebrand it as Dunkin' to encompass its diverse offerings.

Rebranding can be a costly and complex endeavour. Start-ups often lack the financial resources to allocate a significant budget for rebranding and its subsequent communication to the market. Hence, it is crucial to maintain flexibility in the name and positioning, allowing room for pivots and expansions.

As an example, Zepto's founders, Aadit Palicha and Kaivalya Vohra, wanted a short brand name, no more than seven letters, easy to remember, that signalled their value proposition—speedy grocery delivery in ten minutes or less. During the development of Zepto's positioning and naming, Landor's focus revolved around the idea 'as fast as possible'. This helped embody the spirit of speed without confining it to a specific timeframe.

Zepto emerged from a physics dictionary—short for 'zeptosecond'—the shortest amount of time measurable on Earth. This open-ended name met the criteria and signalled speed and time in a novel way. The ten-minute delivery promise was effectively communicated through messages, which, unlike the brand name, could be adjusted as the positioning evolved.

Diligently check what customers think about your brand

Start-ups need to consistently evaluate whether their positioning resonates effectively with their target market. Regular customer surveys, conducted through research agencies or online tools like SurveyMonkey, are crucial to comprehending a brand's perception in the market. They help to evaluate the alignment between communicated brand attributes and customer perceptions.

Besides surveys, a reliable metric for measuring customer satisfaction and loyalty is the Net Promoter Score (NPS). This involves asking customers a simple question: 'How likely are you to recommend our product/service to a friend or colleague?' Consistently tracking NPS enables brands to monitor customer sentiment shifts and pinpoint improvement areas. Lulu emphasized that brands often undergo a refresh when they outgrow existing market perceptions or lose relevance with their target audience. Some opt for evolutionary changes, updating and revitalizing their identity, while others choose revolutionary changes that signal a new direction and commitment to stakeholders.

For example, Kangaroo Kids, a premium preschool brand, encountered heightened competition from both new and established preschool players. In response, it revamped its positioning as 'The Learning Adventure', recognizing preschool as a child's first independent journey. This new approach emphasized the essence of fun, warmth and optimism. Alongside this repositioning, the brand introduced 'Kan' as a playful character, representing the vibrant energy and curiosity of young children, also symbolizing the preschool experience at Kangaroo Kids.

In another instance, Monster.com, a trailblazer in job boards, began losing relevance to emerging competitors like Glassdoor and LinkedIn. Also, job seekers today tend to prioritize purpose and fulfilment rather than traditional nine to five jobs. To adapt, Monster transformed into an end-to-end talent management platform and rebranded itself in Asia Pacific and the Middle East as 'found it'.

Brand transformation through an outside-in approach is better than inside-out

When a company adopts an outside-in approach, it prioritizes understanding the needs and expectations of its customers. This involves actively listening to customer feedback, analysing market trends and adapting the brand strategy accordingly. Conversely, the inside-out approach prioritizes internal perspectives and assumptions about what the brand should be, often overlooking customer needs.

Let's look at an example of an outside-in approach. Mahindra & Mahindra (M & M), an established leader in the SUV market, faced mounting challenges from competitors such as Hyundai, Kia Motors, MG Motors and Tata Motors, who introduced innovative SUV models. Struggling with stagnant growth and declining sales in FY20, the group recognized the need for a brand overhaul. In 2021, M & M introduced a new 'Twin Peaks' logo for its SUVs. This marked the group's shift towards premium positioning and the development of future-ready SUVs. The transformation encompassed product design, technological upgrades and a strategic focus on new markets. Formerly dominant in rural and semi-urban regions, M & M pivoted towards major metro cities, targeting Generation Z, corporate professionals and top executives. They also launched a groundbreaking digital booking site, which generated over $2.3 billion in sales within the first thirty minutes of its launch on 30 July 2022.[1] This strong response demonstrated the enthusiasm of tech-savvy buyers towards M & M's offerings.

Now let us look at an example of an inside-out approach. In 2009, Tropicana replaced the iconic image of an orange with a straw with a generic glass of orange juice on its best-selling orange juice. The decision to overhaul the packaging design was driven by internal considerations, such as a desire for a more modern and streamlined look. However, this redesign did not align with customers' expectations and preferences. Within two months of the new packaging launch, sales dropped by 20 per cent, leading to a loss of $30 million.[2] As a result, Tropicana had to return to the original design.

'One of the most critical errors businesses can make is acting without a thorough understanding of customers' needs and how changes might impact their lives. Regrettably, numerous companies often prioritize their own perspectives over those of their customers,' Lulu pointed out.

Case Studies

How Razorpay Became One of India's Leading B2B Fintech Companies

In the complex world of financial transactions, whether you're making an online purchase or conducting an offline transaction through a card or UPI, a payment gateway plays a crucial role. It verifies the details of the transaction with your bank and facilitates the transfer of funds to the merchant's account. The primary source of revenue for payment gateways is the fees charged to businesses for each transaction processed. However, they may also generate additional revenue through monthly or annual fees for value-added services.

Before the launch of Razorpay in December 2014, several payment gateways were already available in India. However, they primarily served large enterprises, possibly due to the higher transaction volumes that provided greater revenue opportunities. The integration of these payment gateways with businesses required substantial paperwork, including past operational records, proof of physical offices and security deposits. All these documents had to be couriered, often making the overall process take more than a month. Additionally, high setup fees were associated with the integration of these payment gateways.

During this period, many small businesses were seeking to accept digital payments from their customers. Simultaneously, numerous start-ups that required online payment systems were emerging in India. Two IIT Roorkee alumni, Harshil Mathur and Shashank Kumar, believed that the payment gateway integration process for start-ups and small businesses should be simple, taking no more than eight hours. Consequently, they pioneered India's first user-friendly payment gateway, specifically designed to cater to the needs of start-ups and small businesses.

'Payments is not a simple domain. You can't just build an app and launch,' said Harshil. Establishing a payment gateway is a complex venture, requiring a deep understanding of India's diverse and complex financial landscape, building strong technology, complying with various regulations and getting support from banks for secure and smooth transactions. One significant hurdle was Harshil and Shashank's non-finance background. Banks weren't initially ready to trust them. Despite facing rejection from nearly all of the hundred banks they approached, a turning point occurred when a senior banker from HDFC recognized their potential. Harshil recalled, 'This young graduate from XLRI listened patiently, understood our idea and chose to take a bet on us. The rest, as they say, is history.'

They collaborated closely with the bank to identify the necessary documents for start-ups and SMEs in comparison to larger enterprises, negotiating to eliminate redundant documents from the KYC process. Razorpay introduced digital onboarding, enabling businesses to upload their paperwork digitally. This streamlined the process, eliminating the need to physically courier documents and allowing businesses to onboard within two days.

To underscore its commitment to data security and the protection of sensitive financial information, Razorpay has been diligent about obtaining necessary data security certifications since its inception. Right from the start, Razorpay took a distinctive approach by refraining from charging any setup or annual maintenance fees, instead opting only for a transaction-based fee. Furthermore, Razorpay established a 24/7 helpline to provide support to SMEs and start-ups.

However, the primary obstacle faced in onboarding businesses to Razorpay's payment gateway was the significant trust deficit attributed to Razorpay's start-up nature. The founders adopted a strategic approach to address this challenge by piloting the product with a select group of start-ups at Jaipur's Start-up Oasis incubator, the very co-working space from where Harshil and Shashank were operating. Leveraging Razorpay's user-friendly payment gateway, these small businesses found it more convenient to facilitate online payments from customers, thereby enhancing their sales.

Although the pilot was successful, the Razorpay team needed acceptance from multiple banks and small businesses to achieve scale. The real game-changer occurred in March 2015, when Razorpay got selected for the incubation programme of Silicon Valley-based Y-Combinator, one of the top start-up accelerators in the world. This significant development and word-of-mouth about Razorpay's services from the first set of onboarded start-ups at the incubator led to around 300 small businesses and start-ups signing up for the Razorpay payment gateway. Harshil said, 'The Y-Combinator experience helped us in scaling up and also gave us clarity on how we should approach our seed funding process.'

Meanwhile, Razorpay raised funding from some well-known names, including Ram Shriram, an early Google investor, and Tiger Global. MasterCard, the second-largest payment technology corporation worldwide, has a 'Start Path' programme to support different start-ups building technologies in finance and commerce. In 2015, Razorpay was selected for this programme. 'Banks trust the Mastercard brand,' said Harshil. 'So, getting funded by Mastercard helped us quickly tie up with a lot of banks.' Subsequently, Razorpay tied up with Visa, AMEX and other financial services companies. These alliances played a pivotal role in propelling Razorpay's growth and solidifying its position in the market.

Over time, Razorpay onboarded various businesses—from small schools and local grocery shops to SMEs, start-ups and social media influencers running Instagram shops or conducting online courses. However, the growth was relatively slow till 2016. To build visibility and trust in the market, Razorpay needed media coverage. However, many journalists had not even heard of the company. Furthermore, Razorpay had to justify its existence and purpose as another payment gateway.

To address these issues, starting 2017, Harshil visited the financial hubs of India—Bangalore, Mumbai and Delhi. He sought to build relationships with the media to increase awareness and understanding of their brand and services. He found that despite being the second Indian start-up selected by Y-Combinator, majority of journalists hadn't heard of Razorpay. The remaining had a vague understanding, often confusing it with something like Paytm due to the 'pay' in its name.[3] This comparison was inaccurate as Paytm was mainly a payment wallet, while Razorpay was a payment gateway.

To educate the media, Harshil prepared a non-technical, jargon-free pitch to explain Razorpay. He visited all major start-up centres in India to build relationships with local journalists. He persuaded them to spare fifteen minutes, not for any coverage, but just to listen to Razorpay's story and purpose. In the first year alone, he gave ninety-five interviews and achieved decent media coverage.

The Razorpay team realized that large media outlets were primarily focused on covering significant funding news about well-known start-ups. At that time, Razorpay, a relatively unfamiliar brand with a limited customer base and no major funding, struggled to attract the attention of these media houses. So, the team at Razorpay initiated their media strategy by sharing the company's founding story with smaller publications, recounting how two IIT graduates left lucrative jobs in the USA to address payment problems for small businesses in India. They soon recognized that this narrative had a limited shelf life.

The media developed a keen interest in the Digital India narrative, soon after the demonetization event. Understanding that the media was interested in covering companies helping India become more digitally inclusive through unique, industry-first innovations, Razorpay's team started discussing their own groundbreaking innovations and their impact on small businesses. For example, Razorpay was among the first to introduce UPI acceptance in India. Such announcements helped Razorpay secure some media coverage.

Over time, the Razorpay team identified several problems plaguing small businesses and start-ups. Some of these businesses collected money from various sources, from UPI and NEFT to cash. In marketplaces like Swiggy, Ola and Urban Company, the business model involved a third-party service provider, with monetary transactions extending beyond the platform level until the third-party contractor received payment. Furthermore, in the SaaS industry, businesses that relied on a subscription payment model found that customers paid manually each month instead of automatic account debits. There was no single platform addressing all these issues.

In its mission to streamline financial operations for businesses, including the receipt, transfer and management of funds, Razorpay pioneered a series of innovative solutions in payments, business banking and lending. This evolution elevated Razorpay from being just a payment gateway to becoming India's leading fintech company, offering comprehensive end-to-end payment solutions for businesses. Instead of presenting this progression as a series of independent innovations, Razorpay rebranded itself as India's first end to end financial solutions company in 2018. This compelling narrative of Razorpay's evolution resonated strongly with the media, earning widespread attention and acclaim.

Early on, the Razorpay team recognized the importance of retaining media interest, even during periods without significant product launches or funding announcements. To maintain their media presence, they crafted numerous narratives, primarily highlighting the payment challenges encountered by small businesses, start-ups and freelancers. They also touched upon how Razorpay offered solutions to these issues, albeit without delving into excessive detail. These captivating narratives resonated strongly with both the media and their intended audience.

The company had a wealth of fascinating stories within its team. For instance, a school dropout built his career as an engineer at the company, and a village boy from a farming background started as a security guard before transitioning into the HR team. These personal success stories humanized the company and underscored Razorpay's commitment to nurturing talent and fostering growth within the organization.

Moreover, Harshil meticulously tailored his pitch for each city, offering unique insights into the performance of digital payments within specific industries and regions. He expanded his knowledge base beyond start-ups and fintech to encompass the broader business landscape. Frequently, he provided insightful commentary on various national and international business developments during media meetings. Over time, he built a reputation as a trusted source of expert opinion, with journalists often seeking his perspective on the topics they covered.

Meanwhile, Razorpay also maintained its status as a pioneer, actively shaping key milestones within the Indian fintech industry. In 2020, Razorpay achieved the remarkable feat of becoming the fastest-growing unicorn in India. In 2021, Razorpay earned a place on the Forbes Cloud 100 list, honouring the world's premier private cloud companies. By 2022, it had solidified its position as India's most valued fintech company. These remarkable achievements not only solidified Razorpay's position but also garnered considerable media attention for the brand.

In 2022, Razorpay expanded its reach into offline payments by acquiring Ezetap, positioning it as one of the few companies worldwide with a significant presence in both online and offline payments. As of December 2023, Razorpay empowers over ten million businesses, including seventy-four unicorn start-ups in India. With its extensive experience in developing innovative solutions for the diverse Indian market, Razorpay has established itself as a formidable player ready to tackle various fintech challenges in the Southeast Asian markets.

How Chaayos Created Its Unique Positioning in a Crowded Indian Market

Founded in 2012, Chaayos was the brainchild of Nitin Saluja and Raghav Verma, both IIT alumni, who identified a significant gap in the beverage market. Despite India being primarily a tea-drinking nation, with roadside tea stalls abounding, there was a notable lack of upscale tea cafés that catered to tea lovers. In contrast, there was a plethora of upscale establishments dedicated to coffee. As a result, regular tea drinkers were left with limited choices, ranging from homemade to office tea, to roadside chai wallahs or a handful of hygienic branded tea shops.

'What coffee is to the West, tea is to India. Worldwide, tea is the second most consumed beverage after water,' Raghav noted. The apparent void in the market sparked the idea of establishing a tea café that would serve authentic and customized chai in a warm and inviting ambiance.

Before establishing their first cafe, the duo conducted market research, engaging with potential customers, as well as family and friends. Through their discussions and observations, they identified three key insights:

1. People desired a trendy and inviting place to enjoy tea outside their homes. This highlighted a supply gap rather than a lack of demand for such an establishment.
2. People loved a vast variety of tea, ranging from favourites such as Darjeeling, Assam and Nilgiri tea, to various ethnic variations such as kadak chai, cutting chai and Irani chai.
3. In India, people enjoyed consuming snacks such as bun maska, rusks, cookies and pakode with their tea.

Nitin and Raghav embarked on a quest to find the perfect brand name that would not only evoke a connection with chai, but also encompass a broader significance. Their brainstorming led to twelve different names, which they asked their friends to vote on. Of the suggested names 'Chaayos' received the fewest votes, yet the duo settled on it because when said aloud, it fell pleasantly on the ear, and it was easy to remember. Raghav explained, 'As people heard it repeatedly, they began to like it even more.'

To enhance the brand identity, they selected green as their primary colour, inspired by the colour of tea leaves and the natural tranquillity green conveyed. The tagline 'Experiments with Tea' was chosen thoughtfully, to convey the variety and customization, along with new concepts and innovation.

The duo identified their target audience as individuals in the age group of twenty-four to thirty-four years. Interestingly, instead of opting for a mall or market location, they strategically launched their first store within a business park. This decision was driven by the prospect of a consistent clientele who would become loyal, repeat customers if satisfied with the product and experience. Thus, the first Chaayos store was opened in DLF Cyber City, Gurgaon.

Raghav expanded on this saying, 'We wanted to bring together India's modern and traditional sides through our design and concept. So, everything—from the chai served in *kulhad*, to the store design and branding—was a blend of these two worlds.'

At Chaayos, customers were presented with a diverse menu featuring twenty-five flavoured teas and an enticing fusion of traditional Indian snacks that paired perfectly with the tea. Nitin said, 'People get free tea in offices, so industry experts doubted whether customers would pay forty bucks for our tea. However, we were convinced of the demand.' And so, it proved to be. Chaayos' distinctive menu and inviting atmosphere resonated with consumers. Raghav recalled, 'To our delight, people did come. In fact, many came four times a day.'

The duo placed strong emphasis on fulfilling the unique preferences of each customer. Raghav elaborated, 'We decided against using pre-mixed or pre-made tea. Each cup was freshly brewed and customized according to individual tastes.' Nitin added, 'We introduced a concept called *Meri wali chai* (My kind of tea), which allowed customers to tailor their tea exactly to how they enjoyed it or made it at home. They could opt to include ingredients like ginger (adrak), holy basil (tulsi), fennel seeds (saunf), or black pepper (kali mirch), adjust the milk and water proportions, and even experiment with unique combinations.'

The café's distinctive appeal and positive customer reviews quickly attracted a wave of new patrons. Impressively, the first café turned profitable within a month of its launch. Armed with a year's worth of insights from their first café, the duo opened a second one at a different business park in Gurgaon. As neither Raghav nor Nitin was from the industry, for the first few years they focused on building the base and understanding the market. They spoke to many café and restaurant managers, CEOs of food companies, as well as food vendors, to understand how they operated and from where they sourced their raw materials.

By 2015, based on what customers were asking for, Chaayos had created around 12,000 different tea recipes by mixing ingredients in different ways. That same year, the brand started an R&D centre to come up with even more types of tea recipes. They then began Chaayos Academy to train new team members in the company culture. By the end of that year, Chaayos had grown to fifteen cafés all over Delhi NCR.

The duo wanted every Chaayos café to offer a great experience, so they made various systems and ways of making tea. Raghav remembered, 'Back then, everything was prepared by hand. Ensuring our products' taste was the same every time was a big task. We didn't have the technology to help us keep things consistent.' This was when Mohit Malik joined the team as chief technology officer and started working on in-house technology solutions.

To enhance operational efficiency and improve customer service, Chaayos developed a technology system known as Kettle. It facilitated seamless integration between live inventory at cafés and kitchen production, effectively minimizing food wastage. Furthermore, the company implemented a streamlined process to track the duration from order placement to customer delivery. In addition, the performance of each team member was evaluated using app-based workstation screens.

Following three years of research, in 2018, Chaayos launched the chai robot called Chai Monk, to brew every variety of tea consistently. Raghav said, 'Chai Monk is an IoT-enabled bot platform integrated at the point-of-sale. It takes orders and makes the tea in human style without manual intervention.' Notably, Chai Monk can access a customer's purchase history to generate live offers, enhancing the personalized experience for patrons.

Meanwhile, there was a growing demand for delivering Chaayos tea to homes and offices. So, the team developed unique packaging to deliver hot tea. Raghav explained, 'Our disposable container comprises a heat-retaining pouch and outer cardboard packaging, ensuring that the delivered tea remains hot for up to an hour.' Once customers had sampled and liked the numerous tea varieties at the cafés, they wanted to purchase specialized tea mixes and varieties for home consumption and gifting. So Chaayos began an FMCG arm, selling packaged offerings through their cafés as well as various leading e-commerce stores.

Chaayos has strategically forged connections with a range of events and communities. One noteworthy instance is their consistent presence at the Jaipur Literature Festival since 2014. By setting up a tea café, Chaayos firmly established its presence in the literary and cultural sphere. Their cafés have also hosted engaging poetry sessions. Additionally, Chaayos formed alliances with local biking groups, offering them a starting point for their rides. Moreover, the brand found common ground with marathon runners who find solace and vitality in the cafés. Chaayos has also expanded its footprint by collaborating with significant events such as the World Book

Fair, Auto Expo and select IPL matches. These partnerships not only attract patrons but also foster a sense of belonging within these diverse communities.

Chaayos cafés are now present in high streets, malls, business parks, hospitals, educational institutions, metros and airports. All the stores have a colourful ambience and quirky decor. Raghav said, 'No two cafés have the same décor. They look very different on purpose—people visit different places for different needs. So, every café is designed keeping in mind the possible use cases of that place. Also, tea is a high repeat category, as the same customers could visit Chaayos at different places; they ought not to get bored by the same ambience everywhere.'

Discussing the premium nature of the brand, Raghav said, 'Merely labelling something as "premium" doesn't automatically make it so. The real test lies in whether customers can genuinely sense that elevated experience—whether it's through interactions with our team, the cleanliness of our cafés or the way our products are presented. It's the holistic package that truly defines our premium offering.'

With time, the founders decided to reposition Chaayos as more than just a place to work out of or have investor meetings. They wanted to position it as a sensorial place that tea enthusiasts and customers visited to unwind and relax, before walking out refreshed. In 2021, Chaayos developed a new messaging—*Chai + Snacks = Relax*. Raghav stated, 'We believe that with the increasing stress levels in their lives, people need a tea and snack break to aid relaxation. Scientifically, it is also proven that tea contains compounds that assist in reducing stress. This understanding formed the foundation of our repositioning approach.'

As of August 2023, Chaayos caters to a diverse clientele, encompassing individuals from 18–65 years. The brand has successfully established over 200 outlets across tier-1 and tier-2 cities in India. Raghav remarked, 'Our brand isn't created only at headquarters; it comes alive in each store. We've set up good teams and systems, and then we've empowered our team members to provide the right experience and managing P & L for each cafe. Our operations team is known as the Customer Experience Team, and the café manager's title is Café CEO, in which "E" doesn't mean executive, but experience.'

Notably, in line with their commitment to delivering personalized teas through their *Meri wali chai* promise, the brand now boasts an extensive collection of over 80,000 chai recipes. The Chaayos differentiation is not just limited to tea. The team keeps experimenting with the food they offer and has created numerous innovative snacks by mixing various cuisines from India's rich culinary treasure house.

How Icertis Solidified Its Position in the Crowded CLM Market

Icertis was founded in 2009 by Samir Bodas and Monish Darda, serial entrepreneurs renowned for building and selling multiple enterprise software companies. During Icertis' inception, the duo chose not to emphasize the product, the problem being addressed or projected revenue. Instead, they defined their ambition—to build a consequential and enduring company. The duo discussed the possibility of achieving this goal by either initiating a technology wave or riding an emerging one. They recognized that creating a technology wave was challenging, an achievement attributed to visionaries such as Bill Gates, Steve Jobs and Elon Musk. So, they aimed at identifying the right technology wave to ride. During this period, cloud computing was an emerging wave, and the duo decided to explore opportunities within it.

Traditional enterprise software was often bulky and expensive to manage. Companies had to invest in hardware, servers and dedicated IT departments to handle traditional software installation, maintenance and upgrades. On the other hand, cloud computing seemed cost-effective, scalable and manageable for businesses of all sizes. The duo initially focused on developing a cloud-based solution for large enterprises. However, cloud computing encountered various concerns from CIOs in large enterprises, who were hesitant to take risks and invest in nascent technology.

Over a three-year period, the duo concentrated on consulting assignments while simultaneously experimenting with cloud-based products. They realized that developing products to meet the specialized needs of large enterprises would be impractical in terms of scalability. Consequently, they began to develop a platform. To clarify, a platform provides a framework and pre-built components for developers to build and deploy products. However, developing a platform is much more expensive than creating a product, so Icertis took gradual steps in this direction.

In 2010–11, Amazon and Microsoft were heavily investing in cloud technologies. Monish was based in Pune, while Samir resided in Seattle—the heart of the cloud wave and the hub of Microsoft and Amazon operations. At a dinner in Seattle, Samir conversed with a senior Microsoft executive, highlighting Icertis' emphasis on cloud computing. The executive, who was facing contract management challenges within his department, offered to have Icertis build a contract management solution for Microsoft.

Given this opportunity, Samir and Monish did some background research and discovered over 100 CLM (Contract

Lifecycle Management) companies in a fractured market.[*] However, these companies offered solutions built on legacy technology, which were not natural fits for the enterprise since they solved one problem at a time, whereas Microsoft sought a flexible, cloud-focused solution that could handle their global business at scale, which was Icertis' distinctive value proposition. The Icertis solution resulted in 83 per cent faster contract turnaround time and more than a million legacy contracts digitized and converted to live assets. This success led to an increase in engagement with Microsoft. Subsequently, the founders allocated some of the company's revenue to expanding their cloud platform beyond the needs of Microsoft.

By 2014, Icertis had developed products around contract and compliance management, transportation management, fleet management and dealer management, using its platform. As the Icertis platform was hosted on Microsoft technologies, Microsoft stepped in to support Icertis in its go-to-market strategy. Monish recalled, 'We met many potential clients through the Microsoft network.'

That same year, during a morning walk, Samir discussed Icertis' progress with Pradeep Singh, founder of Aditi Technologies. Pradeep told Samir that Icertis' positioning was getting diluted by working on multiple areas. He advised Samir to focus solely on contract management, which seemed a large opportunity since the prospective customers were among the top 2000 companies globally.

---

[*] In a fractured market, no single company holds a significant market share. The market has numerous small players, and the competition is intense.

Samir and Monish became deeply engrossed in exploring the vast potential of contract management. As Monish explained, 'Contracts are foundational to commerce, governing every dollar coming in and every dollar going out of a company. Every monetary transaction within a company—be it employees' payroll, procurement, sales, leasing, or rentals—is anchored by a contract.'

Traditionally, storing and managing contracts was inefficient for large enterprises. They handled countless contracts spread across departments, causing consistency issues. The lack of visibility increased risks and hindered compliance. Additionally, finding relationships between these contracts required laborious manual reviews. Monish told me, 'We believed that by enhancing the contracting process through our ICM (Icertis Contract Management) platform, we could offer businesses a transformative edge.' He recalled, 'At that time, the CLM vendor market was highly fragmented, with many players concentrating solely on either procurement contracts (buy-side) or revenue contracts (sell-side) or even narrower use cases like a specific industry, or region-based contracts. On the contrary, our ICM platform offered a comprehensive suite of tools covering sell-side, buy-side and corporate contracts, encompassing NDAs, employment agreements, MOUs and more. Additionally, ICM offered an intuitive user interface, swift deployment and seamless integration with all major ERP and CRM solutions available in the market.'

Large companies found it cumbersome to juggle between multiple CLM solutions to manage various contract types. ICM's positioning as an easy-to-use, enterprise-level solution capable of handling all contract types significantly fuelled Icertis' growth. Icertis expanded its global presence by acquiring numerous Fortune 500 customers across sectors.

Starting in 2015, the Icertis team began to proactively conduct feedback sessions with customers and esteemed industry analysts like Gartner and Forrester. These interactions played a pivotal role in consistently evaluating how the market perceived Icertis' distinct value proposition and differentiation. Moreover, these discussions served as a valuable platform for Icertis to demonstrate its innovative solutions and growth trajectory to influential stakeholders. Furthermore, the sessions provided Icertis with the opportunity to gather insights and perspectives on fine-tuning the positioning and messaging of its offerings in response to an ever-evolving market landscape.

In 2016, Forrester recognized Icertis' breakthrough platform as a leader in the CLM category. Soon, Icertis also began appearing in influential reports by Gartner. To stand out in a crowded market, Icertis initiated the practice of publishing press releases for every significant customer win. These press releases were highly impactful as they featured quotes from customers about their reasons for choosing Icertis. Collectively, these mentions increased conversations about the Icertis platform within industry circles.

About 2017–18, Icertis ramped up its efforts to educate the market—explaining the changing business landscape, highlighting the importance of enterprise contract management solutions and showcasing its unique vision for transforming commerce. The company's marketing team wrote numerous blogs on relevant topics and became more active at industry events, promoting the benefits of the Icertis approach to contract management.

In 2019, Icertis achieved several significant milestones. It emerged as the top-ranked contract management company on Deloitte's Technology Fast 500—a prestigious list highlighting the fastest-growing companies in North America. Additionally, it secured a spot in the esteemed Forbes Cloud 100 list, which recognized the foremost private cloud companies globally.

Icertis was the first company to grasp the true potential of applying AI (Artificial Intelligence) to contract data. In 2019, it became the only CLM company to be featured in the Forbes AI 50 report—an exclusive list spotlighting America's most promising companies leveraging artificial intelligence (AI).

Within six years, Icertis witnessed an extraordinary revenue surge, leaping from $1 million in 2014 to $100 million by 2020. In this period the company garnered 150 customers, including industry giants like Google, Apple and Microsoft. In the same year, Icertis achieved unicorn status and made history by becoming the first CLM company valued at over $1 billion.

The Gartner Magic Quadrant is one of the most popular and influential research methodologies used to evaluate and compare technology vendors in various industries. In 2020, Icertis was named a leader in Gartner's first-ever Magic Quadrant for CLM. Remarkably, Icertis has garnered recognition multiple times.

As Icertis quickly became the most recognized CLM company in the world, many competitors began copying its messaging and offerings. However, Icertis has always stayed ahead of others in terms of innovation. In 2021, Icertis repositioned itself from solely a contract management company into a contract intelligence company. Consequently, the popular Icertis platform ICM became ICI (Icertis Contract Intelligence). Monish explained this saying, 'Contract management focuses on contract storage, standardization and insights from static contracting data. On the other hand, contract intelligence is contract management powered by AI (Artificial Intelligence). It delivers ongoing and forward-looking insights that drive business excellence by making it easier for companies to increase revenue, reduce costs, manage risks and ensure compliance.'

As of November 2023, the ICI platform supports numerous renowned global brands in managing a vast portfolio of over ten million contracts, amounting to a total value exceeding $1 trillion. These contracts encompass over forty languages and span over ninety countries worldwide. Over a decade ago, CLM software was primarily seen as a digital document repository. Today, it holds a significant position among essential software categories and a fifth system of record[*] for the rules of business. As a market leader, Icertis has played an instrumental role in redefining and elevating the positioning of this category.

---

[*] There are four traditional systems of record in enterprise software—CRM (customer data), SCM (supplier data), ERP (enterprise resource data) and HCM (employee data). By applying artificial intelligence to contract data, Icertis has established contracts as the fifth system of record, capturing a company's entitlements and obligations for all its customers, partners, suppliers and employees.

9

The Role of Design in Building a Strong Brand

Elegance is not about being noticed, it's about being remembered.

—Giorgio Armani, fashion designer
and entrepreneur

Design plays a crucial role in a brand's overall strategy, as it has the power to enhance perceptions and create differentiation. Whether it is a strikingly crafted chair in a furniture store, an elegant package on a retail shelf or a captivating advertisement in a newspaper, good design stands out everywhere and draws attention.

Though visual appeal is important and captures our attention, design encompasses much more than just outward appearances. It is about thinking deeply about people's needs, making things easy to use and finding solutions to problems.

Take a chair, for example. Great design is not just about how the chair looks. The aim is to ensure comfort, durability, ease of production and environmental friendliness.

Similarly, a well-made package is not just pretty. It must be easy to use while keeping the product safe. Making things work well is a big part of design. Whether it is a website, a car dashboard, or a kitchen gadget, design simplifies things and improves the whole experience.

While exploring this topic, I had the privilege of engaging in a discussion with **Ashwini Deshpande, co-founder of Elephant Design, India's largest design agency.** Notably, the *Economic Times* has ranked Elephant Design as the top design agency for nine years. Here are a few lessons I learned from her.

Design is logic first, creativity second

Ashwini explained, 'Although the design may look like a piece of art, designers must carefully understand the logical aspects of consumer decision-making before layering on the creative elements.'

Let's focus on a specific aspect of design—product packaging. The package serves as a customer's first moment of truth with a product. It must distinguish itself from the competitors on the shelf, while effectively conveying the brand's message and product benefits. For instance, while collaborating with MTR on their packaging, Elephant Design faced the challenge of working with a wide range of product categories. While all the products were food-related, customers approached them differently. Some purchases were impulsive, while others were more informed choices or part of a regular grocery list. Each scenario required a tailored approach to customer decision-making.

Ashwini told me, 'When buying ready-to-eat food, taste becomes crucial. On the other hand, when purchasing ready-to-cook food, customers prioritize the recipe's authenticity as it reflects their reputation when serving it. When it comes to buying spices, customers are concerned about the quality and authenticity of the ingredients, desiring knowledge of the chilli or cardamom's origin. By understanding consumers' decision-making approaches, we strategically selected messages and determined their sequence in packaging.'

Packaging also plays a vital role post-purchase. It should be easy to open while protecting the product effectively. As an example, when designing the packaging for MTR's ready-made South Indian batters, the Elephant Design team considered several important factors, including storage-friendliness, ease of transportation and usage convenience. Ashwini added, 'A good packaging experience can enhance customer satisfaction, loyalty and advocacy for the brand.'

Visual experience can differentiate a brand in a crowded market

The visual experience significantly impacts how customers perceive and remember a brand. A brand's visual identity encompasses elements such as the logo, colours, fonts, photography and illustrations, along with their application. Materials such as wood, glass, lighting and stone significantly contribute to shaping a brand's visual experience in physical spaces like stores and offices. If a brand embodies qualities such as taste, nostalgia, goodness, luxury, affordability or any other attribute, the visual experience must adeptly convey these characteristics.

Moreover, in an era of online shopping, brands are not only physically placed on shelves but also displayed on screens, alongside numerous other options. Regardless of the package size, the image on the screen looks the same. This makes it crucial to consider factors such as the size of the logo and how the pack graphics are treated to ensure visual appeal and differentiation from the competition.

Like humans, every brand possesses its own unique personality and visual elements, especially colours play a pivotal role in reflecting that personality. For instance, there is a clear preference for blue and green in the medical industry, as these colours tend to convey calmness and cleanliness—both vital in healthcare. However, if multiple brands within an industry use similar colours, brand boundaries may become blurred.

Ashwini clarified, 'In various categories, certain colours become norms. If a brand adheres strictly to them, it can blend in with the category, but differentiation becomes challenging. Alternatively, a brand can aim to stand out and assert its uniqueness by using other colours with meaning relevant to the category. In such case that brand needs to go the extra mile to establish its credentials. However, this path allows it to create a unique image.'

Let's take the example of water brands. It is challenging to differentiate them solely based on the product, and they often appear similar, with blue-coloured labels. However, Bisleri boldly broke away from this trend by choosing green, effectively standing out as a market leader. Similarly, Himalaya also departed from the expected blue, opting for pink, establishing a distinctive and memorable presence in a competitive market.

The brand owners' ambitions direct the design approach

A founder's ambition in business mirrors a mountaineer's aspiration in conquering a mountain. Just as climbing Mount Everest requires greater resources and preparation than scaling a smaller mountain, a founder's ambition to establish either a niche or mass business dictates the essential values, capabilities, resources, and effort required for that particular entrepreneurial journey.

Ashwini said, 'A founder's ambition forms the square within which a design team operates. You can push the boundaries of that square if needed. However, it's crucial to thoroughly understand the parameters of that square.' She elaborated, 'While many founders aim for business growth, Bhavani and Bharat, the founders of Organic India, started with an aim to improve the well-being of farmers, consumers, and the environment. They saw sales and success as secondary outcomes to a larger, more impactful goal of promoting eco-friendly farming practices. As a result, our design approach centred on prioritizing product authenticity and source story over sales-centric messaging.'

In another scenario, during discussions with a food brand team, Ashwini asked about their aspirations. They responded saying, 'We want our brand to be so beloved that if stores run out of our stock, then customers would prefer to return empty-handed instead of looking for an alternative!' Ashwini described this as the mark of a cult brand—irreplaceable and highly sought after. In this situation, Elephant's design approach aimed to present the brand persona through innovative packaging that would attract and engage potential shoppers in unique ways.

The creative assets of a brand are shaped by its positioning

Developing the creative elements that define a brand—its name, visual identity, packaging and retail design—is an intricate process deeply linked to the brand's positioning. Understanding and defining that position begins with a comprehensive grasp of the users' lifestyles and preferences across diverse categories, and a meticulous examination of the competitive landscape. This in-depth research is essential. At times the desired space in positioning might already be occupied by competitors in the same category or companies in other categories targeting the same market. In response, start-ups often re-analyse their goals or unearth new insights to redefine their brand positioning.

Positioning a brand is not just about its current status but also a commitment to its future trajectory. This commitment requires an ongoing demonstration of the characteristic that defines the brand positioning. For example, claiming to be the most innovative brand demands continuous, visible innovation that can be experienced by its buyers.

However, committing to a specific brand position can raise concerns within the team. Anticipating the team's ability to sustain the chosen attribute over time can also be daunting. Thus, it is crucial to thoroughly evaluate the harmony between the brand's chosen positioning and the team's ability to deliver it consistently over a long period of time.

It is also essential to conduct market tests to validate positioning. Products that highlight positioning around functional benefits, like healthcare devices or medications, often undergo rigorous evaluations, including clinical trials, ensuring safety, effectiveness, and regulatory compliance. These offerings typically demand extensive testing with larger sample sizes to gather sufficient data for licensing and certification.

On the other hand, products emphasizing positioning around emotional benefits, such as soft drinks, may require a significantly larger testing base to genuinely capture their market appeal. This heightened requirement stems from the challenge soft drinks face in crowded markets where differentiation based on ingredients is difficult.

To illustrate relationship between positioning and design, let's look at the case of Epigamia. It aimed to establish its credibility as a healthy snack, positioning itself as the 'Hero of Small Hunger', ideal for 4 o'clock cravings. To align the design with positioning, Elephant Design created a bold and confident visual identity for Epigamia. The package design incorporated vibrant fruit colours, making it easy for consumers to differentiate between flavours, as well as enhancing the overall taste and functional appeal.

Ashwini said, 'Given that the healthy aspect is a significant part of Epigamia's philosophy, we prominently highlighted the product's features such as "High Protein, Low Fat", "All Natural, No Preservatives" on the front of the packaging. This approach ensured that the healthy food image was clearly communicated to consumers and at no point was it confused with desserts.'

Designs must be user, business, and tech-friendly

Ashwini insisted that successful brands maintain their relevance by embracing FOBO—the Fear of Becoming Obsolete. This drives them to remain attentive to evolving dynamics in consumers' lives.

Design, a pivotal factor in a brand's relevance, loses its impact if it does not align with user needs, or lacks cost-efficiency, or does not onboard technological advancements. Ashwini stressed, 'Designers must strike the "sweet spot" between user needs, technology offerings, and business requirements when creating relevant solutions.'

Let's look at an example from the three-decades-long enduring partnership between Elephant Design and Symphony, the world's leading cooler brand. After launching several innovative, category-creating air coolers for over a couple of decades, Symphony naturally attracted intense competition from imitator brands. During its research to create a differentiable product, the Elephant team observed how consumers used coolers. They found that in the off-season, to save space in rooms, people placed their large coolers on their balconies, often using them as clothes drying racks. This was seen by the design team as an opportunity to create an innovative category of compact coolers. Consequently, Elephant Design collaborated with Symphony to develop a very compact, tall cooler, occupying just one square foot of space. This cooler strongly resonated with users and continues to sell in over sixty countries.

Case Studies

How Paper Boat's Brand Identity Was Designed

In 2012, the Hector Beverages team introduced their collection of beverages to Elephant Design and outlined their brand essence—delivering natural, unadulterated drinks from the past in a modern format. The close collaboration between Elephant Design and Hector Beverages led to the development of the brand name, its narrative, packaging structure and visual identity.

Let us uncover the story behind the now famous brand name—Paper Boat. To evoke childhood nostalgia, the teams sought a name that would instantly reconnect people with cherished childhood memories. Drawing inspiration from the universal practice of crafting paper boats during childhood, and the lyrics of Sudarshan Fakir's ghazal, famously sung by Jagjit Singh, *Woh Kagaz Ki Kashti Wo Barish Ka Pani*, the name Paper Boat emerged as the perfect choice.

Paper Boat wasn't merely a beverage; it symbolized a nostalgic journey back to childhood. Understanding the crucial role of packaging in reflecting this sentiment, Elephant Design chose paper-like Doy packs—a deviation from the conventional beverage packaging of glass bottles, tetra packs or tin cans. The Doy packs felt like textured paper, giving a unique and authentic experience while holding and drinking from them. Additionally, the boat-shaped bottle caps enhanced the pack's visual appeal and functionality. Easy to handle and open with just two fingers, these caps were designed for convenience, turning and opening with ease.

While the packaging adopted a modern approach, the drinks themselves were named in a traditional manner. For example, instead of being labelled Mango Pulp, the first drink was called Aamras, invoking a sense of nostalgia, instantly transporting consumers to a familiar world.

Drawing again from childhood memories, the packaging embraced vivid natural colours and delightful fruit illustrations that echoed simplicity and goodness. Moreover, witty one-liners were added to highlight the absence of artificial flavouring. Captivating mini stories were written for each beverage and added to the back of the pack. To distinguish each drink, the design was enhanced with a unique and identifiable brand world, featuring elements such as waves, trees, sky, birds, fish and frogs in various colours.

In 2013, Paper Boat quietly debuted in retail outlets across major metros, as well as on certain airlines, without advertising or promotions. The packs vanished from retail shelves so rapidly that Hector Beverages had to quickly reassess their capacity plans.

The India Design Mark is a prestigious design standard that recognizes excellence in various design aspects, such as form, function, quality, safety, sustainability and innovation. In 2015, Paper Boat was awarded the India Design Mark. In 2018, Paper Boat's design received 'Best of the Best' recognition at the Indian edition of the Lexus Design Awards. Over ten years, many awards and recognitions have followed as Paper Boat continues to partner with Elephant Design on their brand journey.

How CaratLane Made Design One of Its Biggest Differentiators

CaratLane has been a trailblazer in presenting beautiful, wearable and affordable jewellery that can be worn every day and not just reserved for special occasions or kept in bank lockers. The brand's appealing designs have played the biggest role in its popularity and success, helping to establish a distinctive identity and fostering a strong brand recall.

'When someone purchases jewellery with an investment mindset, it is likely that their primary consideration will revolve around making charges or the prevailing gold rate,' said Avnish Anand, CEO of CaratLane. 'We don't aim to attract such customers as we're not in the business of chasing revenue at any cost. Instead, we cater to a distinct type of customer—someone who seeks jewellery for adornment and enhancing their appearance and appreciates beautiful designs.'

CaratLane follows several approaches to launch new designs. A few are outlined here:

First, designers derive inspiration from the natural world, commonplace objects and famous characters. For instance, CaratLane's butterfly collection is a tribute to the life cycle of a butterfly, while their Aranya line is a nod to the untamed jungle. CaratLane has also collaborated with Warner Bros. on a Harry Potter-themed jewellery collection. Additionally, the brand has partnered with franchises like Peppa Pig and Minions, incorporating these characters into its jewellery designs. These strategic alliances have allowed CaratLane to connect with a vast fanbase of these famous characters and offer unique gifting options for children.

Second, designers meticulously craft jewellery tailored for specific occasions or to evoke particular emotions. 'Jewellery design goes beyond aesthetic appeal; it's about infusing the meaning that customers seek. For instance, a piece of jewellery might symbolize someone's first pay cheque or a significant life event, such as becoming a mother,' Avnish explained. 'We ensure our designs resonate with specific occasions and make the recipient feel genuinely special and appreciated.'

Third, CaratLane is constantly trying to marry the traditional with the modern. For example, the mangalsutra, a traditional form of jewellery that holds significant importance for married women in Indian culture, has been reimagined by incorporating black beads into contemporary designs. While the traditional form is usually worn with ethnic attire, the contemporary version can be paired with any outfit. Avnish explained to me, 'We don't want to disrupt traditional codes of jewellery; we just want to infuse contemporary style and make it more wearable.'

Fourth, CaratLane has always employed advanced manufacturing techniques, like 3D printing and stamping, to create aesthetically pleasing designs that are also cost-effective because they require less material compared to traditional methods. For example, while a conventional jeweller might use four grams of gold for a specific design, CaratLane achieves a similar look using just two grams, without compromising the structural strength of the jewellery. Avnish expanded on this by saying, 'Thanks to advanced manufacturing techniques, we're able to provide our customers with beautifully designed jewellery at affordable prices.'

Fifth, designers delve into extensive research, studying emerging trends, international fashion trends and exploring social media platforms like Instagram for inspiration. The generated ideas are then sketched and transformed into prototypes to assess their aesthetic appeal. These preliminary samples undergo stringent evaluation based on criteria such as profit margin potential and wearability safety, ensuring the designs are neither too sharp nor uncomfortable.

Elaborating further on the design process, Avnish said, 'Mithun Sacheti's instincts are integral to our design methodology. He has studied design, manufacturing, and branding so thoroughly that he has developed a "trained intuition". This allows him to discern the finer aspects and understand what will or will not resonate with customers.'

Following the launch of any new designs, CaratLane actively gathers consumer feedback. Initially, the new design is introduced in a select number of stores. The company's technology ecosystem allows it to track how customers are interacting with its new designs both online and offline. They are able to assess factors like how often these pieces are tried on or viewed. This kind of granular data guides the team on which designs to retain and which to discontinue. Avnish said, 'This feedback process ensures that inventory and marketing investments are made only in successful designs.'

The brand is also proactive about adapting its designs based on customer feedback. For instance, when introducing children's jewellery, feedback highlighted the need to include a specific attachment to prevent the jewellery falling off during play. Similarly, feedback from women emphasized the significance of varied earring attachments to accommodate diverse preferences and comfort associated with different variations. In response, CaratLane promptly made the required adjustments, showcasing its dedication to meeting customer needs.

The CaratLane leadership strongly advocates collective appreciation and understanding of the value of design within the organization. Initially, every employee undergoes training in the company's design methodology. Subsequently, all employees, regardless of their role, actively engage in sales conversations at least three or four times a year. This process ensures that the core ethos of design-centricity is instilled in everybody, and the time spent selling helps in gaining valuable customer insights.

Avnish told me, 'We invest significantly not only in crafting exceptional designs but also in presenting them to our customers in the best possible way. The founding principle of our company is that design will never take a backseat to anything else. Not to any model, nor to any brand ambassador. Our designs are the heroes of our story, and we are committed to presenting them in the best possible light. We want people to look at what we provide and say, "This is what I want because I want to look beautiful or feel special"'.

However, Avnish also emphasized that creating beautiful jewellery is futile if the discovery of designs, their trial, and purchase don't occur seamlessly. At CaratLane, a lot of focus is placed on imagery because beautiful jewellery only looks as good as the images representing it. To provide a seamless shopping experience for its customers, the team ensures that jewellery discovery is straightforward, whether customers are browsing through the brand's app, website or in-store. They also ensure that the billing process is swift and efficient. Additionally, the team makes sure that information about CaratLane's services, new categories, newly launched designs and ongoing discounts or promotional schemes is readily available.

In essence, CaratLane's relentless focus on design excellence, paired with its proactive approach to meeting customer needs, has solidified its position as a significant powerhouse in the jewellery retail industry.

How Focus on Design Drove Razorpay's Growth

Razorpay operates within the realm of B2B fintech, primarily because its services and solutions are designed to cater to businesses rather than individual customers. Shashank Kumar, co-founder at Razorpay, recalled the early days, noting, 'When we began our journey, people believed that payment management in B2B was essentially about managing technology and business dashboards, and design didn't matter much. However, whether it's B2B or B2C, at the end of the day, it's a human using your product.'

While designing its products, the company places great emphasis on conducting thorough research and gathering feedback from individuals who utilize its services. An in-house team is dedicated to maintaining continual communication with the users.* Insights derived from these interactions are shared throughout the organization, contributing to a comprehensive understanding of the needs and challenges faced by those using the platform. Feedback from sales, customer support and other customer-facing teams is consistently channelled back to the design, product and engineering departments, fostering cross-functional collaboration.

To further enhance its understanding of the overall user experience, every Razorpay employee actively participates in supporting users on a monthly basis. This direct involvement provides immediate insights into the specific needs and challenges faced by users. Additionally, an individual who utilizes Razorpay's services is invited each month to share their experiences with the entire organization at the all-hands meeting. With its unwavering focus on improving user experience and driving innovation, Razorpay has introduced many industry-first solutions.

Shashank explained that design is not just about 'how a product looks' but also about 'how it works'. This involves the

---

* The term 'user' refers to an individual utilizing Razorpay on behalf of a business, which could be an enterprise, small business, start-up or freelancer.

ease of navigating through multiple options to find the right feature, the user-friendly experience in utilizing any feature and the overall efficiency of the feature itself.

As a testament to its sophisticated design approach, Razorpay manages many complexities in the backend while appearing simple on the front end. For instance, the platform enables businesses to accept payments through various methods, including UPI, NEFT, RTGS, IMPS, debit and credit cards, net banking and mobile wallets. Moreover, it offers multiple products designed to streamline the financial operations of businesses. These include facilitating payments to vendors and employees, providing short-term loans, enabling fund transfers across numerous bank accounts, managing recurring payments in various currencies and processing customer refunds. So, while a user navigates through multiple options on the front end, the multitude of workflows run in the backend, ensuring that every transaction is completed within seconds.

The movement of money is a sensitive matter. Razorpay transfers money from one place to another with a simple touch of a button. Therefore, it consistently upholds the following principles in its design process:

Trust: Users need assurance that their money will securely and accurately reach its intended recipient. They must also trust that their sensitive financial information is well-protected against fraud or theft. As an example of strengthening trust, in the early days of e-commerce, customers would select products on one website but were then redirected to another site for payment. This often led to confusion and a loss of trust. Razorpay addressed this issue by introducing a checkout form that opens directly within the original website or app. This solution, which has now become an industry standard, eliminated the need for redirection and significantly reduced drop-offs at the checkout stage.

Accessibility: The transaction system should be user-friendly, ensuring that people of all ages, backgrounds, and abilities can use it without difficulty. For instance, recognizing the technical complexity of setting up a payment gateway, Razorpay developed a 'NoCode' solution. This allows businesses to create custom payment pages without writing a single line of code or needing support from technology consultants.

Assistance: Users should receive help or support when they need it, instilling confidence and reliability. Consequently, Razorpay provides 24/7 support to its users.

Talking about the impact of design on business, Shashank shared an anecdote. A few years ago, a start-up aimed to integrate payments into their app, assigning the task to a product manager. Being relatively new to the payment landscape, she delved into researching various payment gateways online to make an informed decision. Among numerous established players, one start-up caught her attention. After signing up, experimenting with the features, and consulting with her team, the verdict was clear: Razorpay would be the chosen payment partner for Cure.Fit. Shashank emphasized, 'Cure.Fit naturally leaned towards Razorpay due to its user-friendly design; no aggressive sales pitch was needed to seal the deal.'

The simplicity of Razorpay's design led to a strong influx of organic sign-ups and negated the necessity for a sizable sales team. As more businesses signed up, Razorpay witnessed the effectiveness of word-of-mouth marketing. When inquiries arose in Facebook groups regarding choosing a payment gateway for business, Razorpay swiftly transitioned from being rarely mentioned to becoming one of the top recommendations. The rest, as they say, is history. Today, Razorpay's solutions are utilized by over ten million businesses.

10

Building Consistency through Systems and Processes

Always fight for quality, whether giving or receiving.

—Walt Disney, co-founder of The Walt
Disney Company

When the processes supporting business areas such as supply chain management, inventory control, order processing, and customer support are meticulously streamlined, start-ups can confidently ensure prompt delivery of products or services, maintain required quality standards, and provide exceptional customer experiences. This solid foundation forms the bedrock on which a successful brand is built.

I had the privilege of discussing this topic with **Hari Menon, co-founder and CEO of BigBasket, India's largest online grocery delivery company**. Here are a few lessons I learned from him:

Establish operational foundation before scaling up: People are drawn to branded products and services because of the consistent quality and experience they offer. To maintain this consistency, brands need to prioritize the smooth running of their back-end operations. By doing so they can deliver on their promises while establishing themselves in the consumer perception as trustworthy and reliable service providers.

Since its beginnings in 2011, BigBasket has focused on setting up its processes and operations to meet the three golden metrics of grocery retail:

The first is the fill rate. This measures the extent to which a customer's order is fulfilled. For example, if a customer ordered ten items and the retailer delivered eight, the fill rate was 80 per cent. BigBasket focused on achieving a fill rate of 99.5 per cent, which is considered best in the industry from a customer delight perspective.

The second is on-time delivery. Customers prefer a specific and predefined delivery time slot, chosen when placing an order. Interestingly, BigBasket introduced 100 per cent slotted delivery from day one.

The third is the in-stock rate. This means that when a consumer visits a store, the item they are looking for should be in stock. BigBasket focused on keeping its in-stock rate over 96 per cent. Hari explained this saying, 'Every category has must-have essentials and nice-to-have specialized items. In every city we first focus on building a supply chain for essentials, and then add specialized products over time.'

He added, 'In our first year, we didn't heavily invest in marketing. Instead, we concentrated on establishing our backend operations and limited our marketing efforts to our existing network, which was substantial in Bangalore. Our primary goal was to gather feedback and enhance our operational metrics.' Having successfully achieved the three golden metrics in Bangalore within a year, BigBasket expanded its operations to Mumbai and Hyderabad in 2012. The company operated exclusively in these three cities for the next two years. In late 2014, BigBasket expanded to Chennai, Pune, and Delhi NCR. Having established a solid foundation with tested operational efficiency, BigBasket continued to expand into numerous new cities.

Hari explained BigBasket's growth philosophy to me saying, 'While it can be tempting for venture capital-funded businesses to prioritize rapid expansion, at BigBasket we opted for gradual growth to establish these metrics in every city we operated in. To gather support for our long-term vision from our board members, we would have two monthly board meetings to keep them fully informed about our strategy and ongoing progress.'

As of December 2023, operating in fifty-five cities, BigBasket delivers over 15 million customer orders a month. Hari added, 'Even now, after being in business for over a decade, we hold monthly board meetings, even though the norm is quarterly.'

Any process creation or change must go through a process: Customer feedback, market trends and operational challenges frequently drive the need to create or change processes within a business. Hari highlighted, 'Jugaad, a term reflecting quick shortcuts and band-aid-like fixes for immediate problem-solving, is prevalent in India. While effective in resource-constrained scenarios, prioritizing jugaad over established processes can lead to numerous costly errors in the long run. Therefore, we avoid any kind of jugaad at BigBasket.'

I also learned from Hari that to ensure an effective process it is essential to gather inputs from relevant stakeholders who will be directly impacted by it. Their insights and perspectives provide valuable guidance in crafting a process that meets business needs. To facilitate the execution of a process, it is also important to create clear, concise and easily understandable documentation. It serves as a guide for those involved in the execution process, ensuring consistency and accuracy. Before implementing the process on a larger scale, testing it through pilot projects or simulations is crucial. Based on the results, necessary adjustments can be made to enhance the process's efficiency and effectiveness. Post-implementation, close monitoring is crucial for assessing and enhancing the process's efficiency and effectiveness.

BigBasket's operations revolve around three core areas: procurement, warehouse inventory management, and delivery logistics. The company has dedicated teams responsible for defining processes in each of these areas. Acknowledging the wide-reaching impact of processes across organizational functions, the process creation teams seek inputs from representatives of diverse departments.

Depending on the process's complexity, deadlines are set for implementation, ranging from a few days to several months. Considering the differing factors across regions, such as suppliers' availability, traffic conditions, and order volumes, the teams customize the processes to meet each region's specific requirements. Once established and tested, the process creation teams hand over the processes to the operations team for execution. 'Once we adopt a process, we follow it like robots. If anyone has ideas for improving the existing processes, they can bring these to the process creation team for consideration. But nobody can make even the smallest change without required approvals,' Hari explained.

Defining a process is essential, but success lies in executing it with discipline: Disciplined execution of every process yields numerous advantages. First, it elevates efficiency and productivity by reducing errors, and wasted effort. Furthermore, disciplined execution ensures consistent and reliable outcomes, fostering stakeholder trust. Nevertheless, it is human nature to sometimes bypass or shortcut processes due to challenges or temptations. To illustrate the point, Hari shared one particular incident. At BigBasket, every order used to be packed in crates sealed with finely ribbed plastic cord, similar to those used by airlines. A process was established for opening the crates at customers' homes, requiring the use of a cutter to release the cords. The delivery person was instructed to retain the cut cords for later disposal. However, most delivery executives forgot or did not bother to carry cutters and resorted to forcefully tearing the cords. This practice resulted in damaged crates, scattered plastic cords outside homes, and an unsatisfactory customer experience.

Hari emphasized, 'Through such experiences we learned that merely documenting a process and relying solely on verbal explanations from experienced staff to new employees isn't sufficient. Comprehensive training by a qualified instructor is essential for effective process implementation.' So, to prevent process breakdowns, BigBasket established a training department. Hari elaborated, 'We created a comprehensive training programme, covering every step of the process execution, no matter how small or seemingly simple. Every employee at BigBasket undergoes mandatory New Hire Training (NHT), receiving certification before starting work in the live environment. As processes evolve and new ones emerge, even the trainers undergo regular certification.' To verify that the processes are being followed on the ground, BigBasket has implemented a robust audit mechanism.

The focus of every process should be to improve customer experience: Customers are the lifeblood of any business, and their satisfaction is directly tied to the success and growth of a company. Every business process should be designed with the customer in mind. This means understanding their needs, pain points, and expectations at each touchpoint.

In the context of BigBasket, customer experience can be categorized into four key areas:

First, the ease of placing an order is of utmost importance in the grocery business. Customers typically start each month with a list of twenty-five to thirty planned items. Recognizing the significance of saving time for its customers, BigBasket has developed a solution called Smart Basket. It automatically populates customers' carts with their most frequently purchased items and alerts them if any habitual purchase is missing. Furthermore, for customers who prefer browsing, each product is accompanied by appropriate images and concise yet effective information.

Second, the overall delivery experience plays a significant role. Hari told me, 'We consistently see in the NPS surveys that the biggest driver of overall customer happiness is the quality of delivery experience. This depends on the behaviour of a delivery person, the presentation of the products, and the ability of the delivery person to handle exceptions and complaints. At BigBasket delivery personnel are trained to be patient while customers check their orders. To avoid any conflict, the company operates a no-questions-asked return policy. So, if a customer has any issue with any item in the order, the delivery personnel will take that item back. Also, the delivery personnel are not supposed to contact a customer for any last-mile navigation. Instead, they are assisted by the delivery app and supported by a customer service agent.

Third, the quality of assistance provided in resolving any complaint is a significant aspect of customer experience. BigBasket's goal is to connect a customer with a customer support agent within ten seconds, 98 per cent of the time. 'We take every complaint seriously and constantly push ourselves to provide a better customer experience,' Hari said.

Lastly, the quality of the products themselves is of immense importance. Groceries can be divided into three sub-categories: dry groceries like soap and toothpaste, chilled and frozen items such as ice cream, and fresh produce like fruits and vegetables. Hari emphasized that, 'Quality isn't solely defined by dry groceries. It's best judged by perishable items like fruits and vegetables.' BigBasket has implemented technology and processes to effectively manage the supply chain and delivery logistics for all three grocery categories.

Each process should be empowered by cutting-edge technology: The influence of technology on processes manifests in several ways—it automates repetitive tasks, minimizes manual effort and the potential for human error. Moreover, it enables seamless communication among team members involved in the process. Additionally, technology empowers organizations to analyse and derive meaningful insights from process data, facilitating the identification of bottlenecks, inefficiencies, and areas for improvement.

BigBasket offers both instant order delivery for specific items and preferred time slot delivery, for its entire inventory. Let us explore here the impact of technology on the planning and execution of the latter. When a customer places an order on

BigBasket, they select their preferred delivery timeslot. Based on the customer's location, a designated hub (small warehouse), is assigned to ship the order. An Operations Controller (OC) at the hub determines the number of orders for the upcoming slot and allocates them to a set of vans following specific routes. To properly assign orders to different vans, the OC needs information about the size of each order or the space required in the vans for the crates. The size of the vans varies significantly, with some capable of carrying seventy-five crates while others can only accommodate thirty-five crates. Additionally, since each hub is situated at varying distances from the target customers, the vans must commence their routes at specific times, determined by the distance between the hub and the customers' locations. In Indian cities, road conditions and infrastructure can pose additional challenges. There are often one-way streets and road diversions are not always accurately reflected on mapping platforms like Google Maps. Traffic conditions also vary based on the time of day. Additionally, the service time for each order is not uniform, as some orders may consist of only one crate, while others may have multiple crates. Orders with cash on delivery also require additional time to service.

To address these complexities, BigBasket developed advanced technology that aids its teams with capacity management, including determining the number of delivery executives needed and the number of vehicles required to accommodate the packages. Notably, BigBasket's technology optimizes van routes 20 per cent more effectively than Google Maps, ensuring reliable deliveries within set timeframes and reduced transportation costs.[1] Similarly, there are numerous other cases where technology has assisted BigBasket in becoming a highly efficient company.

Case Studies

How Rebel Foods Built 4000 Restaurants in Forty-Eight Months

Rebel Foods is the world's largest internet restaurant company. It boasts a portfolio of over forty-five brands and a vast network encompassing over 4000 internet-based restaurants across multiple countries. Rebel Foods has successfully served millions of orders to a diverse clientele from various corners of the globe. Their monumental operation involves the management of an extensive array of products, a sizable workforce, and intricate processes. To add to the complexity, the company is in a perpetual state of innovation, constantly experimenting with novel recipes, launching fresh brands, and expanding its presence into new territories. Achieving this consistently at a rapid rate and large scale is no small feat.

A key factor that contributed to their remarkable success was the invention of the Rebel Operating System (Rebel OS) in 2018. This state-of-the-art technological system empowered them to optimize kitchen spaces efficiently, enabling rapid piloting, testing, iteration, and scaling of new products and brands.

The Rebel OS comprises three core components:

Culinary innovation centre: Led by skilled chefs, this innovation centre serves as a hub for creativity and experimentation. Here, chefs craft unique and mouth-watering recipes, while continually enhancing menus across all their diverse brands. Explaining the process behind developing new dishes, Ankush Grover, co-founder at Rebel Foods said, 'It begins with gathering feedback from a targeted customer group. Once the concept solidifies, the dish is introduced within a select number of kitchens. Only when the dish achieves product–market fit, meaning enthusiastic customer adoption is observed, we introduce the dish to a greater number of kitchens.'

Until the product–market fit is achieved, Rebel Foods' culinary teams engage in an ongoing refinement cycle. They tirelessly seek the delicate balance between recipe perfection and economic viability, considering preparation costs, profit margins, customer acquisition expenses, and competitive pricing. Every customer rating is meticulously analysed, with the unwavering goal of not just meeting but surpassing industry benchmarks within the respective food categories. This relentless commitment to continuous improvement ensures that Rebel Foods, offerings are not only delicious but also economically sustainable.

Once the product–market fit has been achieved, chefs break down menus into small Standard Operating Procedure (SOP)-driven steps, meticulously detailing every facet of their preparation. They ensure that each step is thoroughly documented to ensure consistency, even by unskilled chefs during the scale-up phase. Afterwards, the dish is expanded to multiple kitchens.

End-to-end kitchen management technology: Rebel Foods leverages technology and innovation to enhance the efficiency of its kitchen operations, improving various aspects of business such as supply management, cooking processes, demand prediction, and order fulfilment.

One standout feature of their kitchens is the learning displays, which empower chefs by providing step-by-step cooking instructions to preparing a wide range of dishes, obviating the necessity of memorizing specific recipes. Ankush emphasized, 'This means a single chef can create hundreds of recipes for Behrouz, OvenStory, Faasos and other brands.'

Moreover, intelligent kitchen equipment ensures a consistent taste and quality across hundreds of recipes and brands in numerous kitchens. Once chefs input a recipe, including temperature settings, ingredients, and other details, these intelligent appliances take over the cooking process, guaranteeing uniformity of taste and quality.

A noteworthy kitchen technology is the SWAT machine, designed to evaluate dishes based on size, weight, appearance, and temperature. Dishes meeting the required standards proceed to the packing phase, while any discrepancies trigger an immediate alert to kitchen staff, for rectification.

To further enhance efficiency and precision, Rebel Foods has developed an in-house IoT (Internet of Things) platform, which automates cooking processes and efficiently manages inventory, procurement, manufacturing and warehousing. Additionally, Rebel Foods employs an AI (Artificial Intelligence)-based video analytics platform to maintain strict hygiene and safety standards in their kitchens, ensuring top-notch food safety and quality.

Additionally, Rebel Foods gathers and analyses extensive data, encompassing order details, customer behaviour, inquiries and interactions. They utilize data science and machine learning algorithms to make highly accurate demand predictions, which assist in inventory planning for each kitchen. Thanks to these precise forecasts, Rebel Foods has substantially reduced food wastage.

A national supply chain: Rebel Foods excels in its supply chain capabilities, encompassing sourcing, warehousing and safe transportation of various input materials. Ankush emphasized, 'Our supply chain network is the backbone that enables us to scale our brands and products across kitchens and markets, both in India and internationally.' This reliable supply chain enables seamless scaling of successful products and the replication of brands across different markets.

Besides, Rebel OS, Rebel Foods has two other foundational pillars:

Brand/product launch playbook: At Rebel Foods, each brand is overseen by a brand manager, who is responsible for its entire journey—from inception to expansion into new markets, and the introduction of new products. These brand managers take charge of a brand from its very inception, working closely with the Culinary Innovation Centre, to align the product with market demands. Once the product–market fit is achieved, they oversee the scale-up phase.

Ankush explained, 'When we conceptualize a brand, our initial step is to deploy it in two to five kitchens. Seeking feedback actively, we scale the brand only when its rating exceeds the category average. Like a tech product, we avoid investing in marketing until there's a solid product–market fit.'

Since different brands vary in market size and are at different stages in their journey, the allocation of marketing budgets and the selection of media channels for each brand differ accordingly. Ankush elucidated, 'Some of our brands and products remain local, some expand regionally, some go international, and others are launched exclusively during special occasions like Christmas and Diwali.'

As the owner of multiple D2C brands, Rebel Foods capitalizes on its data advantage. With customers placing digital orders, the company consistently acquires valuable customer data and feedback. Rebel Foods even has access to customer phone numbers, enabling direct communication to gather additional insights. This feedback loop, driven by customer input, is vital to creating great products and building strong brands.

Cloud kitchen network: Rebel Foods cloud kitchen network, equipped with advanced infrastructure for diverse cooking processes, fulfils customer orders promptly. When new brands and products achieve product–market fit, this network comes into action, efficiently managing multiple online restaurant brands and ensuring timely deliveries to various locations.

At the core of every Rebel Foods kitchen is a Chief Delight Officer (CDO), a pivotal role comparable in significance to that of kitchen CEO. The CDO's multifaceted responsibilities include assembling and supervising the kitchen team, ensuring exceptional customer and employee experiences, sustaining financial viability, overseeing comprehensive training programmes, and efficiently managing inventory. Central to the CDO's mission is the unwavering commitment to delighting customers, a practice that builds customer loyalty and ensures their continued patronage.

As we envision the future of the food industry, Rebel Foods stands out as a shining example of innovation, technology, and customer-centricity, poised to redefine the culinary world. Their seamless scalability underscores the critical importance of efficient processes and systems that have played a pivotal role in their rapid growth, all the while maintaining a consistent customer experience across a diverse array of cuisines.

How STAGE OTT Created Content Supply

The STAGE team recognized that creating premium dialect-specific content was uncharted territory in India, making proof of concept (PoC) crucial. Given that two of the founders, Vinay and Parveen Singhal, hailed from a village in Haryana, Haryanvi was chosen as the first dialect to focus on. The team began by scouring YouTube and local events to identify talented artists. They then contacted them to record performances, also seeking recommendations for other promising talent.

Having collated 100–150 content pieces, including *shayri*, poetry and comedy, each lasting roughly ten minutes, the team strategically marketed them through a free mobile app using social media. The STAGE team was thrilled to receive an incredible response from the public, resulting in half a million app downloads within a few months.

However, monetizing their content proved more challenging. People hesitated to pay for content on STAGE when they could find similar content for free on YouTube. To overcome this hurdle, the STAGE team decided to create original Haryanvi movies and web series. 'Our belief was that if people in villages could afford and use brands like Dove, Mahindra Scorpio and Royal Enfield, they could also pay for content, provided it was premium and sensible,' Parveen explained.

The STAGE team recognized that following generic Bollywood storylines and producing content in the local dialect would not suffice. They understood the importance of addressing local issues specific to the community. To achieve this, they created cohorts based on popular interests in Haryana, including sport, the army, wrestling, farming, the police, and sensitive but important subjects such as honour killings. Using a model similar to Netflix, STAGE allowed content creators to pitch their stories within the selected cohort/s. Once a project was approved, the actual content production was outsourced to a STAGE-certified production house, with STAGE providing the necessary funding to creators. The artists in Haryana responded with immense enthusiasm to this initiative as STAGE gave them hope by providing opportunities and financial support.

In the first project, the risks were substantial as the STAGE team and the artists lacked experience of film-making. Moreover, there were no dialect-based TV channels or OTT platforms to learn from. The STAGE team established processes and standard operating procedures (SOPs) for various aspects, including costumes, cameras and set construction, to mitigate the risks. They defined stringent quality checks throughout the production process, from scripting to screenplay and casting.

Despite having a modest budget of Rs 4 lakh, the STAGE team successfully produced the very first Haryanvi web series, *Mere Yaar Ki Shaadi*. Parveen noted, 'In Bollywood, celebrities charge crores for appearances, but our cost of production was low because we worked with unknown talent. These artists were content resting under a tree and didn't require fancy amenities like vanity vans.'

It was necessary to pay the artists, camera operators and equipment vendors daily during film production. Since everyone was eager to showcase their talent and worked tirelessly for ten to twelve hours a day, the shoot was completed in just ten days, contributing significantly to the low cost of production. Shashank Vaishnav, co-founder of STAGE, acknowledged that while things did not always go smoothly, nevertheless, everyone's passion and dedication enabled the team to overcome every obstacle. Interestingly, this web series received a tremendous response from the audience.

Over time, STAGE has successfully attracted Haryana-based artists who were previously working in Mumbai, back to their home state. These artists brought with them a wealth of knowledge and experience, contributing to STAGE's high standards of quality and professionalism. Parveen noted that STAGE has funded several notable projects, ranging from Rs 20 to 40 lakh, some of which have become blockbusters. Moreover, the STAGE team has created educational content on progressive topics such as personal finance and fitness.

In addition to producing original content, STAGE has expanded its content library by acquiring the rights to Tamil and Telugu movies, which they have dubbed into Haryanvi. Parveen highlighted that dubbing content was more cost-effective and time-efficient than creating original content. While original content drove subscriptions, dubbed content enhanced engagement and provided viewers with more options.

Recognizing the immense potential of the Rajasthan market, which is three times larger than Haryana, STAGE strategically moved to tap this region, in June 2022. Given the geographical proximity and overlap of dialects and cultures between Haryana and Rajasthan, STAGE was able to dub a significant portion of content produced in Haryanvi into Rajasthani and vice versa. This approach allowed them to quickly expand their reach and impact.

Parveen said that one of the most significant impacts STAGE has had is employment generation for local artists. As of Nov 2023, over 2000 artists in Haryana and Rajasthan earn their livelihood through STAGE.

How Licious Is Setting the Standard for Freshness in the Meat Industry

In 2015, while beginning the journey of Licious, to source the finest meat, co-founders Abhay Hanjura and Vivek Gupta developed an extensive quality assessment spreadsheet and engaged with meat producers to determine if they met these standards. However, they encountered significant resistance, with producers arguing that compliance with such specifications would raise production costs, and consumers would hesitate to buy expensive meat. Many smaller producers faced working capital constraints and were reluctant to experiment. Some considered Abhay and Vivek unconventional, stating, 'Seems you are looking for a gold-plated chicken. Even five-star hotels don't ask for such detailed assessments. Let's not waste each other's time.'

Abhay recalled, 'We were disheartened to witness a food item that holds a special place in consumers' lives being treated merely as a commodity, with producers dictating what consumers should buy, without seeking their input.' He also highlighted, 'The issue wasn't the demand for high-quality meat but ensuring its supply.' It became evident to the duo that the entire supply chain was flawed, which hindered the control over meat quality. Vivek noted, 'A brand offers a consistent and reliable experience repeatedly. We understood that establishing a trusted brand in meat delivery would be challenging without a consistent supply of high-quality meat.' To address this, they decided to establish a supply chain system that would source the finest quality meat and deliver it fresh to customers within a twenty-four-hour timeframe.

To get the desired meat quality, the duo decided to offer producers a 15–30 per cent higher price. While searching for suppliers capable of delivering high-quality meat, Vivek suggested to Abhay that they meet Joe Manavalan. He had previously spent over a decade working as a chef and faculty at The Oberoi Group. Later, Joe ventured into various food-related businesses, and also took charge of JW Marriott hotel in Bangalore. The duo visited Joe's commissary, which he used to run his dessert brand 'Painted Platters'. They were thoroughly impressed by its world-class hygiene standards.

Recognizing Joe's passion for quality and his extensive experience in the food industry, Abhay asked Joe to join Licious as a co-founder. However, Joe's commitments to his existing ventures kept him occupied. Undeterred, Abhay visited JW Marriott to convince Joe. Joe was multitasking and did not respond for thirty minutes. It was then that Abhay said, 'Joe, you have the choice of either sitting behind this boring desk for your entire life or joining hands with us to breathe life into the meat industry.' Joe looked up and gave Abhay his full attention. Joe recalled, 'Initially, my inclination to support the venture was primarily due to my decade-long friendship with Vivek. However, after witnessing the duo's transformative vision for the meat industry, I decided to join them as a co-founder.'

Abhay and Vivek conducted extensive research on the operations of food factories in countries like Japan, Korea and China, where, like in India, fresh food is preferred over frozen. They acquired numerous insights but were unable to replicate any company or supply chain; everything would have to be built from scratch. Explaining, Abhay said, 'Meat is a highly perishable food category. Unlike many other countries, consumer preferences across different regions in India vary significantly. This diversity made a conventional FMCG template unsuitable for our needs.'

Once Joe came on board, he assumed a pivotal role in creating the company's fresh food supply chain, processes, recipes, factory set-up, delivery centres, training modules and packaging. To ensure the highest quality of meat, Licious established direct partnerships with certified meat farmers, fishermen and producers. The company also invested in developing its own poultry farms.

Vivek said, 'The Licious USP is that none of our products are frozen; they are all fresh and devoid of antibiotics, chemicals, artificial preservatives, colouring and flavouring.' The company's state-of-the-art meat processing factory is divided into three segments, dedicated to chicken and white meat, red meat, and seafood. After sorting, the meat undergoes rigorous quality testing and is stored in temperature-controlled rooms.

Licious has a laboratory overseen by doctors and meat scientists. Their responsibility includes testing various elements such as acidity, toxicity, shelf-life and other crucial factors that determine meat quality. Joe explained, 'We store meat at an ideal temperature range of 0 to 4 degrees Celsius. This not only maintains the meat's texture and flavour, but also preserves its essential nutrients.' To maintain stringent quality standards, even the ice used for meat storage is produced in-house through a proprietary machine. Vivek further explained, 'We manufacture our own ice as we found that the water used for ice production in the market did not meet our hygiene standards.' Licious also uses vacuum packing to maintain the freshness of its short shelf-life products. Given the highly perishable nature of its items, it delivers orders within a window of 90 to 120 minutes.

As a result of various comprehensive measures, Licious has successfully established itself as a trusted brand in the meat industry. Its commitment to quality, freshness and hygiene, coupled with innovative end-to-end supply chain management, has enabled the company to consistently meet customer expectations, despite the challenges posed by the perishable nature of its products.

11

The Art and Impact of Brand Communication

Successful brands get into the mind slowly. A blurb in a magazine. A mention in a newspaper. A comment from a friend. A display in a retail store. After a slow buildup, people become convinced that they have known about the brand forever.

—Al Ries, marketing strategist and author

Even an exceptional product can struggle to gain traction if its intended audience lacks awareness of or trust in the brand. Communication becomes key to nurturing brand awareness, trust and favorability amongst stakeholders, including customers, partners, employees and investors.

In my endeavour to delve into this topic, I engaged in a discussion with **Kiran Khalap, co-founder and MD of chlorophyll, India's first end-to-end brand consultancy firm**.

Here are some of the lessons I learned from him:

Maximize impact, even with a limited budget

Start-ups are usually constrained in their communication spending as they have limited or no budgets. Kiran told me, 'The most powerful yet cost effective form of communication is the founder telling the story of the company—why it was founded, what it stands for, its goals.'

A standout example was the 2012 video marketing campaign by Dollar Shave Club, where the founder, Michael Dubin, skillfully conveyed a compelling narrative directly to their target audience. The video garnered millions of views on YouTube and earned vast media coverage.

Kiran gave the example of yet another effective yet budget-friendly communication approach. 'Slurrp Farm, a children's snack brand, smartly included "made by two mothers" on its packaging. The idea was clear—if two mothers could rely on it for their babies, I could place my trust in it as well.'

Another lesson he shared was that a brand's logo is a great communication tool. Kiran said, 'The logo is the most ubiquitous expression of your brand. It peeps out of visiting cards, it smiles from the website, and stares back from the million products your consumers use. In the best-case scenario, your logo communicates to internal stakeholders (employees) and external stakeholders (prospective employees, clients, partners), exactly what your company stands for, so that they decide to join or not join your vision.'

Take for example the logo of Parag Parikh Financial Advisory Services (PPFAS), featuring a tortoise alongside the tagline 'There is only right way'. This instantly creates recall of the timeless hare and tortoise tale, while communicating the message that 'slow and steady wins the race' in the realm of equity market investing.

Also, to effectively reach their audience, start-ups need to be active on the social media platforms that their audience prefers. As revenue grows, they can expand their communication reach and frequency by utilizing online ads, influencers and traditional media, while always ensuring alignment with their business objectives.

Actions speak louder than words

To underscore the impact of communication through behaviour, Kiran shared an insightful experience he had of visiting a Samsonite store in search of a new laptop bag. The salesman inquired about the old bag, but Kiran could not recall where he had purchased it and merely said, 'It is a five-year-old Samsonite endorsed by Richard Branson.' The salesman noticed the old bag's zipper was broken. To Kiran's surprise, the salesman revealed that the model had a lifetime warranty, and if they could not fix the zipper, they would offer either Rs 4500 in cash or a deduction from the current bill. Notably, the salesman did not ask whether Kiran had the receipt for the previous bag.

Kiran reiterated, 'To establish itself as an esteemed brand, a start-up must educate and empower its employees to deliver a brand experience through their behaviour, rather than just through their communication.'

Strike a balance between brand-building and sales-oriented campaigns

When start-ups determine their budget allocation between brand-building initiatives like story-based advertisements,

PR campaigns, and creating experience stores versus sales activation methods such as performance marketing, they often tend to direct greater resources towards the latter. This inclination stems from the perceived cost effectiveness of sales activation and the hope of immediate sales through discounts and promotions. However, it is essential to acknowledge that the impact of sales-driven campaigns tends to be short-lived and diminishes upon reaching a certain threshold.

Conversely, brand-building exercises are instrumental in fostering a positive brand image within the subconscious minds of potential customers and cementing brand equity. This can lead to increased sales and enable premium pricing. Moreover, renowned brands can enter new categories seamlessly and achieve a higher valuation during acquisition by another company.

Let us look at a few examples of brand building oriented communication:

The adhesive produced by Fevicol may not appear different from the competition at the product level, yet distinctive communication sets it apart at the brand level.

Another example is P&G strategically targeting its primary audience—mothers—by positioning itself as the 'Proud Sponsor of Moms' during the 2012 Olympics. This campaign highlighted the pivotal role mothers played in an athlete's success. Consequently, P&G witnessed an impressive $100 million increase in sales that year, while its brand recall surged by 39 per cent by year-end in the US.[1]

Another significant example dates back to 1984, when Apple aired an iconic ad during the Super Bowl. Symbolically portraying the brand as a force challenging the status quo, the ad featured a woman smashing a screen that displayed a Big Brother-like figure. This ad was inspired by the famous novel *1984* by George Orwell. As Kiran recalled, 'This single-release ad perhaps led to the sale of around 1,00,000 computers, even though the ad never showed the product itself.'

People are listening more to their peers than to brands

Today, many brands communicate messages like 'We care for the planet'; 'We do not support any kind of discrimination'; 'We value customer privacy', and so on. Equally, stakeholders hold brands accountable for these promises. If these commitments are broken anywhere, at any time, a reputation crisis can emerge. Kiran mentioned, 'Even a single incident can tarnish the brand image built over a decade. And it takes a lot of time and effort to regain the lost trust.'

Something important I learned from Kiran was that brands should never communicate half-truths. They must always be authentic. In today's digital era, people are no longer just passive recipients of a brand's messages; they actively seek out experiences shared by others through reviews on platforms like Amazon, Zomato and social media. If there is a mismatch between what a brand is communicating and what people are saying about it, then all brands, big or small, can face a reputation crisis.

Moreover, in the world of social media, a crisis can go viral rapidly. So, a brand needs to keep building its goodwill, not only at the product level but also at the corporate level. Kiran added, 'This goodwill acts as a sponge, soaking in the negative while decreasing the impact of the event. A trusted brand survives negativity much faster than other not-so-trusted brands.'

Let us look at some examples. In 2014, Uber faced severe backlash following a rape case in Delhi NCR, which raised questions about its safety measures and practices. Also, in 2015,

Sofia Ashraf's rap video, 'Kodaikanal Won't!' highlighting the negative impact of mercury contamination due to Unilever's thermometer factory in Kodaikanal, went viral. These incidents caused reputation damage to the brands involved.

Kiran stated, 'The first rule in managing such a crisis is don't deny, but don't keep silent either. In skillful post-event communication management, the three stages are, first: reveal what happened; second: explain what actions have been implemented in response to a particular situation, and third: convey what new action has been taken to prevent future recurrence.' He added, 'However, communication must not be restricted to outside target segments like media and customers. It is critical to communicate with the brand's employees first, so they in turn become ambassadors of truth.'

I also learned that in a crisis, a 'third-party' character witness is more powerful than the brand speaking on behalf of itself. For instance, following a worm incident that impacted Cadbury's reputation, the company enlisted Amitabh Bachchan as its brand ambassador, to help restore trust and credibility.

Customize marketing messages to match the market dynamics

Customer preferences vary across markets, and the key challenge today is not just entering new markets, but also strategically connecting with customers in diverse environments. However, people everywhere want to know what a brand stands for. Therefore, the brand message, which embodies its essence and purpose, remains consistent over time. In contrast, marketing messages are often tactical and subject to modifications to cater to specific campaigns, audience segments and market dynamics.

To emphasize this point, Kiran shared the example of Miko, the world's first emotionally adaptive robot that can entertain and educate kids. The brand message from Miko was that it is a smart companion for kids. However, in different markets, parents have distinct expectations from Miko. Through research, chlorophyll identified that in India, parents wanted Miko to prepare their kids for competitions; in the USA, parents desired Miko to entertain their kids, and in the UAE, parents expected Miko to teach their kids the Quran. The brand and product remained the same, but due to varying consumer expectations in different markets, marketing messages and Miko's content were customized accordingly.

Case Studies

How Licious Became One of the Most Loved Food Brands in India

In India, several brands have gained iconic status in various commodity categories. Today, Bisleri is synonymous with water, Aashirvaad is renowned for wheat flour, and Amul is a household name for milk. However, despite a majority of Indians consuming meat, the country surprisingly lacked a prominent national brand in this category. Recognizing this gap, Abhay Hanjura and Vivek Gupta set out to establish a distinguished brand in the meat industry.

The duo went on to demonstrate a profound dedication to every aspect of brand building. When it came to naming the company, they embarked on an extensive brainstorming journey, discarding numerous options such as Pronto Meat, Meatlo and Carnivore Farms. Vivek said to me, 'A brand name is like a permanent tattoo that founders carry throughout their journey. Therefore, crafting it requires meticulous consideration. We wanted to come up with a name that would allow us to explore other food categories, just in case we decided to diversify beyond the meat and seafood category.'

Eventually, they struck gold with 'Licious', a clever wordplay on 'delicious'. Abhay explained, 'Licious is a catchy name that evokes *feelings of hunger and craving*. It isn't limited to a single food category, offering both versatility and longevity.' Moreover, the founders dedicated substantial effort to designing the Licious logo. After multiple iterations, they opted for one that incorporated the signature Licious smile—symbolic of the joy their products brought to their customers.

When they began their journey in 2015, the founders crafted delightful dishes using their high-quality meats and hosted a lunch for more than fifty friends and family. Witnessing the enthusiasm of their guests for the cuisine, the founders encouraged them to spread the word about Licious in their networks. In their first month of operation, they received 1500 orders via word-of-mouth. Despite the pricing being 10–15 per cent higher than the market, the following month saw orders increase to 1800, with 90 per cent coming from repeat customers. Vivek emphasized, 'Our aim wasn't to charge our customers a premium. Instead, our goal was to demonstrate the value. Once customers recognized it, they willingly paid the premium.' Abhay was excited about the high rate of repeat orders, telling Vivek, 'This shows customers trust the quality.' Vivek responded, 'This is a small number. We must achieve this level of repeat transactions even when we have thousands and lakhs of customers.'

During our conversation, Vivek explained, 'In the early days, instead of targeting an entire city, we focused on a specific area as our target market.' For the first six months, Licious only served the Whitefield area in Bangalore. The team conducted events and tasting sessions in residential societies. Abhay was responsible for food preparation, while Vivek distributed pamphlets inviting local residents to their food-tasting stalls. The start-up's mission statement 'We will not sell anything that we can't feed our own families', was prominently featured across communications. As a result of this dedication to quality, people quickly embraced their food, and positive word-of-mouth promotion helped the brand gain popularity.

Building on their initial success, Licious continued to innovate with a strong focus on customer delight. Vivek recalled, 'To get noticed, everything we did had to change the status quo.'

One notable change was the introduction of white paper-based packaging, adorned with customer sketches. This immediately distinguished Licious from the conventional black polythene bags commonly used for meat packaging. Abhay went on to say, 'While other food brands usually focus on product images, we changed the game by featuring our customers' faces. Our packaging design, featuring our customer in their moment of indulgence, holds a special place in the people's mind.' Another novel practice the founders adopted was sending personalized letters to customers—a heartfelt gesture that received warm and appreciative responses.

With the growing popularity of their products, the duo enhanced their marketing efforts by placing billboards in Whitefield, thereby increasing brand recognition. Remarkably, within just six months the company reached the revenue milestone of Rs 1 crore. Vivek explained, 'For us, revenue has never been the sole yardstick to gauge product–market fit. Our primary goal has always been to encourage more repeat orders. If some customers don't return, we don't use discounts to attract them. Instead, we delve into the reasons for their dissatisfaction and promptly address them to delight customers. Also, if we make any mistake, we don't hesitate to accept it and work on making things better.'

In the first year, Licious served approximately 40 per cent of Bangalore, including key areas like Indiranagar, Koramangala, Outer Ring Road and Whitefield. To increase brand awareness, the founders introduced a memorable radio jingle on local stations and placed advertisements in local newspapers. One of the newspaper ads, featuring the tagline 'Meat so delicious that even vegetarians wouldn't want to miss it', did elicit diverse reactions, but the conversations boosted the brand's popularity.

In a mere two years, Licious had firmly established itself as a well-known brand in Bangalore. By the end of 2017, the company was processing about 50,000 monthly orders, with an impressive 90 per cent repeat rate. Notably, it had also managed to reduce supply chain wastage from 40 per cent to just 3 per cent. Vivek told me, 'We were building the entire supply chain from scratch. So, doing things the right way was more important than rushing into scaling business.' Abhay added, 'We had decided not to expand beyond one city until we understood customer expectations, refined our products and operations, and established key business metrics to measure.'

Discussing their learning experiences, Abhay revealed that they initially hired an external company to handle Licious' customer service. However, during a visit to the customer service centre, he noticed that the outsourced team lacked knowledge about meat and Licious products. This realization led to reflection. 'We envisioned building a global brand, but our customer service couldn't even answer basic questions. That day we decided not to outsource any business function,' he said.

In addition to customer service, Licious also managed its order deliveries with an in-house delivery team. Abhay emphasized, 'Since delivery personnel directly interact with customers and serve as the initial point of contact, we wanted them to feel connected to the brand and consider themselves an integral part of the company's operations.'

In 2017, Licious expanded its presence to Hyderabad, followed by Delhi NCR over the next few years. In these new cities, Licious employed various marketing strategies, including newspaper and radio advertisements, as well as sampling activities, to raise brand awareness. However, in Bangalore, where Licious had already established itself, word-of-mouth continued to drive new business.

Additionally, Licious focused on strengthening its positioning as the one stop shop for all things meat and seafood. The team created a range of informative blogs on various topics, including how to prepare different meat dishes, determining the right cuts as per the recipe, etc. The YouTube series 'Licious Meaty Masterclasses', that addressed customer inquiries about meat, explained the Licious quality assurance processes and provided step-by-step instructions for preparing delicious meat-based dishes, further enhancing customer engagement.

Often, customers feel cheated when they don't receive the promised quantity or are provided with poor-quality meat by sellers. In 2018, Licious launched digital ads that highlighted these issues and reinforced its positioning as the ultimate destination for the best quality meat and seafood. The 2019 *Baat Badal De* campaign shifted focus from recipes to the quality of meat. Their ads compelled people to ask, 'Where's the delicious meat from?' and not just 'What's the recipe?'. Abhay pointed out, 'Unlike other food brands in India, that typically show women as cooks, we challenged the norm by featuring men.'

In the same year, Licious introduced its pioneering Experience Centre (now the Licious Kitchen), in Gurgaon, setting a new standard for meat and seafood shopping. This store breaks away from conventional practices by maintaining a knife-free environment and exclusively offering pre-packaged products, sourced directly from the production plant. What sets this Experience Centre apart is the presence of Licious' highly trained Meat Consultants, who are well-equipped to guide customers through the entire lifecycle of meat, and address all inquiries related to product quality. At the Centre, customers can not only purchase Licious signature products, but also take advantage of the innovative 'Endless Aisle' feature. This unique offering allows customers to place orders for items that may not be available in the store. These products can be conveniently delivered to their doorstep through express delivery in ninety minutes. The concept has been such a hit that Licious now has six such Licious Kitchens across Delhi NCR and Bangalore.

In early 2021, Licious enlisted Bollywood actors Anil Kapoor and Arjun Kapoor as brand ambassadors, marking the launch of their inaugural mass advertising campaign on primetime television, significantly bolstering brand awareness and recall.

In the same year, Licious became India's first D2C unicorn and crossed an annual revenue mark of Rs 1000 crore. 'While attaining unicorn status is noteworthy, our most significant achievement lies in reshaping perceptions and transforming any scepticism surrounding meat purchase and consumption into confidence,' Vivek said.

In 2022, Licious underwent a rebranding exercise to capture the brand's evolution from a functional proposition of quality, hygiene and seamless delivery to customers desiring Licious, making it all about taste and the delightful experience of enjoying their Licious favourites. The team reached consensus on the words hearty, gregarious and gastronome (HGG), that aptly captured the warm, generous personality that's passionate about food and meat. Once the three keywords were in place, the team began to look at every brand interface—from logo to packaging and advertising, to check if they passed the 'HGG test'. The new logo featured big, hearty lettering, deliberately opting for imperfections over symmetry. The signature Licious 'smile' was retained but redrawn to make it more realistic.

Later in 2022, Licious introduced the *Nakhra* campaign, featuring Bollywood actor Anil Kapoor. These advertisements cleverly drew parallels between Kapoor's meticulous preparation process as an actor and the Licious stringent quality assurance procedures. The ads depicted various scenarios on a film set, with the veteran actor emphasizing the Licious commitment to freshness, specialty cuts, rigorous quality assessment and reliable service—all of the brand's *nakhare* when it came to their obsession with freshness and safety. A similar campaign was also developed with Telugu superstar, Junior NTR.

Licious has consistently come up with disruptive campaigns to highlight what makes its products special, its distinct positioning and focus on customer delight. For instance, one key aspect that sets Licious chicken apart is its juiciness, surpassing that of regular chicken available in the market. To emphasize this differentiation, Licious launched the 'Juicy, Delicious - Must be Licious' campaign in 2023, showcasing how craveable Licious chicken is due to its juiciness.

Keeping up with the new age media and channels their customers are present on, Licious collaborates with social media influencers, including chefs and food bloggers, to draw engagement with the brand. Abhay said, 'Food is a significant part of people's lives in India. If you look at our communication and product line-up, it revolves around people's personal connection with food. We are focused on positioning Licious as more than just a food brand; it's becoming a lifestyle brand.'

While marketing campaigns play a pivotal role in raising awareness and attracting new customers to the brand, to continually improve conversion rate, the team remains dedicated to enhancing the Licious app's user-friendliness. Vivek underscored this approach, stating, 'Our relentless pursuit is to elevate the app beyond mere food-selling. We want it to awaken the hunger and cravings of our users.'

A crucial aspect of the Licious brand-building effort involves growing responsibly, with a sharp focus on environment and society, actively pursuing global certifications and undergoing audits. Notably, Licious holds the distinction of being India's first meat and seafood D2C company to achieve the prestigious FSSC22000 certification, one of the highest food safety certifications globally.

Since its inception, Licious has remained a purpose-driven organization, unwavering in its commitment to ESG principles. Through efforts such as lowering CO_2 emissions, and conserving water, Licious is dedicated to making a positive impact on the planet. Remarkably, in 2022, Licious became the first Indian meat brand and one of only ten companies worldwide, to attain the SA8000 certification[*] for social responsibility, environmental management, and occupational health and safety, accredited by the British Standards Institution (BSI). Impressively, the brand has achieved plastic neutrality for FY22 and has committed itself to being plastic neutral going forward.

Licious aims to become the most loved food brand in the country. To gauge customer affection, the team employs three key methods. First, they assess social media engagement—a reliable proxy for brand love. Second, they utilize tools like the Brand Equity Index and Brand Power Score, provided by agencies like Nielsen and Kantar, to evaluate public perception, assigning scores on a scale of 0 to 10. These tools facilitate comparisons with competitors in the same category. Lastly, they capture consumer perception by surveying over 1000 customers, aiming to understand their perspectives on crucial image aspects, including authenticity and trustworthiness.

---

[*] **SA 8000** is an international certification standard that encourages organizations to develop, maintain and apply socially acceptable practises in the workplace.

As of October 2023, Licious operates in more than twenty Indian cities, fulfilling over 2 million orders every month. The brand proudly maintains an impressive 90 per cent repeat customer rate, which serves as a clear testament to the loyalty and strong bond the brand has cultivated with its customers. Vivek also noted, 'Our journey has just started. Converting the unorganized meat market to an organized one will take decades. When that transition happens, we want Licious to have the largest market share as a food brand dedicated to helping customers create beautiful and delicious meals.'

How STAGE OTT Created Content Demand

To effectively connect with the audience the STAGE team crafted a catchy and meaningful tagline: *Kyunki boli main apnapan hain* (Because there is belonging in dialects). To reach the Haryanvi audience already present on the internet, they marketed web series posters and trailers through digital platforms like TikTok, YouTube, Facebook, and Instagram.

The team also utilized offline marketing tactics to increase brand awareness. One key aspect of their strategy was using local buses for promotion. By doing so, they achieved long-lasting visibility since the ads remained on the buses even after the advertising deal was over or until another brand replaced it. The humble autorickshaws similarly proved to be an effective marketing tool.

Dainik Jagran, a renowned newspaper, publishes an annual calendar that reaches lakhs of households in Haryana. The calendar plays a vital role in people's daily lives, allowing them to track milk expenses, stay updated with important dates, and mark significant festivals. STAGE effectively utilized the calendar as a powerful advertising medium by strategically placing ads featuring captivating images from their web series on every page. Parveen said, 'A declining Customer Acquisition Cost (CAC) and a growing subscription base indicate that our marketing strategies are working.' Vinay explained that customers come to STAGE for the content and then become the brand's biggest endorsers. In fact, some of the reviewers on Play Store applaud STAGE for saving their cultural pride and dignity.

While enjoying a dinner together one evening, the STAGE founders engaged in a contemplative conversation. Vinay expressed his belief that they were not creating an ordinary company. Parveen said that they were bringing a revolution by challenging the status quo. Smiling broadly, Shashank repeated their combined sentiments, exclaiming, *'Hum company nahi, kranti hain!'* (We are not a company, we are a revolution). The trio instantly found resonance in this powerful statement and featured it on t-shirts for their upcoming company offsite. The team's offsite picture in this t-shirt went viral on social media as people identified with the impactful message conveyed by the tagline.

Vinay also mentioned that usually marketing agencies craft taglines, but when an entrepreneur creates one, each word tends to come from the heart. That is exactly what happened in their case. When the trio appeared on Shark Tank, they proudly wore t-shirts with the tagline they had crafted, which went on to gain national recognition when the Sharks (judges) discussed it.

Vinay said that the STAGE team wears t-shirts featuring the tagline about 90 per cent of the time. Not only does it serve as an icebreaker and draw new people in, but it has also become representative of their brand. When their employees, wearing these t-shirts, walk down the street, they are often asked if they appeared on Shark Tank. 'People might not remember the faces of the founders from the Shark Tank episode, but they always remember the t-shirt with the tagline,' Vinay chuckled. This recognition by the public makes their employees feel proud and serves as a constant reminder of the impact they are making.

Parveen mentioned that STAGE and Kranti have become synonymous, attracting support from the ecosystem. During Yashpal Sharma's visit to the STAGE office, the Bollywood actor enthusiastically shouted with the entire team, '*Hum company nahi, kranti hain.*' Like him, many people have begun to see and support STAGE as a cultural revolution.

A prevalent misconception is that people in rural India are hesitant to pay for premium content due to the abundance of free options on platforms like YouTube. However, STAGE debunked this myth by introducing a subscription service in April 2021, with prices starting at Rs 199 for a quarterly plan and Rs 399 for an annual plan. The turning point occurred in December 2021 with the release of the web series *Safe House*, addressing the issue of honour killing triggered by intercaste marriage—a prevalent problem in Haryanvi society. *Safe House* spurred STAGE's growth, leading to a surge in subscriptions, increased app engagement and heightened brand awareness. Over time, STAGE launched various other web series, further contributing to its popularity.

Vinay emphasized that STAGE caters to its audience using local terminology and processes. For instance, individuals in rural Haryana refer to a STAGE subscription as a 'recharge', coming from the vocabulary for mobile phone recharges. Taking note of this, STAGE also refers to its subscription as a 'recharge'. Many users initially hesitated to use online transactions due to mistrust. To tackle this challenge STAGE introduced a cash-on-delivery option.

By personally collecting payments, STAGE representatives were also instrumental in helping to build trust between the brand and its customers. Interestingly, the in-person visits by STAGE representatives became noteworthy, attracting even non-users to discover the platform.

Vinay reflected, 'When you are exploring a new territory, doubt from others is inevitable. When we initially discussed monetizing our content, many sceptics mocked us, and numerous investors rejected our plan as everyone felt that people in rural India would not pay for premium content. However, we proved that monetization would work, first in Haryana and later in Rajasthan.' He added, 'An entrepreneur has to persevere, even in the face of rejection from 99 per cent of people and keep searching for the 1 per cent who will believe in his purpose. Once some success has been achieved, the non-believers can become believers.'

In 2023, Olympic champion Neeraj Chopra, who hails from Haryana, invested in STAGE. His involvement has significantly boosted the brand's appeal. As of November 2023, Stage has achieved over six million installs and gathered over 5,50,000 paying subscribers. By 2027, the founders aim to launch STAGE in the top twenty dialects of the country, with the potential to reach 200 million-plus households.

How Sirona Created Brand Awareness in an Unmentioned Category

As a pioneering brand in feminine hygiene, Sirona has faced unique challenges:

- **Limited conversations:** The subject of feminine hygiene has been traditionally taboo and rarely discussed openly.

This inevitably left an information void, giving rise to myths and misconceptions.

- **Consumer apathy:** Most women think they must endure their problems silently without expecting solutions and with nowhere to turn, they accepted the status quo.
- **Lack of awareness:** Few women actively sought solutions to feminine hygiene issues, making it challenging to discover products that would help.

Let us delve into some of the innovative marketing strategies Sirona implemented to overcome these obstacles and make a meaningful impact. To enhance consumer understanding of the feminine hygiene category, the brand concentrated on producing informative content about its innovative products, utilizing varied formats such as videos, FAQs and blogs. This content was supported by expert insights, social media influencers and customer testimonials, reinforcing the brand's credibility.

To comprehend Sirona's content focus and messaging, it is crucial to understand the brand's approach to target audience segmentation. Feminine hygiene products typically address a wide range of ages, from pre-teens to women in their fifties. However, as Sirona predominantly promotes its brand online, in terms of demographic segmentation the team concentrates on the eighteen to twenty-five and twenty-six to thirty-four age brackets across tier-1 and tier-2 cities. In terms of behaviour, this youthful demographic actively engages with online platforms, frequently embarking on work and leisure travel, and is open to embracing innovative products.

Furthermore, the team utilizes psychographic segmentation to categorize its audience, based on attitudes, values and lifestyle choices. For instance:

- Hygiene-conscious women prioritize cleanliness and seek products offering comfort and protection.
- Eco-conscious women are increasingly concerned about the environmental impact of feminine hygiene products and prefer sustainable, organic or biodegradable options.
- Convenience-oriented women leading busy lives value products that are portable, discreet, and easy to use.
- Confidence-seeking women want to engage fully in their daily activities without worry or discomfort.
- Brand loyalists develop strong loyalty and trust in a particular brand, sticking with it consistently.

Now let us take a look at the deeper, everyday problems Sirona addresses in its messaging. These include dealing with dirty toilets, managing rashes, preventing leaks during periods, proper disposal of sanitary products, engaging in activities like swimming, travelling and exercising during a period, hair removal, and much more.

In terms of channels, YouTube plays a crucial role in Sirona's marketing strategy, with the brand consistently producing monthly content aligned to consumer search trends and keywords. Sirona has also leveraged the popularity of Instagram Reels, utilizing this format to integrate serious and often taboo topics into fun and engaging trends. This approach has attracted influencers and encouraged active participation from Sirona's employees and customers, who create reels to share their own experiences with the brand.

Moving beyond social media, the Sirona App serves as a one-stop place for content, community and services for women to shop, chat and learn about their period health and personal hygiene. The content educates and provides knowledge regarding various topics of concern to the target audience.

The app provides a bond of unity and support among women, creating a safe community for them to share, discuss and learn without fear of being judged.

Additionally, the period-tracking service on WhatsApp offers a key and convenient utility. This easy-to-use tool helps menstruators across demographics and geographies keep track of their menstrual cycle just by sending a simple 'Hi' to their Sirona WhatsApp Business Account.

Sirona's commitment to breaking taboos and fostering open discussion is further highlighted by its *#PeriodsHiTohHai* campaign. Launched on Menstrual Hygiene Day 2022, the campaign challenges societal norms and aims to normalize conversations around menstruation. The video campaign, which received over eight million views within a year, illustrates its impact.

On India's 75th Independence Day, Sirona launched the Daughter India campaign, a thought-provoking initiative aimed at changing the common citizens' perspective to viewing India not as one's mother but a daughter. This dynamic perspective shift ensures the country receives the care and attention we give our daughters. The campaign was launched with a video and a series of newspaper ads in the north and south markets. In the second phase of the campaign, on Daughters Day—25th September, an engagement activity was launched, encouraging citizens to pledge support for the daughters of India. Over 1000 pledges were received on Instagram. The campaign website was also launched on this occasion, along with contests in schools and colleges, where students shared their vision for Daughter India.

While Sirona holds a leadership position in the women's hygiene category, it remains vulnerable to product imitation by competitors. Consequently, Sirona has strategically focused on differentiation through its packaging and brand personality. It has ensured that its packaging strikes a balance between classic ideas of femininity, such as care and love, with contemporary concepts like freedom and rebellion. This has been achieved by using bold fonts and text to articulate how their products address problems.

Sirona's brand personality embodies trustworthiness, care, modernity and approachability. People trust Sirona because it understands women's needs and communicates clearly about safety and effectiveness. As a genuinely caring brand, it prioritizes women's well-being and fosters a supportive environment. Sirona is also modern and progressive, challenging taboos and outdated ideas about women while engaging openly in important topics for women. Crucially, Sirona is approachable—a brand that listens to feedback and actively builds a friendly community where women can share experiences and learn from each other. Sirona continuously reflects its personality through its visuals and communications, aligning its messaging and imagery with these defining characteristics.

While not all of the marketing activities directly result in sales, they play a substantial role in establishing brand recognition, which continues to influence consumer transactions.

12

Strategies for Sales and Distribution

Superior sales and distribution by itself can create a monopoly, even with no product differentiation. The converse is not true. No matter how strong your product—even if it easily fits into already established habits and anybody who tries it likes it immediately—you must still support it with a strong distribution plan.

—Peter Thiel, co-founder of PayPal

Brand building is essentially a trust-building exercise, and trust equates to a promise. For example, when a company launches a new product and generates substantial hype around it, the company is essentially making a promise. However, if customers visit their local store and don't find the product, it can lead to disappointment, thereby breaking that promise. Furthermore, even if the product is available, if the retailer doesn't speak positively about it, trust can also be undermined. Therefore, distribution and sales are essential components of brand building.

In B2C, distribution and sales strategies are often standardized due to a large audience with similar needs. For example, customers commonly look for similar features and pricing in a smartphone, and they can purchase it through Amazon or local retailers. However, B2B business models can take various forms, including selling raw materials from suppliers to manufacturers, finished products in bulk from manufacturers to distributors, and software directly to businesses. Furthermore, in B2B, customers vary significantly based on industry, company size, location and decision-makers, necessitating a tailored approach to sales and distribution.

I had the privilege of discussing this topic with **Paramdeep Singh Anand (Param), co-founder of FieldAssist, a leading SaaS platform for sales and supply chain automation.** FieldAssist serves over 600 consumer goods brands, including renowned names such as Haldirams', Coca-Cola, Everest Spices, Atomberg and Bisleri. Before assuming the role of CEO at FieldAssist, Param had founded and sold an FMCG start-up.

Here are a few lessons I learned from him:

Keep improving on the three essential dimensions of sales

Param outlined three crucial dimensions of sales: 'pocket', 'brain', and 'heart':

Pocket: It pertains to the financial aspect, ensuring that the offering aligns with customers' budgets and perceived value.

Start-ups often tend to lower their prices to beat competition and attract customers. Param said, 'Getting into a price war is not always advisable.' He drew a culinary analogy, stating, 'Just as salt judiciously used enhances the flavour of a dish, discounts if applied thoughtfully can be beneficial for initial penetration in the market.' He further elaborated that a discount need not be a direct price reduction. For instance, in B2B, it can be given in other forms such as free trials and value-added offerings to enhance customer experience.

Brain: Aspects such as benefits, features, expertise and competitive advantages that provide clear reasons for why a product or service is valuable can appeal to the brain. Param added, 'In addition to these attributes, in B2B scenarios, understanding customers' challenges and speaking their industry language aids in establishing a meaningful connection with them.'

Heart: Emotional appeal is paramount to connecting with the 'heart'. Customers are drawn to a brand that can empathize with them and provide peace of mind and joy. FieldAssist takes this emotional connection a step further by positioning itself not merely as a vendor but as a trusted partner. As Param explained, 'This approach allows us to cultivate deeper relationships with our customers and solve problems collaboratively.'

Param shared another important insight: 'Even with all three dimensions in place, it might require multiple attempts to effectively convey your message to the target audience. Persistence is key! However, it's crucial to diversify your approach with each follow-up. Plan your communication channels, messages and timing carefully. It's essential to never come across as pushy or desperate.'

Success in one distribution channel doesn't guarantee it in another

The implementation of an omni-channel strategy allows brands to actively engage customers across various touch points throughout their buying journey. However, it's important to note that the approaches effective in the online world may not have the same impact in the offline world, and vice versa.

Param elaborated, 'The rise of online channels, including D2C, marketplaces, and quick commerce, has ignited innovation. It empowers new brands to swiftly launch and test their products in the market. Success in the online realm often facilitates acceptance in the offline world, as sellers recognize the existing product demand.' Yet, Param warned, 'Start-ups often wrongly assume success in one channel guarantees success in another; however, strategies and skills differ for various channels.'

Online sales occur within a controlled environment, where transactions can be tracked. This allows brands to understand what's selling and why. Conversely, offline retail channels, such as modern trade, general trade and institutional sales, involve intermediaries like distributors, wholesalers and retailers. It often becomes challenging for brands to collect inventory and sales information at each level and gather customer feedback.

In the offline world, a product must offer high margins for retailers to consider it worthwhile. Moreover, if a product does not sell well, the cost of recalling it from stores can be substantial. Param noted, 'Salespeople interacting with retailers play a vital role in ensuring a brand's products are visible in stores. They can also educate retailers about key messages that could boost product sales. Moreover, they can help identify factors causing dissatisfaction among retailers, enabling proactive resolution of issues and fostering stronger relationships.' He cautioned that those skilled in offline relationship navigation may lack essential digital marketing skills for online success. Brands must recognize and address skill gaps during channel transitions.

Fine tune your offering for different markets

Significant variations can exist in the behaviour and preferences of people across different age groups and cities. For instance, individuals residing in tier-1 cities, particularly younger generations, are often more open to trying new products and providing constructive feedback. Their interactions are predominantly digitized, generating a wealth of data for analysis. Conversely, customers in smaller cities might not be as quick to adopt new products and typically prefer shopping from offline stores.

When introducing a new product into any market, sampling is a common approach used to gauge customer response. Param said, 'Brands need to approach sampling with a clear target audience and objective in mind. They must determine whether the purpose of sampling is to create brand awareness or gather feedback about aspects like taste, packaging, size, design, etc. Without well-defined objectives, sampling could potentially waste money and yield misleading information.'

Param elaborated, 'After evaluating sampling results, brands may need to adjust their messaging, pricing, pack sizes, distribution strategy and SKUs to cater to different markets. Based on the market response, brands can compile a list of "must-sell" products tailored for specific markets and channels. If, over time, these designated products are not being reordered, it becomes crucial to understand the underlying reasons.'

Distribution dynamics become complex with growth

When operating on a small scale, your strategy might heavily rely on direct sales or local retail partnerships. In such cases, your team size is likely small, processes are manageable, transportation remains local, and customers can provide feedback directly.

However, as your business scales up, the distribution network becomes more complex. Transportation time may extend from hours to days, necessitating careful consideration of product shelf life and appropriate packaging. If the supply of raw materials doesn't scale up with expansion, the product might become unavailable in the market, or its quality may become inconsistent, leading to customer dissatisfaction. Moreover, a larger scale requires a bigger workforce, a larger production facility and improved systems and processes to manage inventory and predict demand for effective planning and forecasting.

Param emphasized, 'During expansion, one has to be careful; even a single misstep can have significant repercussions. For instance, if you fail to address retailers' concerns in one city, they might stop purchasing your product. This could result in negative word-of-mouth spreading through their networks, making it difficult for you to sustain your growth in other cities.' Additionally, he advised, 'While pursuing new customers to achieve growth, one should not overlook the existing ones.'

Learn to listen to 'no' from as well as say 'no' to customers

It's natural to face rejections in sales. However, a 'no' today doesn't necessarily mean it's a 'no' forever. Circumstances change, and a customer who rejects your offering today might find it suitable in the future. Param said, 'Keep improving your offering and messaging. Remain open to working with customers who initially rejected you. Don't ignore them merely out of arrogance or ego.' He added, 'We continued to engage with those customers who had rejected us by keeping them updated on our latest developments and expressing interest in theirs. Eventually, some of them became our customers.'

At the same time, Param told me that while the customer is king, not every kingdom may be suitable for every company. Therefore, it can sometimes be necessary to say 'no' to some customers. He explained, 'We initially thought FieldAssist was suitable for all retail businesses, including automotive parts and agricultural goods. However, we later realized that focusing solely on consumer goods would bring the expected growth, so we had to decline customers from other sectors.'

Param mentioned several other scenarios where a company might prefer to refuse customers. For instance, if a customer has not made payments for an extended period, if they constantly change requirements even after months of discussions and pilots, if serving them becomes a loss-making endeavour, or if ethics and values are not aligned. He added, 'It's crucial to manage such shifts without tarnishing your reputation or damaging relationships. Say "no" respectfully and give your customers ample time for the transition.'

Case Studies

How Indigo Paints Grew from a Rs 1 Lakh Investment to Over Rs 1000 Crore in Revenue

India's crowded paint market is filled with industry giants like Asian Paints, Berger and Nerolac, as well as numerous local and regional players. In this competitive landscape, Hemant Jalan founded Indigo Paints in 2000, with an initial investment of Rs 1 lakh. He recalled, 'I ran a small chemical unit in Patna before this. We used to sell calcium chloride, a vital ingredient in cement paint.' Noticing the flourishing success of many small-scale cement paint players, Hemant decided to manufacture lower-end cement paint, usually used for painting garages and warehouses, and providing essential wall protection.

Hemant discovered that the raw materials needed for cement paint manufacturing in Bihar were sourced from Jodhpur. To reduce transportation costs, he rented an industrial shed in Jodhpur and began producing paint there. As he explored potential markets, Hemant avoided the larger cities where prominent brands were highly active. He reasoned, 'We lacked the resources to compete with these established brands for market share. Furthermore, urban customers tend to be very brand-conscious, and at that time, we didn't have the financial means to build a strong brand.' Therefore, Indigo strategically focused on small towns and villages as its target market.

Compared to FMCG products like soap and toothpaste, paint is not an item that customers purchase frequently. This infrequency often leaves customers without the necessary knowledge to make informed decisions, leading them to rely on the recommendation of paint dealers, hardware retailers and painters. Recognizing this dynamic, Hemant began cultivating relationships with these crucial local influencers, highlighting the quality of Indigo's paint and providing incentives.

Jhumri Telaiya, a small town in Jharkhand, was the first market that Indigo tapped into. Following the company's initial success there, orders began flowing in from other small towns. In its first year of operation, the company made about Rs 80 lakh in sales.

Following several years of steady growth, Indigo broadened its product portfolio to incorporate water-based paints such as distemper, primer and emulsion. These products are often used for home painting and wood coating, significantly enhancing the aesthetics of residences. Given the highly competitive market teeming with numerous major players offering similar products, Indigo needed to secure buy-ins from industry influencers like shopkeepers and painters. As Hemant noted, 'Their endorsement doesn't necessarily translate into a sale, particularly if another brand's advertising has heavily swayed the consumer, but a substantial number of people can be influenced by the opinion of these influencers.'

While many companies attempt to sway painters by offering financial incentives, Hemant prioritizes product quality over incentives. He explained his focus saying, 'Painters' businesses thrive on referrals. If a brand they recommend fails to meet customer expectations, it can cost them future business. As a result, they tend to recommend products that they trust.'

To foster trust and convince painters of their products' superiority, the Indigo team began hosting regular meetings with this group. However, painters were biased towards the larger, more established brands due to their past experiences and preconceptions. To counteract this bias and demonstrate the superior quality of its products, the Indigo team initiated blind tests. Hemant described the process, 'We present similar products from Indigo and other leading brands, cover the eyes of painters and ask them to tell us which product they believe is of superior quality. Although this method may not convince everyone right away, it does start to shift perceptions. By repeating this process over time, we have noticed the change.'

Hemant had long desired to create an innovative product to distinguish Indigo's offerings. However, in the first few years no ideas materialized. However, good ideas often come when least expected, and something similar happened with Hemant. 'The first niche product we developed was somewhat accidental,' he admitted. While visiting the office of Sudarshan Chemicals in Pune, one of India's largest pigment manufacturers, he was intrigued by a shade card showcasing metallic pigments—gold, silver, copper and bronze. To clarify, a pigment is a coloured substance used to produce specific shades in painting. Curious about the applications of these metallic pigments, Hemant asked the Sudarshan team where they were typically used. He was informed that these pigments were used mainly in cosmetics such as lipsticks and nail polish, or in the items like buttons, to achieve a metallic appearance. Intrigued, Hemant wondered why these pigments were not used in home paints. The Sudarshan team could not provide a valid reason other than the fact that no one had attempted it before.

Consequently, Hemant requested a sample to experiment with. Eventually, using that pigment, Indigo Paints launched India's first line of metallic paints. Initially, Hemant envisioned that customers would use these paints, especially the golden ones, to create stylish walls in their rooms. Given this usage, the team at Indigo Paints expected the product to sell in small quantities, such as for a single wall, that would perhaps not require more than a litre of paint.

One day, a company salesman in Kerala asked Hemant what reward he could expect to receive if he made Rs 1 crore worth of sales in a year. Amused, Hemant asked what the salesman would like. The staffer requested a Hero Honda motorbike. Hemant agreed.

To the surprise of the Indigo leadership team, they began receiving an influx of orders from Kerala, for their copper shade, with requests for four-litre and even twenty-litre quantities. The orders grew larger each month, leaving the team puzzled about where these customers were using such vast quantities of copper paint. On investigation, they discovered that it was being used to paint roof tiles. In Kerala, it is common for houses to have sloping roofs covered with terracotta tiles that are often painted. Indigo's copper shade had appealed to these homeowners, who were now painting their entire roofs with it. This unexpected trend provided immense publicity for Indigo's copper metallic paint without the company spending anything on advertising.

'This experience taught us the value of remaining open to unexpected applications of our products,' said Hemant. The incident made him realize the significant impact of incentivizing the sales force. In 2009, when Indigo was generating Rs 12 crore in revenue, the company established an incentive programme for its sales force. 'We allowed them to choose their targets and agreed to reward them disproportionately higher if they succeeded. The team started setting high targets for themselves, which changed the business trajectory. We began seeing around 50 per cent yearly growth, and our manpower attrition dropped to almost zero,' Hemant recalled.

'We consistently aim to launch first-to-market products by identifying niche opportunities,' Hemant added. At Indigo, several practices are followed to uncover innovative ideas. One key strategy is direct interaction between senior management and on-the-ground sales people. 'Our sales people engage with painters, dealers and store staff, gathering insights that can spark new ideas,' Hemant pointed out. Annually, Indigo hosts a conference where the sales team convenes for three to four days. Anyone can present their thoughts and ideas directly to the leadership team during these gatherings. As Hemant said, 'Even if some ideas initially seem bizarre, we don't dismiss them immediately. Instead, we allow them to percolate in our minds.'

Another source of inspiration comes from attending international trade shows, which exhibit the latest technologies and raw materials in the paint industry. Unlike most companies that send their Manufacturing Head or R&D personnel to these events, Indigo ensures its sales team also participates. Hemant often attends these trade shows himself, visiting every booth to keep abreast of new developments in the market.

Hemant shared with me an instance when he discovered an idea at one such event: 'Our sales team had informed us that people were looking for robust driveway paint capable of withstanding the wear and tear of cars and motorcycles. Many companies attempted to address this issue using regular exterior paints, but these faded within a fortnight.'

The solution finally appeared when Hemant discovered highway paint developed by an international company at a trade show in Germany. He reasoned that if this paint could endure the harsh conditions of a highway, it could surely withstand use on a residential driveway. Inspired by this, Indigo Paints developed a new type of floor paint. 'To our delight, this paint has become one of our most successful products to date,' Hemant said.

Indigo's dedication to producing innovative products has played a pivotal role in capturing market share, with retailers expressing strong interest in their unique paint offerings. However, Hemant also recognized that brand building was crucial for growth in other competitive spaces, and the necessity of a celebrity endorsement to elevate Indigo's brand status.

Regarding celebrity endorsements, most people instinctively think of film stars. However, Indigo could not use film stars. Hemant explained, 'More than half of our market is based in South India, where each region has its own film industry and superstars. We lacked the resources to hire multiple brand ambassadors for each region.' Then an idea struck him. Why not consider cricket? Cricket remains a passion that unifies all of India, transcending regional differences.

'While selecting a celebrity, it's crucial to establish a connection between the unique personality and imagery of the celebrity and your brand,' said Hemant. M.S. Dhoni's humble beginnings resonated with many Indians, particularly those from small towns. His personal narrative of a small-town-boy-making-it-big had strong appeal, especially for brands like Indigo, who were expanding their market from small towns to big cities. In 2018, Indigo chose M.S. Dhoni as its brand ambassador.

Hemant explained, 'Most brands change their celebrity endorsers every two or three years. However, we have maintained our association with M.S. Dhoni for over six years, as constant change can lead to confusion among customers, who may struggle to remember which celebrity endorses which brand.'

M.S. Dhoni's pan-India appeal helped Indigo Paints achieve significant brand awareness. However, according to the feedback from the sales team, these ads were ineffective in Kerala, a market that contributed 30 per cent of Indigo revenues. Hemant realized that Kerala was the state where cricket was least followed, with Keralites preferring football. Moreover, the Indigo advertisements were primarily conceptualized and produced in Hindi, then dubbed into regional languages. The local population could not relate to the background, attire, or even the translated words used in these ads, which sounded unnatural.

As a result, in 2021, Indigo decided to create a separate ad campaign specifically for the Kerala market. Hemant said, 'We insisted the advertising agency used a Malayali scriptwriter and creative person to ensure the ad would have authentic local flavour. Mohanlal, an undisputed superstar in Kerala, was our first choice for the celebrity. We have even created ads in which M.S. Dhoni and Mohanlal appear together. Our sales numbers reflect the impact of these ads.'

Hemant stressed, 'While celebrity endorsements can be a powerful marketing tool, they require strategic planning and significant financial commitment to be effective.' He pointed out that hiring a top-tier celebrity could cost anywhere from Rs 3–6 crore or more annually. However, that is not the entirety of the expenditure. To ensure your advertisement makes an impact, it needs to be aired multiple times, requiring an advertising budget of at least Rs 25–30 crore. Without this level of investment, the money spent on a celebrity endorser can be wasted, given the clutter in the advertising world.

Hemant added, 'Effective advertising goes beyond crafting a compelling ad. It also involves strategic considerations like the timing in the day and the ad placement during commercial breaks. Your ad's exposure can vary greatly depending on whether it's aired at the beginning, middle or end of a commercial break, or if it's broadcast early in the morning or late at night.'

Indigo has also been actively utilizing billboards for advertising. Hemant explained this strategy saying, 'The success of billboards heavily depends on strategic placement, clear visibility and compelling content.' Although many billboard sellers argue that placing billboards parallel to the road makes ads visible to traffic from both directions, Hemant disagrees, stating that such billboards are often overlooked. 'In countries like India, where driving is on the left, the drivers' natural line of sight veers towards the right. Ads placed on this side are more noticeable,' Hemant noted. He also emphasized the importance of the billboard's angle, stating that those angled at roughly forty-five degrees relative to the road are more visible to individuals in moving vehicles. Furthermore, he advised choosing a standalone billboard over one surrounded by others, to catch viewers' attention. Additionally, ensuring that no obstructions like electrical cables block the view of your billboard is crucial.

Regarding billboard location, Hemant deviates from conventional wisdom. While many billboard sellers recommend high footfall locations like railway stations and bus stops, Hemant believes these might not be the best choices. He explained this logic saying, 'People rushing to catch their bus or train are not in the right frame of mind to absorb your marketing message effectively.' Hemant believes that by applying these principles one can potentially gain 30 per cent, 40 per cent, or even 50 per cent more value from the same advertising budget.

The Indigo team consistently monitors their brand's market performance. Hemant shared that every one to two years, they commission a brand tracking study to compare their brand's perception against other paint brands, helping to identify strengths and weaknesses. Additionally, they interact with dealers to gain insights into customer preferences.

By 2020, Indigo had become a leading brand in small towns and villages. Sensing an opportunity for further growth,

Hemant decided to focus on tier-2 and tier-3 cities. 'A company's strategy is never static; it should perpetually evolve and adapt throughout its journey. Consequently, our focus is shifting towards larger cities,' he explained.

However, the strategy to penetrate these larger markets differs significantly from that employed in the smaller towns. In big cities, painting contractors emerge as a new influencer group to reckon with. A typical painting contractor might manage a team of twenty to thirty painters and undertake contracts to paint entire buildings, delegating the work amongst team members. This necessitated formulating new strategies to incentivize these contractors and win their trust.

Hemant acknowledged this challenge stating, 'The silver lining is that we have managed to establish a strong foothold in the interiors of India, which is a notoriously difficult market to penetrate. Now, as we set our sights on a different market replete with new competition and influencers, we acknowledge that the game's rules will be different. We are prepared to learn and adapt accordingly.'

The company, which commenced its operations with a modest investment of Rs 1 lakh, has surpassed an annual revenue milestone of Rs 1000 crore. As of December 2023, Indigo Paints is the fifth-largest paint company in India.

How Atomberg Cracked the Distribution Code

In the course of Atomberg's journey from 0 to 10 crore in annual revenue, the key to success was identifying a specific segment where their product would serve as a painkiller (must-have), rather than just a vitamin (nice to have). One of the main advantages of Atomberg fans is their energy efficiency, which directly translates into significant cost savings. For example, if someone has many fans in use, the savings could amount to lakhs of rupees on a monthly basis. This cost-saving factor made Atomberg fans a compelling offering for businesses like factories and schools (B2B segment).

To determine where to begin within the B2B segment, Atomberg conducted an in-depth study of the existing BLDC fan market. They discovered the presence of an existent competitor in southern India, and some customers in the western region. The decision-makers behind these purchases were already familiar with BLDC technology, which made the process of introducing Atomberg fans easier.

However, the challenge remained in convincing these decision-makers to choose Atomberg fans over the competition. The team emphasized that their fans had a 30 per cent higher efficiency rate than those of any competitor. This meant that customers could enjoy a better return on investment (ROI). Additionally, Atomberg, being located in the western region, could provide superior service, which became an attractive point to these customers.

Next, the team identified businesses that were either in the process of transitioning to solar energy or considering making the switch. Such businesses were already conscious of the need to reduce energy consumption. Atomberg positioned its fans as a solution to help them achieve lower energy consumption. Shibam Das, co-founder at Atomberg explained, 'We specifically targeted customers in clusters like industrial areas, where one customer's energy savings could influence others to become Atomberg customers as well.'

In larger institutions, the Atomberg team uncovered the presence of dedicated sustainability departments. Recognizing the importance of these departments and their commitment to environment friendly practices, the team decided to engage with them instead of approaching the procurement department.

Remarkably, they established a collaboration with Tata Power for their energy-saving programme. Through this partnership, Tata Power incentivized its customers to transition to energy-efficient appliances, including Atomberg fans. This collaboration resulted in sales of over 7000 fans in Mumbai alone. Notably, Atomberg gained significant visibility as Tata Power included the Atomberg brand name on their electricity bills. This association opened many doors, allowing Atomberg to enter prestigious organizations such as ITC, Infosys, Reliance, Hyatt Hotels, Aditya Birla Group, Indian Railways, IIIT Hyderabad, IIT Bombay and many others.

In India, 90 per cent of fans are used in households, making the B2C market larger than the B2B.[1] In 2016, the team made a strategic decision to enter the B2C market. However, establishing offline sales channels was challenging due to the brand's limited recognition, making it difficult to attract distributors and retailers. As a result, the team shifted its focus to online platforms, with Amazon as the primary choice, followed by Flipkart.

To instil confidence in their brand, Atomberg introduced extended warranties. Nonetheless, customers could question the value of a warranty if they had doubts about the brand's long-term viability. To build trust, the founders—being IIT Bombay alumni—strategically emphasized their association with this prestigious institution, on the product packaging. Additionally, each product box contained a handwritten thank-you note from the founders, expressing gratitude to customers for choosing the Atomberg product.

However, the team did not stop at these gestures. If a customer purchased a product and was dissatisfied, they went above and beyond to ensure their satisfaction. This commitment, combined with consistent investment in online ads and positive customer reviews on Amazon, set in motion a growth flywheel. Within two years, Atomberg had become the top fan brand on Amazon.

Simultaneously, Atomberg began promoting its own website to showcase new products. Shibam said, 'We launched new products on our own website. For approximately six months, we focused on gathering consumer feedback and improving our products. Afterward, we introduced these new products on Amazon and Flipkart.'

By 2018, the brand had achieved an annual revenue of Rs 50 crore. Shibam recalled, 'We were growing in e-commerce but the online market was hardly 2–3 per cent of overall fans. Expanding our online customer base would have required either offering substantial discounts or making significant investments in advertising to convince offline customers to transition to online purchasing—both of which would have incurred high costs. Consequently, we strategically decided to diversify into offline sales channels.'

In the initial phase they centred their attention on five specific states—Kerala, Maharashtra, Tamil Nadu, Karnataka and Telangana. Several factors drove this strategic choice. First, the majority of the brand's online sales originated from these states, offering the potential for offline customers to have references from existing online customers. Additionally, these regions exhibited a strong preference for regional TV channels, making TV advertising more cost-effective and targeted.

The Atomberg team took a strategic approach, treating distributors with the same respect and attention they gave investors. They highlighted their online success to demonstrate the potential for similar growth in offline channels. This resonated with distributors, who showed interest in supporting Atomberg. However, securing distributors was just the beginning of building a strong offline distribution network. The team recognized the importance of engaging with retailers to solidify their market presence.

Gaining entry to modern trade retailers such as supermarkets and retail chains presented formidable challenges due to their stringent requirements and brand preferences. Therefore, the team opted to initiate their distribution efforts by focusing on general trade, encompassing independent retail outlets instead. Retailers have specific concerns, such as having confidence in the products they sell. To establish trust among retailers, the Atomberg team leveraged positive online reviews as a testament to their product quality. They also collected information about various retailers and ran online ads, specifically targeting them. These ads highlighted the awards that Atomberg had won, which helped in increasing retailer confidence in the brand.

Shibam shared some insights, saying, 'During our initial visits, retailers didn't show interest in our brand. So, we kept going back to build connections. We spent six to seven months to get into a few promising stores. However, we realized that getting into more stores would be tough without strong retailer relationships, which takes time to build. That's when we decided to "buy" those relationships by hiring sales people from our competitors, who already knew the retailers well.'

While Atomberg's on-ground sales team came from the appliances industry, they strategically brought in a distribution leadership team from FMCG companies. Shibam explained, 'This choice was driven by the recognition that FMCG companies excel in distribution strategies, and we wanted to align ourselves with their distribution practices rather than those prevalent in the appliances industry.'

Rather than rapidly expanding the number of retail outlets, the team focused on boosting sales of a select group of retailers. They organized fan health check camps in residential societies to raise awareness about energy wastage in existing fans. Once people became aware of the problem, they sought solutions, leading to increased inquiries from local retailers. As these retailers experienced growth, they began sharing their positive experiences with their peers. Shibam said, 'Retailers often attend events where their peers from multiple cities gather, so word-of-mouth extended beyond a single city.'

Advertisements on regional TV channels built brand awareness and brought traffic to the Atomberg website. To generate demand for retailers, the team incorporated a store locator feature on the website's landing page. When website visitors clicked on the store locator, their contact information was sent to the nearest retailer, and the retailer's contact information was shared with the potential customer. As sales using this method increased, retailers gained greater confidence in the brand.

Typically, retailers have connections with local electricians. The Atomberg team gathered contact information of these electricians and hosted specialized events for them. During these interactions the Atomberg team gave the electricians the respect they deserved, while also providing knowledge about the advanced features of their products. This approach resonated with the electricians, who felt appreciated for their expertise while also gaining knowledge about the Atomberg products. As a result, they began recommending the brand to their customers and taking on Atomberg fan installation projects referred by retailers.

Atomberg's leadership team spent a significant amount of time in retail stores, interacting with consumers at the point of purchase and pitching their products with various messages. Whichever message worked best was transformed into a performance-driven advertisement on Google and Facebook. Conversely, if a pitch did not yield positive results, the team excluded similar creatives from their performance marketing campaigns. Arindam Paul, Chief Business Officer said, 'This approach was like a live testing of which messages connect and which don't.'

Customer data is required for mining insights. Online channel customer data is readily available, but with offline channels, retailers possess the customer data. Atomberg implemented a clever strategy using its warranty programme to acquire this valuable customer information. Customers were simply required to provide a missed call, and in response the Atomberg team would follow up with a call to collect their data and activate the warranty.

To eliminate any confusion with retailers, the team ensured consistent pricing for their products across both online and offline channels. Arindam elaborated, 'Each channel has its cost structure. For example, in online channels, we avoid the expense of a sales team but have higher online marketing costs to build brand awareness. On the other hand, offline channels require a sales team. We strategically managed these cost components and margins to maintain uniform pricing. Moreover, during discount campaigns, we implemented measures to prevent online channels from significantly reducing prices below a certain threshold.'

Having achieved an annual revenue of around Rs 500 crore, the team embarked on expanding its distribution across India. Sharing his learnings as advice for others, Shibam said, 'I believe it's not prudent to invest significantly in marketing without a solid distribution in place. The key principle in marketing is consistency. Fluctuating wildly from, say, Rs 500 crore in one year to zero the next due to funding constraints is an unproductive strategy. Rather, a gradual and consistent approach, like starting with Rs 50 crore in the first year, then Rs 75 crore the next year, eventually reaching Rs 100 crore in the third year, while aligning these investments with sales and distribution strategies, can yield better long-term results.'

During their national expansion, Atomberg ran a few campaigns on Hindi and English TV channels and even sponsored a few cricket matches. As of September 2023, the brand has surpassed the annual revenue run rate of Rs 1000 crore. As Atomberg continues to reach new heights, their story serves as an inspiration for businesses aspiring to make their mark in highly competitive categories.

How Fractal Won Marquee Clients as a Start-Up in a New Field

In an age where terms like 'analytics' and 'AI' have become household buzzwords, it is worth noting that when Fractal began its journey, these concepts were relatively obscure in the business world. Securing initial clients is a formidable challenge for any start-up. In this narrative, we explore how Fractal not only contributed to building a new category but also masterfully persuaded renowned brands to become their very first clients.

Srikanth Velamakanni and Pranay Agrawal, both alumni of IIM Ahmedabad, had acquired valuable experience working with prominent names in the financial services industry. However, driven by their passion for mathematics and consumer behaviour, they co-founded an analytics firm in the year 2000, along with a few other IIM Ahmedabad alumni.

During this time ICICI Bank had established itself as a major player in the personal financial services (PFS) sector. However, they still faced a significant obstacle—the lack of suitable mathematical models to support their risk assessment decisions. To tackle this challenge, they reached out to Fair Isaac Corp, a prominent US-based credit company, to adapt their existing models to the Indian context.

Leveraging his network within ICICI, Srikanth met with the PFS leadership team, proposing that Fractal be engaged instead. His persuasive pitch centred on the idea that harnessing Indian data and crafting customized models would give ICICI superior results compared to adopting a global model based on foreign data.

Naturally, ICICI's team inquired about the Fractal team's prior experience. Srikanth responded, 'We are a start-up; this is our first venture.' The next question from the ICICI team was, 'Why should we trust you?' Srikanth's proposition was straightforward, 'We are willing to invest three to four weeks to research various credit scoring techniques. Subsequently, we will provide you with a comprehensive report detailing how to construct these risk models. You can entrust this project to us if our knowledge and expertise meet with your satisfaction.' It was a fair proposal and the ICICI team agreed.

Following a month of diligent effort, the Fractal team presented a comprehensive thirty-two-page white paper. Although the ICICI team was impressed with Fractal's approach, they nevertheless hesitated to entrust a new team with the project implementation. To address their concerns and minimize project risk, Srikanth proposed that Fractal would undertake the work for ICICI without any payment, on the condition that if they found the Fractal performance satisfactory, ICICI would provide a recommendation. This engagement proved highly successful, as Srikanth not only secured the coveted recommendation from ICICI, but also paved the way for future paid collaborations.

At a corporate event, Srikanth had the opportunity to meet the Chief Economist of Hindustan Unilever (HUL). Intrigued by Fractal's work with ICICI, the Chief Economist invited Srikanth and his team to visit the HUL office. Srikanth recalled, 'Our primary focus was the financial services industry, and we had not initially planned to enter the FMCG sector. However, we could not turn down this opportunity as we were also keen to explore the possibilities of analytics.'

At the time, HUL was actively running the Repeat Buyer Survey (RBS) initiative in collaboration with the research agency IMRB. This programme involved the collection of every product wrapper used in people's homes. Researchers periodically gathered these wrappers and documented when each product had been used. This RBS data encompassed information from 30,000 consumers across India. The Chief Economist asked Fractal to derive valuable consumer behaviour insights from it.

This period coincided with the 2001 recession, leading to significant shifts in people's behaviour. Consumers were switching from premium brands to more affordable alternatives, adjusting product quantities, and modifying their purchase frequencies. They also became more receptive to promotional offers, among other changes. Leveraging the RBS data, Fractal developed tailored strategies for HUL brands to remain pertinent to consumers.

Having successfully collaborated with HUL, the Fractal team approached HDFC. Knowing of Fractal's work with ICICI, the HDFC leadership agreed to a meeting. Instead of promoting the Fractal brand, Srikanth and his team focused on educating HDFC about the potential of analytics. After multiple workshops their efforts paid off and HDFC recognized Fractal as a thought leader in analytics. Consequently, Fractal built risk models that helped HDFC identify low-risk customers for loan distribution. In 2007, during the financial crisis, these models proved invaluable, enabling HDFC to outperform other banks in India, with lower default rates.

Back in 2002, after HDFC, the Fractal team pitched to Citibank. However, the Citi leadership informed Srikanth that they already had 150 PhDs in New York, working on analytical models. Undeterred, Srikanth challenged the Citibank leadership to give Fractal a difficult project and compare their performance with their team of PhDs. Srikanth recalled, 'Perhaps I sounded a bit foolish, but I firmly believed that having a PhD didn't grant anyone a monopoly on achieving superior results.'

Taken aback at first, Citibank assigned Fractal the task of creating a model for cross-selling credit cards to their personal loan customers, and vice versa. When Citibank later ran campaigns based on the Fractal models, the results aligned precisely with Fractal's predictions. Srikanth said, 'They were super shocked that our models were so accurate. And that's how we actually won their respect. It was a confidence booster for us as well. When you are a start-up in a new field, everyone doubts you, but if you prove yourself, you gain confidence in your own capabilities.'

With a handful of esteemed Indian clients in their portfolio, the Fractal team set their sights on breaking into the US market. However, they quickly realized that the American market was far more advanced in analytics as compared to India. Fractal was not seen as a cutting-edge analytics provider by American clients. Instead, they perceived Fractal's focus as being split between consulting, technology and analytics, which diluted the company's positioning.

On their return to India, the Fractal team gathered for extensive deliberations. They sketched a triangle on the drawing board, designating 'business', 'analytics' and 'technology' to its three corners. It quickly became evident that the market already housed formidable players like McKinsey in business consulting, and the technology sector was saturated with numerous IT companies. In contrast, the analytics field was still emerging and less crowded. Srikanth recollected, 'Prior to this, we were juggling multiple facets for our clients. While Indian clients appreciated our versatility, it was our encounter with the American companies that made us realize the importance of focus. We understood that we needed to position ourselves as specialists in analytics.'

The next crucial step for the Fractal team was defining their target clientele. Srikanth explained, 'One can spend time trying to sell analytics to smaller companies or giants like Google. We chose to focus on pursuing companies similar to Google because, if successful, the potential rewards would be significant.' To determine their clients, Fractal implemented a '10-20-30' strategy. Srikanth clarified this saying, 'The clients Fractal decided to serve needed to meet at least one of three criteria—either they had to have a minimum of $10 billion in revenue, or possess a market capitalization of $20 billion, or have a customer base of thirty million consumers.'

With this strategy in place, Fractal deliberately chose to decline work from many renowned start-ups and small businesses. Srikanth elucidated, 'While we hold deep respect for the accomplishments of the businesses we've had to turn down, we remain committed to our strategic approach.'

In 2006, Fractal approached P&G in the US—the world's largest FMCG company, proposing a research collaboration.

But even after two years of discussions, progress was slow. However, in 2008, P&G decided to evaluate Fractal, along with twenty-five other companies, for a global analytics partnership specifically focused on marketing mix modelling—a statistical approach to measure and optimize the impact of marketing strategies on product sales and performance.

Srikanth vividly recounted the pivotal conversation, saying, 'During our meeting with the P&G team we expressed our gratitude for the opportunity, but we candidly admitted our lack of prior experience in marketing mix modelling, which initially took them by surprise. However, what we conveyed next was crucial. We informed them that although we lacked practical experience, upon being considered for this work we had dedicated one month to intensive research in this domain. We showed them the three relevant books and twenty-five research papers we had referred to develop a comprehensive approach to address their challenge.'

The P&G team appreciated Fractal's honesty and proactive approach to acquiring expertise in a new area. Fractal eventually secured the project after several rounds of selection, alongside twenty-five other firms. Srikanth emphasized, 'Our willingness to acknowledge our limitations, combined with our commitment to acquiring the necessary knowledge, has been instrumental in our growth.'

Every client engagement at Fractal resembles a captivating story, acting as a magnet that attracts new clients. Srikanth underscored this saying, 'It's worth noting that we don't position Fractal as the hero in these stories. The true heroes are the client team members who place their trust in us. They emerged as heroes within their organizations, advocating for and introducing our innovative techniques and problem-solving approaches. Their careers flourished, and their success naturally enhanced our own growth and reputation.'

The project with P&G, known as Business Sphere, became a turning point in Fractal's journey. It not only garnered acclaim, but also earned Filippo Passerini of P&G the prestigious CIO of the Year Award from *Information Week* in 2010. Srikanth still takes immense pride in the groundbreaking work they did, especially considering Business Sphere is now deployed in over fifty P&G offices worldwide.

Building on this achievement, Fractal strategically shifted focus from smaller Indian assignments to larger-scale projects with American and global clients. As of August 2023, approximately 99 per cent of Fractal's revenue is derived from global clients. Highlighting the significance of preparation before each pitch, Srikanth explained, 'We never go to a meeting without being well-prepared, and we're not just there to sell our analytics solutions. Our learning begins with thoroughly examining the financial data of the key companies we want to serve. We scrutinize their balance sheets and income statements to understand their business dynamics and revenue sources comprehensively. Once we've established this conceptual understanding, we tap into the insights of industry experts who possess a deep contextual understanding. When we meet with clients for the first time, we mainly listen to them and save our ideas for later conversations.'

Fractal's remarkable journey, from modest origins to its current status as a global analytics leader working with 135 Fortune 500 companies, stands as a testament to its unwavering commitment to learning, adaptability, and a clear strategic vision.

13

Managing Brand Portfolio

Products are made in a factory but brands are created in the mind.

—Walter Landor, branding pioneer

As a company grows, it often enters different categories or market segments and sometimes acquires new brands. This can result in the development of a portfolio of brands within the same company. Often, these brands then operate independently, as seen with P&G's Ariel and Tide, using the 'house of brand' strategy. Alternatively, they may adopt the primary brand's identity, like TATA Steel and TATA Motors, following a 'branded house' strategy. Some companies use a blend of these approaches.

Brand architecture refers to the strategic process of organizing and structuring a company's portfolio of brands. It involves defining the relationships between the corporate brand and the individual brands within the portfolio, while also establishing a framework for how the brands are positioned, differentiated and interconnected.

In my endeavour to delve into this topic, I engaged in a discussion with **Lulu Raghavan, President of APAC at Landor, the world's largest brand consulting firm.** Here are a few lessons I learned from her:

Create as few brands as possible

'Developing and managing new brands demands significant management time, substantial financial investment, and the allocation of marketing and operational resources. Hence, it's advisable for start-ups to refrain from creating a new brand until they've generated substantial revenue and garnered significant repeat customers with a single brand,' Lulu advised.

Start-ups undergo a significant amount of exploration, pivoting and expansion. Hence, selecting a brand name with a broad meaning helps to accommodate future evolution. For example, while Amazon began by selling books, instead of choosing a restrictive name like books.com, Jeff Bezos opted for a versatile name, allowing for future expansion into other categories.

Lulu emphasized another point saying, 'When considering brand extension, it's crucial to thoroughly evaluate the suitable categories for extending a master brand.' For example, due to its association as a dairy brand, Epigamia could broaden its offerings from Greek yogurt to other dairy-related products like milk shakes and smoothies.

While strategic advice for start-ups commonly suggests establishing a single master brand, there are exceptions to this approach, based on specific business models and acquisitions. For instance, Rebel Foods leverages the cloud kitchen model to run multiple food brands using shared resources such as kitchens, chefs and delivery infrastructure. Similarly, FirstCry has capitalized on its extensive customer base and reach to create private-label brands like BabyHug. Additionally, Honasa Consumer, the parent company of Mamaearth, has expanded its portfolio by acquiring brands like Dr. Sheth's. However, it is essential to note that these examples involve established start-ups with significant resources and a proven track record with their initial brands. One must carefully consider their unique circumstances and resources in creating or acquiring new brands.

Business strategy drives brand architecture

Creating brand architecture requires deep understanding of the customer perceptions and expectations associated with each brand. Lulu noted that by understanding each brand's distinct positioning, value proposition and weighing the advantages and disadvantages of extending an existing brand versus creating a new one, companies can make well-informed decisions regarding their particular brand architecture.

For instance, the Taj Group of Hotels, one of the oldest and most revered brands of the House of Tatas, realized in 2004 that it needed to re-examine its portfolio. The Taj name was used across properties in different ways, such as Taj Business, Taj Luxury and Taj Leisure, encompassing a range of two-star, three-star, four-star and five-star hotels. This created a mismatch of consumer expectations and diluted the Taj brand with varying quality products and services. To overcome these challenges, the TATA Group collaborated with Landor to introduce three new brands: Vivanta by Taj for upscale hotels, the Gateway Hotel for premium hotels, and Ginger for budget hotels. While these new brands catered to specific market segments, Taj Hotels maintained its luxury status. In addition, the Indian Hotels Company Limited (IHCL) was established as the umbrella brand, overseeing and encompassing these individual brands.

Effective stakeholder management is crucial in brand architecture exercises

Although primarily a rational and analytical process, brand architecture often becomes an emotional exercise due to organizational dynamics. In companies with multiple brands, it is natural for certain brands to get greater resources, leadership attention and media coverage. This discrepancy has the potential to de-motivate employees working with the less-prioritized brands. Moreover, it can give rise to ego clashes and foster envy amongst teams associated with different brands.

The brand architecture exercise also influences external stakeholders such as customers, vendors, suppliers and partners, who are likely to approach the company's employees with various queries regarding the change—asking why it is happening and how it will affect them, and so forth. Such changes also prompt inquiries from the families and friends of employees. Thus, it is essential that all employees are comfortable and confident about answering such questions.

Lulu told me, 'Employees are the most powerful brand ambassadors. The CEO should help them understand that brand architecture is not about restructuring the internal organizational chart but rather about the company's face to its markets. The rationale and the narrative should flow from the CEO to the company's management, then to employees, and further to partners, vendors and suppliers.'

As an example, the Taj brand has long been regarded as a status symbol. During the brand architecture exercise, the primary challenge faced by the management was earning the confidence of employees, particularly those who would no longer bear the 'Taj' name on their business cards. It was crucial that these staffers felt reassured and confident in embracing the new brand identities. To achieve this, Landor and the IHCL leadership team conducted workshops and training sessions to actively engage employees and reinforce belief in the new brands. Landor also collaborated with IHCL's leadership in supporting the numerous partners who were transitioning assets from the Taj to other brands.

Furthermore, prior to communicating the change to customers, Landor validated the promises associated with all the hotel brands. This process ensured that the actions of employees, partners and vendors aligned with the commitments made to customers.

Defining and managing brand promise is crucial

Even seemingly minute details can significantly impact how customers perceive a brand. Hence, implementing new brand architecture requires a clear definition of the target customer, brand promise, and customer experience. Lulu highlighted this, saying, 'The entire organization has to be unified to deliver a seamless customer experience across all touch points.'

In the context of a hotel, there are numerous points of contact or moments of delight in a day. So, when IHCL created different hotel brands, defining the brand experience at each touchpoint was paramount. This involved implementing new uniforms, silverware, talk lines, music as part of the sensory experience, staff behaviour patterns and even the choice of words used in communication. For instance, at a no-frills hotel like Ginger, there were no bellmen; guests wheeled their bags in and checked into their rooms independently. In contrast, Taj offered a more formal and personalized service, escorting guests to their rooms. Similarly, Taj typically maintained a larger staff-to-room ratio when compared to Vivanta by Taj. Moreover, guests were addressed by surname at Taj but by their first name at Vivanta by Taj.

Developing a luxury brand demands a keen eye for nuanced detail. For Taj, this meant prioritizing elements like superior linen quality and distinguishing between hand-knotted and hand-tufted carpets. Even the choice of paper and pens provided to guests were meticulously curated to reflect excellence.

Brand architecture never remains static

As a company expands and enters new markets or introduces new offerings, it may become necessary to adapt the brand architecture to align with the company's strategic goals and evolving vision. Furthermore, shifts in consumer preferences, competitive landscape and industry trends, can also lead to adjustments in the brand architecture. These changes might involve repositioning existing brands, establishing new sub-brands, or even consolidating multiple brands under a unified umbrella.

For instance, in the late 2010s, the IHCL brand architecture underwent modifications in response to escalating competition and evolving business dynamics. The 'Taj' name was removed from 'Vivanta by Taj'. Concurrently, the Gateway brand was phased out, and many hotels were repositioned as Vivanta properties. Moreover, the company introduced a new brand called 'SeleQtion', comprising boutique hotels, renowned locally. While these hotels did not carry the Taj or Vivanta branding, they fell under IHCL management. Notable examples included the President in Mumbai, and the Ambassador in New Delhi.

Note: *The examples of Taj highlighted in this chapter may not fully reflect the current state, given that IHCL has updated its brand architecture.*

Case Studies

How Indigo Paints Refined Its Brand Architecture

In 2011, over a decade after its inception, Indigo Paints achieved a turnover of Rs 50 crores, providing the company with surplus cash for brand-building initiatives. Seeking guidance, Hemant Jalan, the founder of Indigo Paints, consulted with Kiran Khalap, co-founder of chlorophyll, one of India's most respected brand consulting firms. Kiran pointed out the inconsistencies in how Indigo's brand name was represented in different places and raised concerns about the company's strategy of maintaining multiple brands such as Indigo, Indigo Platinum, Shagun and Flora. He urged Hemant to define clearly what the Indigo Paints brand stood for. Reflecting on this, Hemant knew Kiran was right. 'Kiran made us realize that we were possibly doing everything wrong from a branding standpoint,' he acknowledged.

Hemant admitted, 'As a small company, survival was our main focus, not strategy. We tended to mimic the strategies of major industry players like Asian Paints. They had a diverse portfolio of brands like Royale, Apcolite, Tractor and Utsav, each catering to different price points and customer needs. We believed that this was the right approach, so we followed it. We didn't consider the implications of this strategy.'

Kiran emphasized to Hemant that as a smaller brand, Indigo Paints would have significantly lower advertising budgets than established brands. Hemant recalled one of Kiran's observations, 'In the noisy, crowded world of advertising, creating brand recall in the consumer's mind is a significant challenge. Through advertising you are essentially trying to rent out one cubic millimetre of the human brain. This tiny space in the consumer's brain is considered Earth's most expensive real estate. Building identities for four or five different brands would be far more difficult and much more expensive.'

To convince Hemant to collapse multiple brand names and focus on one, Kiran also provided compelling examples, one of which was Amul. Kiran explained that though Amul spanned numerous product categories, it operated under a single brand name. He emphasized that Amul only advertised some of its products individually. When the brand 'Amul' was promoted, whether for chocolates, milk, butter or any other product, there was a beneficial ripple effect across their entire product range.

Hemant was convinced but soon realized that persuading his team would be a new challenge. When he shared the decision to transition from a multi-brand to a single-brand strategy, he encountered significant resistance from his sales team. They firmly believed that imitating Asian Paints was the best strategy. Hemant had to persuade them that Asian Paints had started in a different era and operated in a different orbit. They did not fully understand the reasons behind Asian Paints' strategy, therefore it was unwise for Indigo to copy them.

To illustrate his point, Hemant decided to conduct an experiment in front of his sales team. He invited individuals not involved in the paint industry, including his wife and friends, to serve as participants. Hemant then listed twenty paint brands and asked these guests to identify which brands belonged to Asian Paints, Berger or Nerolac. As he had anticipated, most struggled to correctly associate the brands with their parent companies. Once the experiment had concluded, Hemant turned to his team and posed a question, 'What's the purpose of having multiple brands if consumers can't associate a brand with a specific company?' The room fell silent as Hemant's words resonated with his team, underscoring the validity of his argument.

Reflecting on the past, Hemant acknowledged a crucial realization, 'Copying big players without giving thought to it was a mistake. Just because someone else does something in a certain way doesn't mean we should blindly follow it. Large organizations have different strategies and budgets, which small organizations don't have. So, one should not mimic others without applying critical thinking.'

As a result, Indigo Paints consolidated all its brands under the unified name 'Indigo'. In this alternative approach, products at various price points were distinguished as the Platinum Series, Gold Series, Silver Series and Bronze Series, emphasizing specific product names on the packaging such as Tile Coat, Metallic Emulsion, Floor Coat, etc.

The chlorophyll team organized workshops with the Indigo Paints team to unveil the unique aspects that set the company apart. Kiran recommended Hemant stay away from generic offerings and instead focus on growing Indigo's niche products like metallic finishes for walls, and special coats for floors and ceilings. 'His point was that Indigo was competing against large players with well-known brand names. However, Indigo possessed certain unique products that no other competitor offered. As there was no advertisement noise around these products, even a small advertising budget could lead to significant noticeability. Furthermore, because all of Indigo's offerings share a common brand name, any positive recognition for these unique products could create a "rub off" effect, enhancing the overall brand image,' Hemant said.

Hemant also credits chlorophyll with designing the Indigo Paints' eye-catching logo of a zebra with coloured stripes and the tagline 'Be surprised!', to showcase how different they were as a company. Sharing the story behind Indigo's iconic brand identity, Hemant said, 'The chlorophyll team recognized that even though we were small, we were innovative in coming up with unique paint products to meet needs that no one else had thought of. Our differentiation was not limited to just our products but also extended to the way we functioned. For instance, the method we used to incentivize our sales force, our entire thought process, and our organizational structure were all completely different from any other paint company.'

chlorophyll suggested the brand identity should reflect this uniqueness and innovativeness of the company. They came up with three ideas for various ways to depict this. 'One was a zebra with coloured stripes. The whole team instinctively liked this design, so we decided to go with it,' Hemant recalled with a smile. 'This new identity helped us improve our brand recognition. Our packaging became so popular that dealers everywhere wanted at least the can, if not a dealership.'

Between 2012 and 2020, Indigo Paints only advertised its niche products, which gave the brand a lot of visibility. Over time, these niche products gained prominence, attracting interest from larger players who attempted to enter the market. However, by this point these products had become synonymous with Indigo. Competitors struggled to capture market share unless they were prepared to invest substantial amounts in advertising to create brand awareness—a step they hesitated to take due to the relatively small market size of these niche products. Consequently, for all these products, Indigo retained its position as market leader.

Once Indigo Paints had established strong brand equity through its niche products, the company shifted its focus to advertising products in more competitive categories. Hemant explained this transition saying, 'Our goal was to transfer the goodwill we had earned from these niche products to our wall paints. We orchestrated an engaging rap song-based advertisement with a compelling message—if you can trust us with your floor coat, why not trust us with your wall? And if our ceiling paint has won your trust, why wouldn't our wall paint do the same?'

'The branding strategy worked for us,' said Hemant. Within a decade the company had experienced substantial growth, increasing its revenue from Rs 50 crore to over Rs 1000 crore.

How the Brand Paper Boat was Extended to Achieve Growth

Launched in 2013, Paper Boat achieved phenomenal growth for a few years. However, after 2016, the growth rate slowed, and the burn rate began to increase. Neeraj Kakkar, co-founder of Hector Beverages (the parent company of Paper Boat) said, 'It's nice to see people liking your brand on social media, but it's not very helpful if this appreciation doesn't translate into revenue growth.' The situation prompted the team to ponder why the dip was happening despite garnering significant praise from consumers and media. On careful analysis, two significant challenges came to light.

First, producing their specialized drinks with their authentic taste, flavour and colour proved to be a time-consuming and costly process. For example, one of the famous drinks of the brand was jamun. There was no organized farming of this fruit in India. Consequently, the team relied on small, isolated tribes in Uttar Pradesh and Bihar to source the fruit. This led to uncertainties in the availability of the fruit and impacted production volumes.

Second, the total addressable market (TAM) for premium non-alcoholic beverages in India, excluding energy drinks such as Red Bull, where consumers were willing to pay more than Rs 20 for a single-serve drink, was relatively small, at approximately Rs 200 crore. In contrast, the TAM for mass non-alcoholic beverage drinks in India was much larger, estimated at around Rs 10,000 crore. This segment included popular brands such as Frooti and Dabur Real, offering single-serve drinks priced at Rs 10. Moreover, the Rs 200 crore TAM was not growing rapidly, as consumers in tier-1 cities, having high purchasing power, were moving away from drinks containing added sugar. Also, the majority of the population in tier-2 and tier-3 cities was price sensitive.

The Paper Boat team concluded that to achieve their aspiration of becoming a Rs 1000 crore company, they needed to address a different market segment. As a result, they decided to diversify their product offerings to cater to both the mass and the premium segments.

Neeraj said, 'If you launch a new product which is very close to the brand's core promise, then you are adding a coin in the brand piggy bank. However, if you are launching a product which is far from the brand's core promise, then you are taking a coin away from the brand piggy bank.' Paper Boat wanted to launch products close to its identity, but specialized Indian ethnic drinks have niche markets, and every drink entails a laborious investment in processes, as well as time. Thus, the team began looking for categories where consumers were not getting the right value or the most hygienic product, but still desired an Indian ethnic offering. They identified a demand for chikki and aam papad, which had no large branded players in the market. So, the company decided to extend the Paper Boat brand beyond drinks to foods. But even while venturing into food products, Paper Boat remained true to its goal of offering traditional products in a modern format.

Neeraj said, 'While extending the brand, you must protect the core brand identity. If you have to get into an offering different from your core offering, it's better to launch a sub-brand* or an independent brand based on how different the category is.' To expand its customer base, the company introduced two beverage sub-brands: Swing—a regular fruit-based drink targeting the mass market, and Zero—a zero-sugar sparkling drink that catered to the premium segment. Both sub-brands were endorsed by Paper Boat to provide credibility though they were not the core offerings of the brand—ethnic recipe-based Indian drinks.

Doy pack had long served as Paper Boat's distinctive packaging choice. However, it was not compatible with carbonation, rendering it inappropriate for aerated drinks like Zero, which are packaged and distributed in plastic bottles. Moreover, for larger pack sizes, especially one litre or more, the Doy pack was not suitable. So, Paper Boat began using tetra packs to accommodate the greater volume requirements.

Neeraj stressed, 'When designing brand architecture, it's essential to consider the variety of brands, products and packages in your portfolio, as well as their pricing, distribution channels, and alignment with customer needs. For example, people opt for two-litre bottles for specific reasons, while 200-ml bottles suit different occasions. Customers who purchase from kirana

---

* A sub-brand leverages the reputation of the main brand while striving to establish its distinct identity in the market. For instance, the Apple iPhone serves as a sub-brand under Apple. In contrast, a new brand is an entirely separate entity with no direct connection to an existing brand in terms of identity. For example, Android is an independent brand owned by Google.

stores have different price preferences than those transiting through airports. Moreover, the offerings may vary in popularity between offline and online channels. Substantial analysis is required to determine the right match of offerings, placements and price points.'

Along with the examples mentioned above, Paper Boat successfully launched multiple other offerings, including dry fruits, as part of its brand extension strategy. As of July 2023, the revenue run rate of Hector Beverages stands at Rs 800 crore. This noteworthy achievement underscores the effectiveness of the expansion strategy, resulting in not only a remarkable surge of growth for the company but also profitability.

How Rebel Foods Became a House of Restaurant Brands

Drawing inspiration from brands like McDonald's, renowned for their burgers, and Domino's, famous for their pizzas, Jaydeep Barman and Kallol Banerjee embarked on a journey in 2011, to establish a global quick-service restaurant (QSR) brand for an Indian dish. Their focus was on rolls and wraps, and they named their brand Faasos.

They followed the traditional approach of building a food business—identifying prime locations, creating top-quality products, ensuring cost-effective service, establishing their brand, and making decent money. Four years later, Faasos had expanded to around fifty locations, received customer love and achieved solid sales per outlet. But the business was not profitable, even at the outlet level. Several factors contributed to this situation. First, the restaurants were situated in prime locations, leading to exceptionally high rents. Second, demand was high during peak hours, such as lunch and dinner times, and on weekends, but otherwise low. While meeting the high demand needed a larger workforce, the staff remained underutilized during off-peak periods.

While conducting their sales analysis, the founders discovered that despite having high street locations, 70 per cent of their orders were for delivery. So, they asked their customers a simple question through a text survey, 'Have you ever seen or been to a Faasos outlet?' A whopping 74 per cent responded 'No'. This led to a re-evaluation by the founding duo, who wondered if they really needed to be located on the high street. They piloted a kitchen on the second floor of an industrial complex, with 80 per cent lower rent and much larger floor space. This proved to be a successful experiment. Faasos revenue rose while its chief expense—rent—decreased significantly. Within just a couple of months, Faasos became a profitable brand. Jaydeep said, 'It was a light bulb moment for us. Our pilot had proven that like books, travel, fashion and electronics, customers were increasingly ordering food online. It seemed possible to build a "delivery-focused" food brand without depending on expensive locations.'

In 2016, the team decided to expand the Faasos offerings and introduced pizzas. Yet, despite the team's confidence in the quality of its pizzas, customers did not buy them. After collecting feedback, it became clear that customers hesitated to buy the Faasos pizzas as the brand was primarily known for its wraps. Jaydeep said, 'This was our second light bulb moment. In food, customers believe one brand = one flagship product.'

Sagar Kochhar, co-founder of Rebel Foods, elaborated, 'In the food space, customers often associate brands with specific categories, and they are hesitant to believe a single brand can excel in multiple culinary styles. For instance, McDonald's is renowned for its burgers, Domino's is known for its pizzas, and Starbucks for its coffee. Yum Brands owns KFC, Pizza Hut and Taco Bell, but each brand maintains separate outlets, supply chains and management.'

Having witnessed the successful transformation of Faasos through the cloud kitchen model, the team pondered the introduction of new 'delivery-only' brands following a similar approach. Jaydeep said, 'Suddenly the canvas expanded tenfold. We could utilize the same fixed cost structure to launch multiple brands, creating multiple revenue sources, one after the other. We were going to become a "single kitchen, multiple food brands" company.'

Sagar explained their expansion strategy saying, 'Food is a high-frequency category, with people eating at least three times a day, and approximately thirty times a month, providing about ninety potential instances for food ordering.' He further elaborated, 'Food is also a high-involvement category. Each order involves a significant investment of time as consumers carefully consider their choices, starting with the desired cuisine and concluding with selecting a specific brand or restaurant.'

Sagar shared a few other fascinating insights. In life we often make choices between luxury and value, such as opting for business class or economy flights, choosing between a Mercedes or a Maruti, or deciding on a five-star hotel versus a budget one, and we tend to stick with our choices for extended periods. However, this is not the case with food. In a single week people might transition from enjoying a humble Rs 20 vada pav to indulging in an extravagant fine dining experience, and everything in-between. Food preferences also vary based on factors like dining alone or with a group, regular or special occasions, and specific cravings.

Moreover, for each occasion people turn to an expert food provider. For instance, they may choose Domino's for a home pizza party, opt for Barbeque Nation for an upscale dining experience, visit a local Udupi restaurant for South Indian breakfast, head to Starbucks for a coffee meeting, or grab a quick burger at McDonald's, among other options. Capitalizing on this consumer insight, the team aimed to launch multiple food brands for different consumption occasions. Sagar said, 'We believed that by building brands around various consumption occasions and price points, we could cater to the same customer multiple times in a day, week, month or year. It was akin to creating a Unilever that seamlessly integrated into people's daily lives in various ways.'

To begin their second brand, the team researched into food categories experiencing high demand but having fragmented players and no national category leader. Pizza and biryani emerged as trendy items consistently ordered by customers. In the pizza category, competing with established brands like Domino's seemed challenging, while the biryani category lacked a dominant national player, with local brands offering limited choices. Therefore, they decided to launch an online biryani brand that could go national.

Sagar said, 'We aimed to build a brand, not just another label. A brand embodies a distinct identity.' To achieve this goal the team not only perfected the recipe and created many varieties of biryani, but also focused on shaping the brand's positioning, narrative and tone—elements intended to leave a lasting impression on consumers.

To enhance the brand appeal, they positioned their offering as 'royal biryani' and named it Behrouz. They carefully crafted a captivating narrative, artfully presented in cinematic and graphic formats, depicting the brand's recipe as a 2000-year-old culinary treasure from the mythical Persian kingdom of Behrouz, where wars were fought to safeguard this cherished recipe. This engaging story was adapted as both long and concise versions, for sharing across various communication channels, both offline and online.

Furthermore, they designed visually appealing packaging. Further, for large orders, they even delivered biryani in metal *handis* with candles for an enhanced dining experience. They defined unique names for their products, accompanied by explanations. For instance, they rebranded Mutton Dum Biryani as Dum Gosht Biryani. Additionally, Behrouz Biryani collaborated with TVF (The Viral Fever), to produce a web show titled *The Royal Palate*, inviting the audience to go on an immersive journey with Chef Kunal Kapur, to uncover the culinary secrets of royal families.

People in different parts of the country have varying taste preferences. For instance, Lucknowi biryani and Hyderabadi biryani have unique flavours and cooking styles, influenced by their regions. Sagar said, 'The cloud kitchen model allowed us to experiment at a lower cost and gradually build scale in line with market expectations. We could customize our biryanis to match the local palate and taste preferences across different regions of the country.'

In 2017, following the successful expansion of Faasos and Behrouz into ten cities with 100 cloud kitchens, the team decided to enter the pizza category with a distinctive approach. They conducted consumer research, asking participants to associate the first thing that came to mind with 'pizza'. Surprisingly, approximately 60 per cent of respondents mentioned 'cheese'. However, no pizza brand prominently highlighted cheese at that time in their marketing efforts. This valuable insight led the team to introduce a pizza brand named Oven Story, featuring four unique cheese variants.

What set Oven Story apart was not only its focus on cheese, but also its introduction of unique toppings. These included exotic vegetables, prawn, broccoli, pesto feta, Schezwan, caramelized onion and more, diverging significantly from the typical pizza toppings available in the market.

In 2018, the company introduced the umbrella brand Rebel Foods, encompassing Faasos, Behrouz and Oven Story. Towards the end of that year, the team began creating new brands tailored to diverse cuisines and various food consumption occasions. Sagar explained, 'We identified market gaps, crafted distinctive identities for our new brands, established a strong online presence, and generated interest through effective marketing strategies.'

Today, Rebel Foods has successfully launched brands like Mandarin Oak (Chinese), Firangi Bake (pasta & lasagnas), The Good Bowl (rice bowl), Sweet Truth (indulgent western desserts), Lunch Box (wholesome office meals), and The Biryani Life (positioned as affordable biryani for everyday consumption). These brands have been created using the same kitchen infrastructure to cater to a range of orders—from single servings to group meals—and to various meal preferences, whether regular, indulgent, occasional or anything in between.

Despite Rebel Foods' diverse range of products, spanning biryani, desserts, wraps and meals, gaps still remained in meeting the varied needs of their customers. Some even pointed out, 'You don't offer burgers.' This inspired the team to think innovatively and explore partnerships with third-party brands.

Sagar said, 'We realized there was no need for us to enter every category ourselves. Numerous excellent brands, both in India and worldwide, have been established over decades, and these brands can leverage our Rebel Operating System* for expansion.'

In 2019, Rebel Foods introduced Rebel Launcher, a programme designed to integrate food brands showing high growth potential into its network, facilitating expansion. Rebel Launcher comprises three subsets:

Accelerator: The company extends its expertise and provides selective investments to promising food brands that are operating on a small scale. One notable example is SLAY Coffee, which, by leveraging Rebel Foods infrastructure, boosted its monthly revenue from Rs 1 lakh to Rs 80 lakh within just six months.

Platform Service: The company collaborates with established brands, enabling them to expand into new cities, locations and, occasionally, international markets. Notably, during the pandemic, Rebel Foods welcomed renowned brands like Naturals Ice Cream and Mad Over Donuts into Rebel Launchers.

Licensing: The company secures licensing rights for renowned global brands and manages their expansion. In 2021, Wendy's, the second-largest burger chain in America, partnered with Rebel Foods to establish 250 cloud kitchens across India, achieving rapid growth from just a handful of locations.

To ensure its brands reach a wide audience, Rebel Foods established its own delivery network and formed partnerships

---

* The Rebel Operating System is explained in another case study.

with platforms like Swiggy and Zomato. Sagar explained the reasoning behind establishing their delivery service, saying, 'People often crave a variety of dishes when ordering in groups. However, on food delivery apps, they can only order from one restaurant at a time. This can lead to varying delivery times and separate fees for multiple orders from different restaurants. In response, we introduced the "EatSure" platform, offering food court on an app experience, allowing users to order from various restaurants on the Rebel Foods network in a single order without incurring additional delivery charges.'

Rebel Foods is expanding the EatSure brand offline by opening smart food courts in various locations. In these unique spaces, customers can place orders from various brands on the Rebel Foods network through the app, eliminating the need to stand in queues to place orders. Orders from multiple brands can also be collected together, streamlining the dining experience. The brand is also establishing different formats of EatSure food courts on college campuses, sports events like IPL, as well as at corporate offices.

Since 2019, Rebel Foods has been expanding its presence beyond India, venturing into markets where cuisines, consumer behaviours and competitors vary significantly. Ankush Grover, co-founder of Rebel Foods, explained that as the company expands into different markets, it continually seeks to identify the 'white space'—the gaps and needs in each market. He stated, 'Each market presents its unique set of opportunities and challenges, with varying white spaces that require distinct brand offerings.'

To effectively approach these diverse markets, Rebel Foods employs a straightforward framework for geographic expansion. This involves a two-dimensional evaluation, considering market size along one axis and supply maturity along the other. For example, the United States represents a sizable market with a highly mature supply side, offering a wide range of cuisines and well-established brands. This necessitates an entirely different approach compared to a market like Saudi Arabia, which is substantial in size but lacks supply-side maturity.

Rebel Foods also strongly emphasizes selecting the right leader for each market. They carefully assess the leader's ability to grasp the nuances and effectively navigate the complexities of that particular market. The founding team consistently holds monthly discussions with leaders across diverse regional and international markets to ensure alignment and success.

As of September 2023, Rebel Foods operates a network of over 4000 internet restaurants across multiple countries, including India, the United Arab Emirates (Dubai, Abu Dhabi, Sharjah), the United Kingdom and Saudi Arabia. With more than forty-five owned and partner brands in its network, Rebel Foods has established itself as the world's largest internet restaurant company.

14

Unveiling the Dynamics of ESG, CSR and Social Responsibility

The common question that gets asked in business is, 'why?' That's a good question, but an equally valid question is, 'why not?'

—Jeff Bezos, founder of Amazon

ESG broadly covers how a company affects the environment, treats employees, deals with suppliers and customers, engages with local communities, and how well it's managed ethically and transparently. On the other hand, CSR broadly includes activities that help society, like volunteering and donations. Both ESG and CSR initiatives can play a significant role in brand building as they help positively shape the public perception of a company.

I had the privilege of discussing this topic with **Ambi Parameswaran, one of India's most respected brand strategists and founder of Brand-Building.com, a brand advisory firm. Earlier, he was the CEO of FCB Ulka Advertising, one of India's top ad agencies.** During his nearly four decades of career, he contributed to building brands such as Santoor, Tata Motors, TCS, Tropicana, Zee TV, Sunfeast, Wipro, Thermax and ICICI. He is a best-selling author of eleven books and served as a member of the Board of Governors of IIM Calcutta from 2007 to 2017.

Here are a few lessons I learned from him:

Prioritize ESG; CSR initiatives can be implemented at a later stage

In today's business environment, ensuring good governance and minimizing harm to the environment and society is paramount. Therefore, start-ups should make ESG considerations a priority from the outset.

However, CSR initiatives can be considered once the start-up reaches a certain scale. Ambi elaborated, 'Start-ups face numerous pressing demands, such as delivering results for investors, ensuring timely salary payments to employees, and meeting customer expectations. If a start-up is not yet profitable and primarily relies on investor funds, allocating money in areas like innovation, marketing and operations would take priority over CSR.' He added, 'However, if start-ups are inclined to contribute to a social cause without spending money, they can offer volunteer time to their employees. But in the early stages of a business, when employees are already working tirelessly to meet business demands, it may not be feasible for them to get involved in CSR activities.'

Sometimes, the overlap between ESG and CSR could occur when a company's initiative directly impacts its business operations and a broader societal benefit. For instance, initiatives like recycling water and converting waste from local communities into energy for use in your company can be seen as fulfilling both CSR and ESG objectives.

Don't expect any direct benefit from CSR activities

Ambi said, 'Companies should engage in CSR because it's beneficial for society, not because it might enhance their brand or bring in any financial returns. Any benefits, if they occur, would likely be indirect.' For instance, if a pencil company mentions on its packet that for every packet sold, one pencil is donated to underprivileged children, then it is communicating its social impact. This might or might not affect how customers perceive the company.

Ambi suggested, 'If you are engaging in CSR, do things related to your business.' For example, if a company is involved in making stationery, then a CSR cause like cleaning toilets doesn't connect. However, if that company does something around school education, like distributing drawing books to underprivileged kids or creating a scholarship for children, there is a connection. He emphasized, 'Engaging in connected CSR activities may not guarantee brand benefits, but there's a possibility of gaining some.'

If not connected to business, CSR efforts should at least be connected to the area where the company operates. For instance, if a company operates a manufacturing plant in a remote part of Maharashtra, it should focus its CSR efforts on neighbouring villages. Providing necessities like schools or toilets not only benefits the communities directly but may also indirectly benefit the company as employees from these villages might take pride in their company's contributions. On the other hand, conducting CSR activities in distant regions, such as Karnataka, might present challenges in measuring the direct impact of the initiative.

Commit to a cause for the long term

Many companies contribute to CSR activities without a consistent strategy. They switch CSR initiatives yearly, such as supporting girl children one year, hospitals the next, rural development the third year, donating to the Prime Minister's fund the fourth year, and supporting sports in the fifth year. Ambi suggested, 'Such random acts of giving back can dilute the potential impact. Instead, companies should establish a CSR policy and select a cause for long-term support. This approach allows for measurable improvements over time and demonstrates the company's sustained commitment to a specific cause.'

Collaborate with trusted NGOs

Start-ups might lack the expertise to manage CSR initiatives independently. Collaborating with an NGO provides the necessary expertise for effective CSR implementation. While partnering with an NGO may involve a management fee, it's justified by the value they offer, such as handling logistics, monitoring donations, and providing impact reports.

Ambi suggested that when choosing an NGO, consider those rated positively by agencies like Pratham and those aligned with your chosen cause. For instance, if your

CSR initiative targets education, collaborate with NGOs specializing in that area. Additionally, if a company plans to donate smart pads to schools, a reputable NGO ensures proper implementation, reducing the risk of misuse and enhancing the initiative's impact.

Start-ups should be mindful of their impact on society

Ambi contended that every start-up inherently contributes to society by generating direct and indirect employment and enhancing consumers' lives. As start-ups play a crucial role in society, it is essential for them to consider the ethical and social aspects of their decisions. He said, 'If a company is doing things that negatively affect society, then no amount of CSR could save its reputation.'

Regrettably, some companies neglect their social responsibilities. For instance, they resort to mass layoffs due to financial constraints. Ambi recommended exploring alternatives such as temporary salary reductions instead of immediate layoffs. Some companies neglect to deposit their employees' Provident Fund (PF) contributions. Ambi said such acts are unpardonable. He added, 'If a company cannot care for its people, how can it engage in CSR? In fact, start-ups must ensure that they build caring organizations before focusing on CSR. Charity begins at home.'

Case Studies

How Zoho Is Impacting Underserved Talent in Rural India

Zoho is recognized as one of India's most profitable technology companies. It has never taken external funding and competes head-to-head with big names like Salesforce, Google, Microsoft and Oracle, offering businesses cloud-based software at a lower cost. And here is something inspiring—Zoho helps people from rural areas find jobs in the technology sector.

In 2005, Zoho launched Zoho University, now known as Zoho Schools of Learning (ZSL), beginning with just three professors and six students.

Zoho actively visits government-run schools in Tamil Nadu for student enrolment into ZSL, conducting aptitude tests and interviews. According to Sridhar Vembu, co-founder and CEO of Zoho, 'We disregard their school grades, focusing more on assessing their mathematical skills and aptitude. Our primary goal is to identify students with a strong drive and determination.' Students from all kinds of backgrounds, including from small towns and socio-economically disadvantaged backgrounds, are part of ZSL. 'Numerous individuals possess untapped potential but lack opportunities because nobody is willing to take a chance on them. They don't receive the chances they deserve,' Sridhar said.

ZSL employs a comprehensive approach, commencing with a three-week training programme to evaluate the students' real-world capabilities. Successful candidates are then granted seats in the twenty-four-month programme, along with a monthly stipend of Rs 10,000. Each year, approximately 200–250 students join ZSL, which includes the School of Technology, the School of Design, and the School of Business. Technical School covers subjects such as structured problem-solving, programming languages, web and mobile technologies, foundational mathematics, and communication skills. Design School focuses on design principles, tools and communication skills. Business School includes subjects like business principles, English and soft skills, mathematics, entrepreneurship, product management and marketing. Situated within Zoho's Chennai and Tenkasi offices, in Tamil Nadu, ZSL's proximity to both employees and management facilitates consistent syllabus updates. Additionally, students can immerse themselves in the office culture and interact with employees.

On completing a year, students undertake internships at Zoho, based on their performance and interview results, as well as the stream of interest. They then receive rigorous training. Remarkable performers are subsequently offered permanent positions, receiving salaries equivalent to those of college graduates. Thanks to the robust preparation provided by the programme and the zealous participation of the students, almost all the students get placed at Zoho.

By August 2023, around 15 per cent of Zoho's current workforce consisted of ZSL alumni. One notable example among them is Abdul Alim. Sridhar shared the story: 'Abdul started at Zoho as a security guard. One of our employees noticed him using a computer at the reception desk and recognized his passion for programming. Abdul subsequently enrolled in ZSL and has grown into a valued programmer within the Zoho Charts team.' Besides hiring from ZSL, Zoho also hires locally in its offices based in villages, tier-2 and tier-3 towns. That is how it creates job opportunities for the local youth.

Like that of many of Zoho's employees, Sridhar's own journey is an inspiration. Born in 1968 in a village in Tamil Nadu's Thanjavur district, Sridhar went on to earn an engineering degree from IIT Madras in 1989. After that, he pursued his MS and PhD at Princeton in the USA, followed by a thriving entrepreneurial career there. However, in 2019, Sridhar made the pivotal decision to return to India for good. Rather than embracing an urban lifestyle, Sridhar focused on rural regions, establishing his office in a village in Tamil Nadu's Tenkasi district. This unconventional choice was motivated by his aim to create job opportunities for rural talent within India's flourishing technology sector. In these villages, Sridhar has also established R&D centres where the work is not necessarily related to Zoho.

Sridhar observed with characteristic humility, 'While Silicon Valley may not notice my absence amidst its abundant talent and brilliance, my presence in rural India can create a significant impact. That's why I've chosen to be here for rural revival. Many talented people in rural areas are often overlooked as there are few job opportunities in their own villages. So, they move to larger cities, leaving their families behind. This influx makes cities crowded and expensive to live in, especially for newcomers. The high cost of living and expensive real estate in cities is neither good for the employees nor for companies.'

Starting with a single canter in Tenkasi, Zoho has expanded to thirty offices in non-urban locations globally, with a significant presence in Indian states such as Tamil Nadu, Kerala, Andhra Pradesh and Bihar. Sridhar envisions that providing well-paying jobs in rural regions not only elevates the quality of life for employees and their families but also plays a pivotal role in fostering the economic growth of these areas.

Rooted in the belief that software can be built from anywhere, Zoho plans to open 100 new offices around the world in small towns and villages.

Though Zoho workers are generally sought after in the industry, the company's attrition rate is low. Sridhar said, 'If you want to build key technologies, people should be proud to call your company their home. When you take care of employees, when you invest in them, when you invest in skill and talent creation, they are going to give back something in return. What do employees give back in return? Their commitment. Their loyalty. Their love and affection.'

How Zerodha and Its Founders Are Giving Back

The Indian government has mandated that companies allocate 2 per cent of their average net profits, computed over the preceding three years, towards CSR initiatives. Zerodha, however, has chosen not to conform to this standard by refraining from assigning a specific percentage to its philanthropic endeavours. Instead, the company has intensified its commitment to giving back each year. In 2023, Zerodha donated Rs 110 crore, which accounted for 4.17 per cent of its profits from the preceding three years, to various social causes.

Zerodha embarked on its giving back journey around 2016, when the company began experiencing substantial financial success. Founders Nithin and Nikhil Kamath were conscious of the disparity that existed in society, with immense wealth concentrated in specific pockets. At the same time, a significant portion of the population grappled with profound existential challenges. Driven by this awareness, they decided to back entrepreneurs with innovative ideas and non-profits dedicated to alleviating societal hardships.

In 2016, Zerodha started a for-profit entity—Rainmatter—a fund to back fintech start-ups. Nithin said, 'We recognized that nurturing India's capital market participation required actions beyond establishing a discount brokerage firm, and we couldn't do everything. Thus, we set out to create an ecosystem of diverse, high-quality fintech products through multiple start-ups.'

He added, 'We are patient long-term investors and aren't looking for quick exits. We aim to build a good, sustainable, long-term business, not just to generate rapid returns. Moreover, we see this fund as our giving-forward initiative. The profits from the investments go back to supporting more entrepreneurs and non-profit initiatives.' Subsequently, the fund extended its scope to include the health and storytelling sectors.

Around 2019, the Zerodha leadership team felt giving back for social causes through non-profits was going all over the place, and impact measurement was becoming difficult. So, they decided to create a structured non-profit entity to give back to social causes. Consequently, Zerodha started the Rainmatter Foundation to support organisations and projects focused on climate action and a healthier environment.

Nithin said, 'I think climate change will affect the bottom half a lot more than maybe the top 1–3 per cent of the planet. In the future, questions will be asked of successful businesses and people, "What did you do about it when you had the money and influence to make a difference?" We want to be part of the group that will be able to justify their contribution.' He added, 'We do not see this as charity but as an investment in our own future and well-being. And one of the reasons I think we are very vocal about this is to nudge others to think this way.' The foundation has committed $100 million in funding and grants to individuals and organisations working in the climate space. It is also considering establishing seventy acres as private forest land.

Beyond the Rainmatter Foundation, Nikhil also initiated The Young India Philanthropic Pledge (YIPP), which brings together many start-up founders to support initiatives like education in government schools in Karnataka. They have provided aid during floods in Assam, while undertaking various other projects during the pandemic, including the preparation and distribution of more than 20,000 meals daily, free medical assistance using twenty ambulances, and providing free treatment at a mini-hospital for Covid-19 patients. In 2023, Nikhil emerged as the youngest philanthropist on the EdelGive Hurun India Philanthropy List. Notably, he has pledged to donate 50 per cent of his wealth toward causes encompassing climate change, education and healthcare.

The philanthropic endeavours of Zerodha and its founders have not only enriched society but significantly strengthened goodwill for the brand and its founders. Moreover, these initiatives motivate employees who wish to associate with an organization dedicated to meaningful causes and attract customers inclined to align with socially conscious brands.

How Sirona Is Combating Period Poverty

Period poverty is a complex and challenging situation wherein girls and women face significant challenges in accessing or being able to afford essential menstrual hygiene products like sanitary pads. The consequences of this lack of access to menstrual supplies can be profound, leading to unhygienic practices, an elevated risk of infections, missed school and workdays and restricted participation in daily activities. Furthermore, persistent cultural taboos and stigma surrounding menstruation in various societies frequently aggravates the problem.

In response to these pressing challenges, the Sirona Hygiene Foundation was established in 2020, as the social responsibility arm of Sirona. The foundation remains unwaveringly committed to the cause of promoting sustainable menstrual health and combating stigma associated with menstruation. Its primary mission is to eradicate period poverty in India by providing access to menstrual cups and offering training to over 10,00,000 underprivileged women through its flagship project—Lakhon Khwaishein.

Deep Bajaj, co-founder and CEO of Sirona, commented passionately, 'Our foundation's main goal is to make sure that every woman and girl can have a healthy life without feeling ashamed because of their periods. We want to discuss it openly, clear any misunderstandings and help women manage their periods safely and confidently. We want to change the old ideas and rules about periods. By educating more people, we can get closer to ending period poverty.'

To show support for the foundation's noble endeavours, Sirona contributes Re 1 for every product sold. The collected amount helps fund initiatives that focus on improving menstrual health and hygiene for underprivileged women across India. Alongside the distribution of free menstrual cups in vulnerable communities, the foundation has conducted webinars in schools, colleges and social clubs in the past year, educating over one lakh girls and women about menstrual health.

The foundation has partnered with more than fifty organizations such as Raintree, PVR Nest, TYCIA, SOS Children's Villages of India, Sangam World Centre, World Association of Girl Guides and Girl Scouts and many others. These collaborations allow the foundation to reach the right beneficiaries and address menstrual health challenges comprehensively. They conduct thorough training sessions to help people use menstrual cups correctly and provide follow-up support for continued usage.

As of August 2023, Sirona has generously donated over 10,000 menstrual cups to underprivileged girls and women as part of Project Lakhon Khwahishen, marking a significant milestone in the journey towards ending period poverty.

The Sirona Hygiene Foundation is not only a force for positive change but also a valuable asset for the brand itself. By championing the cause of menstrual health and hygiene, Sirona has demonstrated its commitment to social responsibility and its role as a catalyst for meaningful change. This alignment of brand values with a pressing social issue enhances Sirona's reputation and fosters the positive image that the brand is not just about selling products. It is about making a difference and leaving a lasting impact. This engagement with a cause that resonates with people deepens customer loyalty and attracts a wider audience of supporters and advocacy.

Acknowledgements

First and foremost, I am thankful to God for giving me the strength to embark on the journey of writing this book. Looking back, finding time with so many renowned leaders in the Indian start-up ecosystem seems like a miracle.

Next, I would like to thank Manish Khurana for entering my life and motivating me to write this book. I am deeply grateful to the team at Penguin Random House India who believed in the idea of a book on start-up branding. Thank you, Milee Ashwarya, for your support. Thank you to the editor, Saba Nehal, for making my book more engaging, and the designer, Aakriti Khurana, for giving the book a beautiful look. Additionally, I am appreciative of Rhea Gangavkar for her invaluable editorial assistance. I want to thank my wife, Pooja, for being a constant motivator. I am grateful to Anoushka Rai, my student at FLAME, for always being there to help me with her insightful review comments. I am also thankful to my parents, Surendra Pamnani and Kanchan Pamnani, and my sister, Honey Pamnani, for their moral support.

Numerous kind-hearted people have supported me in this journey. Thank you, Seth Nesbitt, for becoming the first reviewer of the book's initial abstract and table of contents.

Thank you, Prajakta Bhosale at Licious; Minal Pashte and Isha
Dhoble at Epigamia; Dinesh Pai at Zerodha; Vishnu Acharya,
Hepsibah Rozario, Arun Chetty and Anu Saraswat at Razorpay;
Praval Singh and Nanya Srivastava at Zoho; Mariya Kapadia at
Rebel Foods; Seth Nesbitt at Icertis; Anika Wadhera at Sirona,
Surbhi Sood at Paper Boat, Gunjan Wathodkar at SUGAR;
Soumitra Choubey and Jhanvi Thakkar at Meesho; and Srinath
Narasimhan at Fractal. I am deeply thankful to the founders who
contributed to the brand case studies and to the brand experts
and leaders who provided valuable insights for each chapter.

Special thanks to Anand Lunia, Vineet Malhotra, Sameer
Arora, Arun Diaz, Ajit Nagral, Vibhu Nagral, Prakash Iyer,
Sandeep Singhal, Srinivas Rao Mahankali (MSR), Prashant
Jadhav, Vivek Singh, Vargab Bakshi, Shripad Nadkarni, Sharad
Sarin, U.T. Rao, Ameen Haque and Mahalakshmi Ajaykumar
for always being there to help me.

I am grateful to Achintya Goyal, Chandralekha Maitra,
Jivraj Singh Sachar and Sanket Srikanth for their invaluable
support throughout this journey. The list of people who have
helped me in my life is long. So, I may not be able to mention
all the names. But I am grateful to every person who has played
a role in my journey. Thank you, everyone!

Notes

Chapter 1: Investor Outlook on Start-Up Branding

1   Vikram Chaudhary, 'Duolingo India stats 2022: English, Hindi top languages Indians learn', *Financial Express*, 6 March 2023, available at https://www.financialexpress.com/jobs-career/education-duolingo-india-stats-2022-english-hindi-top-languages-indians-learn-3000619/; Abhishek Baxi, 'Tech Startups, Take Note: More Indians Access the Internet in Their Native Language than in English', *Forbes*, 29 March 2018, available at https://www.forbes.com/sites/baxiabhishek/2018/03/29/more-indians-access-the-internet-in-their-native-language-than-in-english/.

Chapter 2: Building a Start-Up's Belief System

1   'Icertis CEO and Co-founder, Samir Bodas, Honored by Goldman Sachs for Entrepreneurship', Icertis, 18 October 2023, available at https://www.icertis.com/company/news/dispatches/icertis-ceo-and-co-founder-samir-bodas-honored-by-goldman-sachs-for-entrepreneurship/.

2   Deep Bajaj, 'What's impeding an eco-friendly shift in menstrual waste disposal? Stigma, ignorance, and accessibility', *Times of India*, 1 August 2023, available at https://timesofindia.indiatimes.com/blogs/voices/whats-impeding-

an-eco-friendly-shift-in-menstrual-waste-disposal-stigma-ignorance-and-accessibility/.

Chapter 3: Building a Start-Up's Culture

1 'Why Fractal Analytics Limited is a Great Place to Work', Great Place to Work, available at https://www.greatplacetowork.in/great/company/fractal-analytics-pvt-ltd.

Chapter 4: Leveraging Insights to Uncover Hidden Opportunities

1 Manu Balachandran, 'How Shan Kadavil is building FreshToHome into a proficorn', *Forbes India*, 15 March 2023, available at https://www.forbesindia.com/article/take-one-big-story-of-the-day/how-shan-kadavil-is-building-freshtohome-into-a-proficorn/83707/1.
2 'Meat – India', Statista, June 2024, available at https://www.statista.com/outlook/cmo/food/meat/india#revenue.
3 'Decoding Licious' Organic App Growth Playbook', Inc42, 7 April 2023, available at https://inc42.com/features/decoding-licious-organic-app-growth-playbook/; Sohini Mitter, 'How on-demand meat delivery startup Meatigo is changing the way India buys and eats non-veg food', YourStory, 13 January 2021, available at https://yourstory.com/2021/01/meat-delivery-startup-meatigo-india-eat-non-veg-food.

Chapter 5: Category Creation and Selection

1 '10 businessmen to watch out for in 2016', *Economic Times*, 31 December 2015, available at https://economictimes.indiatimes.com/biz-entrepreneurship/10-businessmen-to-watch-out-for-in-2016/2-anil-ambani-chairman-reliance-group/slideshow/50388312.cms.

Chapter 6: The Importance of Segmentation

1 Esha Roy, 'India's population 142.8 crore in 2023, crosses China's: UN population report', *Indian Express*, 20 April 2023, available at https://indianexpress.com/article/india/

india-population-up-un-sowp-report-life-expectancy-fertility-rate-8564123/.

2 'Kraftshala expands its marketing launchpad programmes, adds new course in digital media', *Telegraph*, 3 December 2021, available at https://www.telegraphindia.com/edugraph/news/headline-kraftshala-expands-its-marketing-launchpad-programmes-adds-new-course-in-digital-media/cid/1841718.

Chapter 7: Achieving Product–Market Fit

1 Sagar Malviya, 'Juice brand Paper Boat loses steam, sales down 12.5%', *Economic Times*, 19 January 2018, available at https://economictimes.indiatimes.com/industry/cons-products/food/juice-brand-paper-boat-loses-steam-sales-down-12-5/articleshow/62562762.cms?from=mdr.

2 'How podcasting is growing in India', *Financial Express*, 31 July 2022, available at https://www.financialexpress.com/business/brandwagon-how-podcasting-is-growing-in-india-2612119/; Pankaj Doval, '90% of new net users non-English', *Times of India*, 26 April 2017, available at https://timesofindia.indiatimes.com/business/india-business/90-of-new-net-users-non-english/articleshow/58371769.cms.

3 'Meesho adds 8 new vernacular languages to tap 377 million potential user base', *Economic Times*, 12 August 2022, available at https://economictimes.indiatimes.com/tech/startups/meesho-adds-8-new-vernacular-languages-to-tap-377-million-potential-user-base/articleshow/93513613.cms.

4 Ibid.

5 'Meesho Becomes India's Fastest E-com Platform to cross 1 mn Sellers Milestone', Indian Retailer, 30 March 2023, available at https://www.indianretailer.com/news/meesho-becomes-indias-fastest-e-com-platform-cross-1-mn-sellers-milestone.

Chapter 8: Dynamics of Brand Positioning and Transformation

1 Harshith K.N., 'Gone in 30 minutes! Mahindra Scorpio-N bookings cross 1 lakh in just 30 minutes', *Times of India*, 30 July

2022, available at https://timesofindia.indiatimes.com/auto/cars/gone-in-30-minutes-mahindra-scorpio-n-bookings-cross-1-lakh-in-just-30-minutes/articleshow/93231874.cms.

2   Marion Andrivet, 'What to Learn from Tropicana's Packaging Redesign Failure?', Branding Journal, 30 November 2023, available at https://www.thebrandingjournal.com/2015/05/what-to-learn-from-tropicanas-packaging-redesign-failure/.

3   Harshith Mallya, 'Jaipur based RazorPay becomes the second India focused startup to be selected for YCombinator', YourStory, 23 March 2015, available at https://yourstory.com/2015/03/razorpay-raises-usd120000-ycombinator.

Chapter 10: Building Consistency through Systems and Processes

1   T.N. Hari and M.S. Subramanian, *Saying No to Jugaad: The Making of Bigbasket* (New Delhi: Bloomsbury India, 2019).

Chapter 11: The Art and Impact of Brand Communication

1   Ravi Balakrishnan, 'P&G's largest ever global campaigns "Thank You, Mom"', *Economic Times*, 25 April 2012, available at https://economictimes.indiatimes.com/pgs-largest-ever-global-campaigns-thank-you-mom/articleshow/12850617.cms?from=mdr.

Chapter 12: Strategies for Sales and Distribution

1   Meha Agarwal, 'How Home Appliances D2C Brand Atomberg Went From Zero To $100 Mn ARR', Inc42, 23 April 2023, available at https://inc42.com/startups/how-home-appliances-d2c-brand-atomberg-went-from-zero-to-100-mn-arr/.

Scan QR code to access the
Penguin Random House India website